M000238387

SAILING THROUGH RUSSIA
FROM THE ARCTIC TO THE BLACK SEA

Published by
Maxine Maters & John Vallentine
2016

www.sailinginrussia.org
www.tainui.org
info@sailinginrussa.org
jvallentine@gmail.com

All rights reserved. No parts of this publication may be reproduced, transmitted or used in any form by any means – graphic, electronic or mechanical, including photocopying, recording. Taping or information storage and retrieval systems or otherwise – without the prior permission of the Publishers.

© John Vallentine 2016
© Maxine Maters 2016

John Vallentine and Maxine Maters have asserted their rights under the Copyright Design and Patents Act 1988 to be identified as the authors of this work.
All photos by John Vallentine and Maxine Maters except where stated.
The cover image is a photomontage created by Libby Blainey.

First edition 2016
A catalog record of this book is available from the British Library
ISBN : 978-1-5262-0258-1

The book is structured around the blogs written by John Vallentine and Maxine Maters while sailing in Russia and includes practical information for cruisers.

Caution
Every effort has been made to ensure the accuracy of this book. It contain selected information and thus is not definitive and does not include all information on the subject in hand; this is particular relevant to the plans and charts which should not be used for navigation. The authors believe that their selection is a useful aid to prudent navigation, but the safety of a vessel depends ultimately on the judgement of the navigator who shall assess all information, published or unpublished.

Plans and charts
We would like to thank iSailor for its generous support with this project. In particular, we are grateful for permission to reproduce iSailor chartlets in the text. Please note that these maps remain the property of iSailor and are not to be reproduced without specific permission. It goes without saying that the charlets are for general guidance only and are not to be used for navigation. While we have made every effort to ensure the accuracy of waypoints reproduced in the chartlets, any errors are ours and not iSailor's.

Correctional supplements
This cruising guide will be updated at intervals by information published on the internet at our websites www.sailinginrussia.org and www.tainui.org

This work has been corrected to December 2015

Printed by Zrinski in Croatia

DEDICATION

To our predecessor Miles Clark, with
admiration and thanks. He made our journey so
much easier and more interesting.

PREFACE

The Russian Federation has decided to allow foreign vessels access
to its inland waterways as of May 2012. These brief notes should be
regarded as no more than an introduction to the inland route from
the White Sea to the Sea of Azov, based on Australian yacht Tainui's
experience in 2013. They are addressed to adventurous sailors
considering an alternative route south from Arctic Norway to the
Mediterranean.

In 2013 Tainui completed a 4 month voyage from Archangel'sk to Azov.
She was preceded by Wild Goose (Ireland,1994) and Aenigma (UK,
2000), both flying Russian flags. In 1998 two Dutch yachts travelled the
shorter route south to Azov from St Petersburg, also carrying Russian
flags. As far as we know Tainui is the first foreign-flagged vessel of any
description to have gained access the Volga-Don waterways in 100
years.

JOHN VALLENTINE

A retired Australian physician, John Vallentine has been ocean racing and cruising for almost 50 years. He says has won his battle with youthfulness but not with adolescence.

MAXINE MATERS

One-time publisher of The Moscow Times, Maxine is Dutch but has lived in Moscow for 25 years and dreams in Russian. She loves sailing and does enjoy a crisp chenin blanc.

TABLE OF CONTENTS

ABOUT THE SKIPPER : JOHN

I am a retired doctor. I left Australia 7 years ago and am half way through the world's slowest circumnavigation. My Sydney-Hobart racing days are long over and I like to keep comfortable on board, even if it means not going so fast. My old friend Christine Hampshire joins me when we drop anchor in some lovely place and the chardonnay is chilled. The rest of the time I have similarly old men join me for the long, cold, wet and uncomfortable bits.

In 2005 we sailed from Sydney down to the subantarctic islands (Macquarie, Campbell, Aucklands etc) then via NZ and the Chatham Islands to Patagonia, where we spent two superb and very remote seasons. After a slow trip up the east coast of the Americas, with long stops in Brazil, Cuba and New York, Tainui spent a further two seasons in Newfoundland and Labrador before crossing the North Atlantic via Iceland, Faroe and Shetlands to Scotland.

Last spring we sailed to St Petersburg via Gdansk, back west through Finland and Sweden, then up the Norwegian coast to Svalbard. Tainui was hauled out in Tromsø Norway last winter for a much-earned rest while I earned some cruising money working in Central Australia.

Tainui is a well-travelled 40 year old Peterson 46. She is heavily built and comfortable – GRP with timber deck and centre cockpit. Because we have so much gear on board there is limited space and no hot showers. But the galley is good with fridge but no freezer, the music system excellent (classical, bluegrass, jazz and blues especially) and the heating system adequate (just). All navigation systems, radar, etc are good. I don't steer much – we have a good wind vane and an autopilot.

Tainui is my 5th offshore yacht and the only one which I feel no need to replace - indeed I cannot imagine a better cruising vessel. I am 65 years old but feel much older during long night watches in bad weather. I get seasick often.

I have a folder of devoted, patient crew who keep coming back to Tainui despite her skipper. My two gorgeous daughters also know Tainui well and are to join Tainui again, further down the Volga. It is a rare pleasure to have them aboard, trapped and unable to avoid open, extended conversation with their adoring father.

My time is divided between Tainui and remote indigenous medical practice in Central Australia. As I get older I have gotten into the habit of laying Tainui up for the winter, wherever she may be, and returning home to re-engage with my long-suffering partner Chris, and deal with the inevitable mortgage bloat.

Future plans? - well, I suppose I have another 6 or 7 years of declining but adequate competence in me, before senescence and gravity win over. I would like to see Tainui home to Australia in that time. And I want to visit South Georgia and Kerguelen Land on the way.

As we say in Tainui - "and then you die".

ABOUT THE FIRST MATE : MAXINE

Maxine is originally from the Netherlands but has lived in Russia since time immemorial. At least, she says, that is how it feels.

When Gorbachev became president, it became easier for foreigners to obtain Russian visas and off Maxine went to see whether the USSR was really so different. She did not intend to stay for more than 20 years but somehow it just happened. At one point Russia even tried to prohibit her entry but a Russian court ruled in her favour.

Maxine, a lawyer by training, became involved in legal and then newspaper publishing.

Maxine has been sailing since childhood on her family's boat. Now however, she is committed crewperson. She decides on a route and chooses skipper and boat accordingly. And that is how she ended up in s/y Tainui, organising the voyage through the Russian inland waterways.

INTRODUCTION

The inland waterways of Russia are vast, with an intricate system of interlinked rivers, canals and navigable routes for commercial vessels. There are more than 90,000 km of them! Over half of these passages are fully buoyed and lit, carrying river cargo in excess of 100 million tons annually. Of these routes, it is the Volga and Don Rivers (and the great canal connecting them) which carry the bulk of commercial traffic. They are the subject of this guide. Other great rivers (such as the Kama, Lena, Yenisei and Ob), await future exploration by more intrepid sailors.

The Volga is the longest river in Europe, almost four times the length of the Rhine and twice the length of the Danube.

A voyage down the huge Volga-Don system is remote only in the sense that for over 2,000 miles you will see almost no pleasure craft, no foreign yachts and at most only one or two Russian cruising yachts. But you will be accompanied by an endless, fascinating parade of commercial vessels of all sorts – huge double barges, push tugs, 5,000 ton bulk carriers, oil tankers, floating cranes and Russian cruise ships.

Leaving aside the physical enormity of the journey from the White Sea south to the Sea of Azov, the bureaucratic issues involved in smooth passage of yachts down the waterway cannot be stressed highly enough. There are 6 separate authorities controlling various sections of the rivers and, when it exists, communication between them is far from seamless. You will spend a great deal of time and effort with each, explaining over and over again who you are, what you are doing, where you are going and why.

You will be a novelty and your presence will not fit comfortably within the rigid processes governing regulation and passage of the almost entirely commercial shipping along the way. Nowhere is this more apparent than in Azov, where exit formalities posed significant difficulties for Tainui (see section Azov).

Tainui's journey was smooth, thanks largely to the tireless efforts of her Russian-speaking crew Maxine. She and her bemused and often helpless skipper took every opportunity to ensure smooth transition between the various maritime jurisdictions. We found that the following techniques were pivotal:

1. The establishment of informal, personal contacts within those departments (particularly navigation authorities, lock keepers and dispatchers) with which we dealt along the way. This was particularly useful in Belomorsk, Yaroslavl, Nizhniy Novgorod and Azov. On each occasion, at completion of formalities we urged these contacts to pass on our details to their successors down river, so that we were known about and expected when we arrived at subsequent ports.

2. The garnering the assistance of local sailors and the office bearers of boat clubs we visited en route. Always interested, hospitable and helpful, they forewarned their downstream contacts of our arrival. This meant that we were commonly met on arrival at the next port, marina berths (where present) were arranged and, at times intrusively, local press alerted to our arrival. Many of these folk are listed in the contacts section of the guide and each has expressed willingness to assist future yachts and sailors.

For foreign masters, waterways administration along the Volga seems fragmented, inefficient, unpredictable, fluid and at times quite opaque. This is one of the many reasons why each transit will be unique.

You and your vessel will be objects of curiosity and delight for local people along the way. And the Volga and Don Rivers are wonderful waterways - by turns majestic, mysterious, grand and subtle.

Vardo

Barents Sea

White Sea

SOLOVETSKIY ISLANDS

Belomorsk

Archangel'sk

Belomor Canal

SWEDEN

FINLAND

Gulf of Bothnia

Lake Onega

Vytegra

Vytegra

ALAND

St Petersburg

ESTONIA

Rybinskiy Reservoir

RUSSIA

Novgorod

Kineshma

LATVIA

Yaroslavl

Cheboksary

Tver

Nizhniy Novgorod

Kazan

LITHUANIA

Baltic Sea

Moscow

Central

Russian

Oka

European Plain

POLAND

Upland

Don

Plain

Samara

BELARUS

Saratov

Marxs Engels

Warsaw

Volga R

CZECH REPUBLIC

UKRAINE

Don R

SLOVAKIA

Kiev

AUSTRIA

HUNGARY

Carpathian Mountains

Volga R

KAZAKHST

MOLDOVA

ROMANIA

Volgagrad (Stalingrad)

CROATIA

Sea of Azov

Azov

SERBIA

Dinaric

Kerch

BOS.& HERZ.

MACEDONIA

BULGARIA

Black Sea

GEORGIA

Caspian Sea

ALBANIA

Sinop

AZERBAIJAN

Baku

GREECE

ARMENIA

TURKEY

TURK

INTRODUCTION

Like Russia itself, the Volga is much loved and a source of great pride for Russians. Over and over again we were asked for our opinion of this great river. Fortunately, it was impossible for us to speak of our impressions in other than glowing terms.

For cruising yachts the seminal work is Wallace Clark's account of his brother Miles' ground-breaking journey in Wild Goose In 1994 ("Sailing round Russia", published by Wallace Clark). While this book is required reading, things have changed very much since Miles' trip. Also flying a Russian flag, Barry Woodhouse later took his UK yacht Aenigma down the Volga in 2004. We hope that these notes will be of assistance to those who follow Wild Goose, Aenigma and Tainui.

Looking back on this journey of ours we have found there is too much to hold in mind at once. It has been a rich and rewarding experience. The rivers are indeed beautiful, but our overriding memory is of the warmth, generosity and friendliness of the wonderful people we have met along the way. Finding perspective will require space and time.

Tainui's Journey

VARDO TO ARCHANGEL'SK

HOW WE STARTED OUT : JOHN

Spitzbergen is about as far as you can get from Australia. Wherever you go from there, you are heading home. But which way to go?

As we counted polar bears, dodged icebergs and photographed beluga whales, I began to think about getting south from Norway via the Volga River instead of back down that beautiful but endless Norwegian coast. In St Petersburg my friend Vladimir Ivankiv had told me that 2 Russian flagged vessels (Aenigma and Wild Goose) had completed the journey in the last decade, so I knew that it was theoretically possible.

In 40 years of sailing Tainui has been blessed by regular crew, family and friends, who all seem to want to come back for more. Crew requirements for the Russia journey were stringent however - fluency in Russian, ICC and CEVNI licensing, navigational skill, freedom to commit to 4 months aboard, and a sanguine attitude to the whole plan falling through in Archangel'sk if we were not allowed into Russia. Not to mention enthusiasm and a patient forbearance with my idiosyncracies.

So I placed a notice on one of the crew finder websites, not hopeful of finding anyone, let alone the right person. I described the boat and her skipper as honestly as I could, then set out the requirements listed above. One more essential was added to the list - "must love Mozart and Schubert".

The following day I received a brief note from a Dutch woman living in Moscow. Her reply - "And what about Shostakovitch?" I knew I was on a winner.

Over the years I have come across many boats who regularly seek crew via the internet. One high latitude hermit has had 23 successive female crew members, none of whom came back for a second trip. Internet dating is not something I have ever previously contemplated or, until this trip, needed. I doubt I would do it again, but on this occasion I can say it was a great success.

Maxine Maters is a Dutch lawyer who completed her postgraduate legal training in Moscow. She has lived in Russia for 25 years and became the publisher of The Moscow Times in 2004. She thinks and dreams in Russian. A keen sailor since early childhood, Max is adventurous. She has always leapt at any opportunity to let go fore and aft.

This was 8 months before we set out from Tromsø. A long email correspondence followed, during which Maxine's interest in the journey, her practical search for solutions to the bureaucratic hurdles we faced obtaining the necessary approvals from Russian authorities, her humour and her optimism confirmed my initial assessment.

Tainui having been bedded down for the winter in Tromsø, I headed home to the Australian desert to deal with that inevitable mortgage bloat, the bane of every cruising sailor's life. Idle, theoretical research gathered momentum after I gained Maxine's interest in the project.

For 8 months we explored the process by which we could make it happen. We were empowered by a decree issued by Russian Prime Minister Medvedev in 2012, affirming his government's intention to allow access to Russia's inland waterways for foreign vessels after 100 years.

The application process was lengthy and frustrating. The main problem we faced with our Russian respondents was silence. I think our plans were too far into left field for the bureaucracy to cope with. And this despite a formal decree by the Russian Prime Minister. The main problem is that there is a gulf between senior level intention and its practical expression by workers at the coal face.

My first requirement was a 3 month business visa, needed for foreign skippers and crew. There is just no mechanism allowing easy attainment of this. The list of hotels we planned to stay in, the towns we intended to visit, the dates and means by which we were travelling couldn't be put into the rigid visa application. Purpose of travel? Cruising doesn't make sense to the authorities. And of course you can't get a visa without a formal invitation from a prescribed organisation inside Russia. The way I got round this was not entirely dishonest. I formed a company called "Maritime Research" and my stated intention was to research a book on marine transport on the inland waterways. I do intend to produce a simple guide for those who wish to follow, so I did not feel I was being deceptive. I said I was interested in the exploits of the Vikings on the Volga in the 10th century, and that is not entirely untrue either.

I dutifully listed all the ports we planned to visit and the dates as accurately as we could guess them. Off went the application and.... silence. New applications were submitted, enlisting the dubious assistance of the Russian Yachting Federation and a government organisation called Rusarc, which organises local cruising between St Petersburg and Archangel'sk. Still silence.

Ultimately I was granted an invitation from the Ministry of the Interior to apply for a business visa and the visa was granted me in Sydney without demur, just a week before the deadline for my return to Norway. Maxine lives in Moscow and didn't need a visa. My worry all along had been that nowhere in my application was there any mention of our planned mode of travel - Tainui. I worried about that right up until we found ourselves well inside territorial waters, with the apparent blessing of all the right people. And then our wonderful adventure began.

MORE ON INTERNET DATING : MAXINE

As a sailor and long-term resident of Moscow, I was obviously intrigued by John's post on the crewseeker site. After the first email exchange of text and pictures, we skyped. On my computer screen appeared Captain Birdseye, beard and all. Both e-mails and call made a good impression despite the whiskers, but hey?

We agreed it all sounded good but there remained a risk in embarking on such a trip without ever having met each other. Still, with Birdseye in Australia and me in either Moscow or London, we realised it was a risk we would have to take. Obviously we did discuss it. What if we met and there was no click? What if we fell out halfway through?

Looking back, planning and organising the trip was tedious but not too difficult. It meant organising a Russian visa for John, getting hold of paper charts and a Russian VHF, and finding some more Russian speaking crew. But before all of that was in place, in particular John's visa, we went through quite a few emotions together over the phone and email. For me the most astonishing part was the ease with which we slipped into planning and organising, all against a background of mutual trust which miraculously had established itself out of nowhere. Somehow it felt right from the start.

I did not set out planning to do the whole trip. Three months on a yacht with a skipper I didn't know and perhaps some other crew was something I had difficulty getting my mind around. I vaguely imagined coming on board at intervals and somehow managing the whole process from Moscow or something. I had sailed with other skippers whom I had found through crew sites before but never for more than a fortnight. John, too, kept looking for other Russian-speaking crew who could take my place during time-outs.

In the middle of May 2013 I flew to Tromsø, Norway, to meet John and Tainui for the first time. At the last minute I got cold feet and asked my partner Dirk to come along. On the third morning after some more beers, Dirk flew back to London and John and I set off in the direction of North Cape. Little did I know that I would not disembark until Kerch, on the Crimea, exactly FOUR months later.

TROMSØ, SATURDAY : JOHN, 4 MAY

I don't like arriving back at Tainui after extended absence. Long, freezing winters tend to play havoc with plumbing, pumps, haberdashery and electrics despite the most meticulous winterization. I'm not sure why. This time the Skattøra Marina yard has done a sterling job keeping her dehumidified and warm, so there is no mould and she smells fresh. But still, down below I am reminded of those space stations in hibernation – everything is dead, unloved and it is all a bit forlorn. Add to that the jet lag, the mess of my half-unpacked bags and the nuisance of living aboard a boat high and dry, and you have a recipe for black moods. I have one. But everything will fall into place – it always does.

It is sunny but cold here, with residual snow banks in the marina, and snowy mountain peaks all around glistening in the hard light. One oddity about arctic Norway is that summer arrives much later than you'd expect it to. In 2 weeks it will be midsummer's day and it is already light for about 20 hours out of 24. But there is more snow expected and by any sane measure it is only early spring. Autumn is the season for warm, still weather.

Skattøra Marina

VARDO TO ARCHANGEL'SK

My major worry at the moment is the diesel engine. By the end of last season our dear old Ford was losing serious amounts of fresh water coolant – up to 1 litre every 4 hours. I had hoped this was just a heat exchanger problem but yesterday we pressure tested the unit and there is no leak. There being no external loss and no evidence of coolant leak into the engine oil, that leaves head gasket and exhaust manifold. The latter is the most likely. I replaced the manifold at huge expense in Maine a couple of years ago and I dread the likely delay we face in getting another one imported. I have 10 days to sort it out before the crew arrive. We have some 2000 miles of motoring down the Volga and Don rivers, if the authorities grant us permission to enter the inland waterway system. A dead engine we cannot tolerate.
All fingers are crossed.

Our plan is to depart Tromsø on 16 May, weather permitting. We should clear out of Norway at Kirkenes or Vardø and I hope to start Russian entry formalities in Archangel'sk on 1 June, if the ice has cleared from the White Sea.

From Archangel'sk it is an overnighter to the Solovetskiy Islands, a world heritage site soon to be closed to most marine traffic, they say. Then across to Belomorsk to enter the Barents Sea Canal, one of Stalin's more notorious construction exercises.

That all seems so far away. For now, I have to deal with jet lag and engine coolant loss.

WHERE HAS ALL THE COOLANT GONE? : JOHN, 6 MAY

I am running in treacle. Silly, boat-in-foreign-country things like getting a SIM card that works, downloading AIS and Iridium software drivers for the new Windows 7 computer, living on the hard without water and 10 miles out of town. And without a word of Norwegian. All of that is normal, but this engine coolant loss problem has me and Sentrum Diesel stumped. Pressure testing confirms a steady loss at 1 bar. But the exhaust manifold is quite dry and the heat exchanger/header tank pressure tests normally. There is no external loss and the oil is not milky. Where on earth is that water going?

It is still cold and icy. Winter comes and goes late in northern Norway. Nonetheless, new anodes have been installed, sails are bent on and stowage is progressing satisfactorily. My new folding bicycle is a godsend and I get into town daily for R&R, which saves my sanity. Spirits have risen even though coolant levels have fallen. As Christine would say, just do one day at a time.

LIFE'S RICH TAPESTRY : JOHN

It is snowing and there is a good layer of the cold stuff on the decks. The gale force winds have abated but it is grey and very cold. At least, for an Australian! I expect the view across the fjord to the mountains is quite grand – if there were not a power outage here at the marina I would admire it. It is very chilly in the cabin however, and as things stand, I would happily exchange Life's Rich Tapestry for a warm blanket.

We have pressure tested the engine to within an inch of its life. There was initially a leak as predicted, but with no apparent external loss. I went round and re-tightened all the hose clamps and – blow me down – the pressure no longer drops. By my calculation the loss would have been of the order of 4- 5mls/min. It should have been visible but wasn't.

As with all things boat, whenever you look for problems you find them. In the course of my coolant loss detective work I discovered a worn shaft bearing in the coolant pump. It hasn't failed but probably will, so I will install another here in Tromsø. This one was only 3 years old – Martin brought it across to Patagonia from Nelson – and I am suprised it has failed after perhaps 2,500 hours. I am surprised also that Sentrum Diesel has been able to locate a replacement so quickly. Mind you, it will cost the odd peanut or two.

I have charged our propane tanks with 25 kg of the smelly stuff, which should see us through the summer. The MaxProp has had its annual grease packing, Tainui's bottom has been painted and shiny new anodes are attached. These are zinc, of course, but I believe I should be considering sacrificial aluminium for the 3 month fresh water trip, but I probably won't do anything about it, knowing me.

BACK INTO THE WATER : JOHN, 14 MAY

Some injudicious yard work with the travel lift led to a bent ProFurl yesterday afternoon. We cancelled the launch so we could dismantle the foil and straighten the bent section Mercifully, the bend was round and fixable and all went well this morning. The yard felt bad about things and brought in a cherry picker to save me going up the mast. They have also offered to buy me a new foil section.

I can recommend Skattøra Marina as a place to overwinter. George, Bjørn and Stig are hard working, professional and very friendly. I have another connection with Tromsø – when I first went to sea in 1966, I was in "Norbu", a Norwegian coal ship built in Tromsø and crewed by locals. I mentioned this to Bjørn Jacobsen, the yard manager here, who told me that Norbu had in fact been built and owned by his father. A small world.

Norwegian customs have removed constraints to laying up in Norway and the customs permit is easy to get. Last winter in Tromsø cost me around $4,000 including travel lift, water blasting and snow clearance. The only problem is the 10km haul into town. There are few buses and no local services other than fuel, water, gas and an engineering facility. No shops.

My new little Brompton folding bike has earned its place on Tainui. If my bum stops hurting I will give the bike a "gear that works" plaudit.

We're back in the water at the top of the tide tonight. At last! The only uncertainty now is whether we've fixed the coolant problem. If not, it'll be off with the head and the exhaust manifold. Sentrum Diesel have been good, albeit a bit preoccupied with bigger ships. I know they'll rise to the challenge if the leak continues. Maxine arrives tomorrow with Dirk, her partner, who is coming to check me out. We should get away a couple of days later.

MISTY AND GREY : JOHN, 18 MAY

Finally, finally Maxine and I said goodbye to Dirk, let go our lines and motored out into Tromsø Sound, on our way. A calm, misty day.

Our route winds north and east through protected waters with magnificent snowy peaks on all sides. Time at last for John to slip into a coma in the saloon with Max at the helm.

We crept into Skjervøy at 11 at night. A pretty, snug little harbour with rows of drowsy fishing boats, neat cottages and snowy mountain slopes. Today it was cold, and when the fitful northerly freshened it became quite bitter. Snow-clad peaks loomed then disappeared through swirling mists. It was good to have Henry Ford ticking over at 1,400 rpm and the bus heater punching warmth into the saloon. The sad news is that our coolant leak hasn't been fixed – still 1 litre every 4 hours. Where on earth is it going? We can find no external leaks. When cold, the system passes pressure testing at 15psi, so we are dealing with an internal, temperature-dependent problem. We're off to Hammerfest today, where I will try a hot pressure test on the system.

Skjervøy

HAMMERFEST

After a lazy start from Sjervøy we motorsailed into a freshening headwind, past spectacular snow-clad peaks and glacial valleys and into the big sound south of Suroey Island. This is a grand ampitheatre of sharply etched peaks and valleys, glistening in a late-blooming evening sun. For Maxine, sundowners were Farida's leftover single malt. I stuck with G&T. Happy hour saw us through till our arrival in Hammerfest at 2330h. Admittedly closing midnight on a cold grey Sunday you should be careful judging a town, but for us it was not reminiscent of Paris or Rome. In the small hours, and I thought deeply asleep, I felt a change come through with fresh ESE breezes. Interesting how attuned you become to variations in weather, boat motion and sound after time afloat.

Today, Monday, the skies are cloudless. Weather precludes travel and I would get an mechanic to look at our engine coolant problem, but it is yet another public holiday. There seems to be a relentless succession of them.

Hammerfest

Honningsvåg in flat water

NORTH CAPE, NEAR AS DAMMIT

"Near as dammit" because here at Honningsvåg the Hurtigruten ferry stops to allow tourists to travel by road 35km north to North Cape, the northernmost tip of mainland Europe.

We removed the exhaust manifold in Hammerfest and we think we found the leak – an obscure welch plug on the under side of the unit. Resealed and fingers crossed. Today it has been warm and sunny. We motor-sailed (and sometimes just sailed) north to Mountains have given way to rolling, snowy hills. In Magerøysund reindeer dotted the rocky shores towards Honningsvåg, waiting to swim across to their summer pastures on the island. Apart from an occasional fishing boat we had this huge landscape to ourselves all day. Such a privilege. Crunch time comes tomorrow morning, when I check the engine coolant level. But now, to bed.

Honningsvåg harbour

VARDO TO ARCHANGEL'SK

Here we are in Honningsvåg. Maxine, with her curious Flemish sense of humour, pronounces this "honey fuck".

This morning there was no coolant in the header tank. We have stripped off the head and the gasket looks OK. The exhaust manifold and header tank pressure test well. We conclude that there must be a crack in the head. So it must be sent down to Bodo for close examination. Of course there is an airline strike, so it must do the 1,000 km trip by road. And there is a weekend coming up. And Pasha and Max will be waiting to join the boat in Archangel'sk. And there is a weather system approaching. And our Russian visas are non-negotiable.

In the meantime, we sit. And sit. Gins and tonic assist. Tainui is tied up at the marine engineering wharf, against dreadful black tractor tyres, with an intermittent surge as fishing boats pass by. It is warm and sunny. The snow is melting fast and I expect the hills will soon be green. A 3m baby orca, which has taken up residence in the bay just outside the harbour, is a real novelty for the locals. We are the only sailing boat here, and an object of curiosity for all. Old men sit on the wharf, smoke their pipes and look benign and very ethnic. Neat, drab-coloured cottages extend up the rocky hillsides. Purposeful red and blue fishing boats come and go. King crab, cod and halibut are the stock in trade.

The port is very pretty. If there were not a pressing urgency about getting into Russia, a bloke would have to be pretty relaxed. Maxine is a tower of enthusiastic strength, while I just retreat into the forecabin to sulk and sleep.

THINGS ARE LOOKING UP : JOHN

The weather is gorgeous! The long fjords are serene. Steep mountains etch sharply against skies of deepest blue. We have made a 7 hour trip down to Central Troms to get the engine head pressure tested. The birch forests are greening, wild flowers line the roads and mountain streams rush urgently with the spring melt. Reindeer are getting fat and you could hardly want for a better place to fidget while summer rushes on. Lately Archangel'sk has seemed a long way off, but Nordic Motors has done Tainui proud – there is no crack in the head and our coolant loss can only have been an internal leak through the head gasket. Maybe the trip can continue, after all.

Now for the long, lovely drive back to Honningsvåg, where we can have the engine reassembled.

Off Thursday morning, weather permitting. This engine business has been extremely expensive, Norway prices being what they are. I can only hope our coolant loss will become just a fading memory, like all those other problems which make long distance cruising what it is. Maxine has been splendidly optimistic and good-humoured. Without her sharp wit, enthusiasm and patience this last week would have been truly miserable for this impatient old curmudgeon.

And the baby orca is alive and well, accepting fish scraps from local lads in small boats. How exciting!

In Tromsø we saw Sami people in national dress for the Norway Day parade. But here in Finnmark it is a privilege and a delight to meet Sami like this woman, who have dressed up for no reason other than to go shopping. This lovely woman was flattered and delighted to pose for me.

Sami people are still actively herding and farming reindeer and you have to drive with care to avoid hitting them (reindeer, not the Sami, I mean).

VARDO TO ARCHANGEL'SK

NORTH CAPE : JOHN, 31 MAY

We left Honningsvåg 3 hours ago. Finally. Unbelievably. Now, North Cape is on the port quarter and we have a close fetch across smooth seas with 11kts of wind. For company we have a dozen fulmars, who think foolishly that there are fish to be had here. The Barents Sea horizon is sharp as a knife and our next mark is 20 miles ahead. Maxine, eternal seeker after something better, is complaining that it is too bright. She wants clouds so she can sleep! Really!

Leaving Honningsvåg was a bit sad. We got attached to the place and I worry about our little killer whale. The Professor (our engineer, Mr Odd) finished the engine at 6 and farewelled us affectionately after more than a few beers. I should have been more careful and I am now feeling a bit seedy, but there you go. It is 135 miles to Vardø, where we refuel and clear Norwegian customs. I will let the engine run for a good while, still unable to accept that those coolant problems (like my credit bank balance) might be behind us. From Vardø it is a 500 mile trip along the Kola Peninsula into the White Sea. Weather omens look good for the moment and 4 days might just do it. I think there is a fat blocking high sitting over us, keeping much vile weather well below the Arctic Circle and over mainland Europe.

Like the barometric pressure, our spirits are high.

VARDO TO ARCHANGEL'SK

VARDØ – FRONTIER TOWN : JOHN

A languid 18 hour motor sail in bright midnight sunshine and here we are.

In Vardø harbour Tainui has the only tall mast in a veritable forest of workmanlike varnished fishing boats. Cod, king crab and halibut seem plentiful and this is a busy port. But certainly not for cruising yachts. Russia is right next door and there is new, incomprehensible Russian VHF traffic on the radio. It is a short day sail to Murmansk and 500 miles along the Kola Peninsula coast to Archangel'sk.

We have 2 problems – first, customs and immigration here are closed for the weekend. Second, and vastly more worrying, is that our coolant loss persists despite everything. I am at a complete loss. Re customs formalities, we are going to take the Hurtigruten ferry to Kirkenes at 4 am to do the Norwegian exit paperwork there.

As for the coolant leak I can only say to hell with it – we press on and feed the system with water every 4 hours for the next 3,000 miles of motoring. I just wish that one of the many engineers who have looked at the old Ford engine could have solved the problem for us. We've pressure tested the header tank hot and cold 3 times, pressure tested the exhaust maninfold coolant jacket similarly, taken the cylinder head off for pressure testing and resurfacing and installed a new head gasket. To the satisfaction of all the engineers, the cylinder head itself is fine, as are all those other components. Heavens, we've spent enough time and money on it.

From Central Australia Chris emails me the suggestion that we just stop buggering around and get a new engine. But that's a month's work, involving cutting out the cockpit sole, importing a new donk, fabricating bearers and brackets, finding an adapter for the Borg Warner gearbox and putting it all back together. The Vikings didn't have to do that!

Chris is a committed primary care physician. For many years she has been the other half of my adventure. Like my commitment to the sea, hers to that other ocean – the Central Australian desert – has become an insurmountable challenge for us. After her offspring (and books and art and good music and the call of the pied butcherbird) comes remote indigenous medical practice. Despite our separation she remains constantly in the background, providing acerbic and usually accurate comment on my foibles.

All alone among the fishing boats

LUCIANO BERIO IN VARDØ : JOHN

One of the great delights of cruising is the occurrence of unexpected, intense friendships. While we were refuelling Tainui this morning a young Vardø couple introduced themselves and we fell into conversation. Per has been planning a RIB boat voyage to Arctic Russia. Felicia is a high coloratura soprano with a love for the music of Messaien and Berg. We sat in the sun, tippled and discussed her next performance, Berio's Folk Songs. A lovely young couple whose 15 month old has ice blue eyes and a deep suspicion of bearded old Australian men. (Chris would say that's hardly new or surprising). Talking about Berio on the oil wharf in Vardø – how extraordinary!

I have made similar friendships here with serious birders wearing Wellington boots and expensive binoculars; quiet, weatherbeaten fishermen; professional photographers; Americans doing secret things at the radar installation, and even a rock singer from Oslo. As we talked, the seagulls nested furiously under the eaves of a nearby building.

We took the Hurtigruten ferry down to Kirkenes yesterday to clear customs and immigration down at the Russian road border. With difficulty. The fresh-faced young officials were reluctant to stamp our papers because we were not immediately crossing the road border into Russia. Finally we reached a compromise with them, in which they wrote free text on our papers and passports, with impressive but meaningless stamps superimposed. Vardø is a port of entry supposedly, but there are no officials here. Even the police are only in town every second week.

We stopped for a swim in the dark, icy waters of a pretty lake before hitch-hiking back to Kirkenes for the 5 hour ferry trip back to Vardø. Now it is cloudy and there is a fresh SE wind, right on the nose, so we will wait for tomorrow's northerly and in the meantime do some laundry.

The staff at Vardø Hotel, so hospitable, have allowed us showers, washing, wi-fi and almost permanent installation in their lounge room.

If visiting cruising yachtsmen have problems in Vardø, they should contact lovely Eric at the hotel. He seems able to sort out most things.

I will talk to Chris tonight until my phone card is empty, then cast my Norwegian SIM card into the briny. I hope that is not inviting disaster.

Tight quarters manoeuvering

HOMAGE TO HOLLAND : JOHN

Russia has to thank Holland for teaching Peter the Great about ships and the sea.
My gratitude is directed to Maxine for all that she has done to make this trip possible, and
to Dirk, the love of her life, for all the work he is shortly to be doing in Tainui. But gratitude
also is due to Willem Barentsz, Dutch navigator, cartographer and Arctic explorer, whose
expeditions into these waters in the 16th century made all this business of ours possible.
He is remembered here in Vardø as this picture attests.

Thanks to all of you.

Willem Barentsz

VARDO TO ARCHANGEL'SK

OFF AT LAST! : JOHN, 3 JUNE

We are at sea – finally – beginning a journey which Christine has irreverently called "Biggles does Russia". We slipped out of the glassy harbour this morning, out from under the imposing bum of the Hurtigruten Finnmark, past the splendid graffiti on the waterfront storehouses and into the bay.

I am reminded of a photograph in the Vardø museum of a storm in this same harbour and am grateful that for the twin luxuries of a flexible timetable and good weather forecasts.

The top secret NATO radar installation domes stand bold to starboard. We have a lovely warm and cloudless day, an 8 kt northerly and a steady barometer. Lumpy seas do not prevent one of us downing a palate-cleansing ale. We have about 5 days at sea, touch wood.

Our track will keep us out of Russian territorial waters until the passage from the Barents Sea into the White Sea, but we will report in to Russia Coast Guard as we pass each of their defined coastal waypoints.

Fair winds all!

Storm over Moloene. Foto: Arne Store

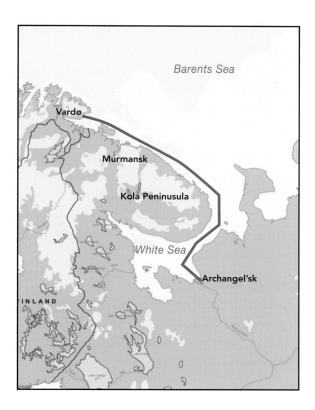

DEPARTURE FROM NORWAY

The fishing port of Vardø would seem the logical spot from which to set off on the 480 mile journey east to Russia from Norway. Unfortunately, customs and immigration functions there are the responsibility of the police department, whose officers are themselves only in Vardø a couple of times a week. It is much easier to clear out at Kirkenes, although this adds some 70 miles to the Archangel'sk rhumb line.

Before you leave Norway you will need to forewarn your Russian shipping agent of your ETA in Archangel'sk. 5 days is a generous allowance for the passage. Your agent will need to have complete details of vessel and crew, which he will provide to the Dvina River Traffic Authority, and to customs and immigration.

MURMANSK

Looking at the charts you would expect Murmansk to be the logical place to clear into Russia. Entry here would break the 500 mile Barents-White Sea journey and save the long detour east to Archangel'sk in the White Sea.

Unfortunately, as the centre of Russia's Arctic naval fleet Murmansk and its bureaucracy have well-earned reputations for soviet obfuscation and pedantry. We have heard numerous stories of innocent vessels beset with administrative problems, delay and even arrest here. Those yachts who have visited Murmansk say it is not worth the effort. In any event, Tainui sailed past the entrance and proceeded direct to the White Sea.

VARDO TO ARCHANGEL'SK

CHILLY BARENTS SEA : JOHN

It has been a slow, uncomfortable passage along the Kola Peninsula from Vardø. Persistent 20 knot headwinds and cold rain, with no room to tack as we are so close to Russia's 12 mile territorial waters boundary.

Passing the approaches to Murmansk we strayed 1/2 mile into Russian waters (the other tack was such a dead loser) and were promptly, politely and firmly asked to remove ourselves by the coast guard VHF operator. Needless to say, we did as he asked. There followed an endless series of radio calls from the Coast Guard, requesting our every imaginable detail apart from shoe size. It was a relief to give them contact details of our shipping agent in Archangel'sk. I hope Yuriy will authenticate and endorse our details for them.

There is a series of Federation defined waypoints along the 12 mile limit of this low, snowy and windswept coast, at which vessels are to report in to Russia Coast Guard. At each of them we have tried repeatedly to check in on channel 16, without success. Two merchant vessels have confirmed our signal clarity and strength, so there is not much more we can do. Even Maxine's lucid, patient Russian language has not milked a response from them.

Yesterday the seas were confused and irregular, forcing poor Tainui to hobby-horse at barely 3-4 knots into the chaos. It must be vile here in winter storms. We have kept the engine idling for warmth and autopilot charging. Today the seas are flat. It is cold and grey but the rain has stopped. So has the crashing, banging and my mal de mer. Maxine is immune to seasickess of course. Among the many seabirds around us are northern fulmars, terns, guillemots. I have been trying to find the glaucous gull, elusive spotters prize of the birders we met in in Vardø. Apart from the birds and 2 passing ships the sea is grey and empty (like the skipper).

Now, on day 3, we are abeam Nokuyev Island. We have good current with us and the wind has backed to the NNE to allow us to sail our course at 6-7 knots over the sea bottom, under main and yankee. Our mysterious fresh water coolant loss continues. In fact it has increased to around 1.3 litres every hour. We have a long and expensive list of all the things it couldn't be, with nothing left to blame. I will dye test the coolant under pressure in Archangel'sk, to see if UV light will point us in any useful direction. Mr Ford (our engine) is himself running smoothly. Tomorrow we turn south into the White Sea approach. It is now ice free. I have my fingers crossed...

THE KOLA PENINSULA

The coast of the Kola Peninsula is featureless and uninviting, comprising snowy hills, tundra and permafrost. We marked a series of emergency anchorages on our charts but without first-hand experience of any of them we leave descriptions to those who follow.

In May and June, thick but patchy fog is common. Cold easterly winds predominate, as was our experience. Summer weather in this part of the Barents Sea is generally similar to that you might encounter en route from North Cape to Svalbard.

Winter is another story. The Kola's coastal waters experience storm force winds and huge seas with appalling regularity - due, we were told, to the juxtaposition of relatively warm water and very cold land. Like the Bering Sea, this is not a place to be sailing in winter! Masochists might try it eventually, but it will not be us.

RUSSIA COAST GUARD REPORTS

We assiduously attempted VHF communication with coast guard stations every 24 hours (in Russian, of course) but not once did we get a response. Exasperated, Maxine called a passing freighter and asked it to relay our position. Immediately, the coast guard's response could be heard loud and clear. The problem was neither with our signal nor our radio language skills.

It is important to remain outside the 12 mile limit along the entire Kola Peninsula. Your movements will be tracked all the way by the naval and Russia Coast Guard radar stations. The point here is that they know all about you but do not enter easily into the sort of two-way communication which might reassure.

Our Archangel'sk shipping agent had given us a list of waypoints at which we were expected to call up Russia Coast Guard and report in. These are listed in the appendix. Assiduously we did so, but our reports were met with silence.

Our second direct radio contact with Russia Coast Guard occurred as we entered the strait separating the Barents and White seas. During a brief moment of inattention to navigation we were set east to within 10 miles of Morzhovets Island. Immediately we were asked by the coast guard to explain our course alteration to the east. One of us explained in her impeccable

VARDO TO ARCHANGEL'SK

INTO THE WHITE SEA : JOHN

We have 18 hours to go until Archangel'sk, gods willing, and should take our pilot on board for the final approach tomorrow at 2pm. The pilot is one of the many bureaucratic burdens we are having to put up with. Reporting in to the navy and the Russian coast guard every 6 hours or so by radio, to operators who have no English and are generally unwilling to respond to our calls, has been wearisome. So we have started calling up passing ships, of which there are very few, and asking them to relay our position reports for us. Each VHF conversation takes about 25 minutes of patient Russian for Maxine, without whom I could certainly not have managed. We can hear the relay ship conversation with the coast guard and it is clear that the latter have heard all that we have said. It has been gloves, beanies, scarves, and 3-layer thermals cold. 2 degrees with wind chill.

The Barents Sea is a lonely grey place and it is good to be out of it, into the White Sea. Exactly the same view from the balcony, but psychologically a relief. It has been a long trip from Norway, made worse for me by low-grade, non-vomiting seasickness. Miss Perfect does not suffer from that vile malady, needless to say. There has been much crashing and banging, of the sort Chris (and I suppose any sane person) would have loathed. Winds on the nose and slow progress.

We have been motor-sailing into fresh headwinds and have had to stop the engine every four hours, wait for it to cool down then top up the coolant chamber. The leak is steady and remains concealed from rational assessment. We have enough coolant to get to Archangel'sk, and I will be glad when we arrive. Now the seas have abated and we are sailing fast with engine on idle for warmth.

Maxine had been terrific on navigation and radio communications and is eternally enthusiastic and cheerful. I am glad she is here. On board she is a bloke, really, and a good one. This afternoon I hove to to reef the main and then flopped into the cockpit for a rest. Up came Max rugged up to the nines, with a bottle of Jacobs Creek chardonnay under one arm and and two glasses in the other hand. A delight, until she started complaining that Tainui's toilet compartments don't have under floor heating.

The channel from the Barents Sea into the White Sea is about 40 miles wide and the tide runs at 2-2.5 knots. So the seas kick up when wind is against current. We have only seen 2 ships in the last 24 hours and our conscientious seabirds seem to have deserted us. Still, in bright sun the seas now sparkle and the whitecaps are dancing. It is good to be here.

Russian that we had both fallen asleep and were heading back onto the rhumb line. As during the previous communication we had to repeat all our details - ship name and port of registry, last port, destination, number of crew, crew names, etc.

We have since been told that communication between the various regional departments of Russia Coast Guard along the Kola Peninsula is poor.

WE ENTER RUSSIA : JOHN, 7 JUNE

After a fast 12 hour sail to the pilot station at the fairway buoy we sat for 3 hours on a glassy sea, waiting for permission to enter the Dvina River. We have just tied up at Archangel'sk customs wharf after a long trip upstream against a 4 knot current. Low wooded shores, tea-coloured water, sand flats and only an occasional commercial ship. Clearly we are the first and only cruising yacht to have arrived this year. A ferry boat blew its siren, people waved and workmen at the customs wharf – a huge shipping wharf with tire fenders 6 feet in diameter – took our lines and welcomed us warmly.

Russia Coast Guard seems finally to have accepted that we exist and they kindly gave us bearings, range and crossover instructions all the way up. The sun is shining and it is warm. As always, it is very strange and exciting to arrive in a new port after time at sea. Even if the travails are not of themselves newsworthy. Maxine warns me to expect major uniformed officialdom for our entrance formalities. In the meantime we wolf down fat omlettes with mushrooms and sip rum with lime juice.

Arrival formalities turned out to be surprisingly uneventful. Certainly easier than Brazil, Cuba or Svalbard I must say. It helps to have a shipping agent here and I am happy to recommend ours, Yury Klyutkin, for future visitors. Customs have granted us permission to keep Tainui in Russian waters for 4 months (longer than my business visa). We are assured that our entrance to the Belomorsk Canal should be hassle-free, although time will tell.

Two further very friendly and helpful contacts here are Alex Galitsky and Sasha Laschenko, local sailors warmly recommended by Barry Woodhouse (UK) and also Vladimir Ivankiv (St Petersburg).

Archangel'sk sits on a flat island among many others in the Dvina River estuary. The trip up from the river mouth is long and tortuous. It is important to run with the 4 knot tide (which we didn't).

As we entered the town harbour at 8 pm, little yachts sailed over to welcome us and guide us to the tiny, ramshackle yacht club. Our new Muscovite crew Pavel (Pasha) and Max (Maxim) took our lines and a familiar contact (Sasha Laschenko) stopped by to welcome us. With little delay we repaired to the bar at the grand, monstrous Meridien Hotel. Then, after an interesting pork with fetta sauce, came deepest sleep.

continued next page

APPROACH TO ARCHANGEL'SK

wpt	64 57.2/040 05.3

This marks the pilot pickup point, near the fairway buoy at the mouth of the North Dvina River. We had splendid weather and fine sailing here, but with a 4 knot ebb outflow this can be a very unpleasant spot in fresh south-westerly winds.

Vessels need permission to enter the North Dvina River. Your agent should already have provided the Port Control Authority with your ETA and ship details, so you will be expected. While in theory all foreign vessels require a pilot to enter the North Dvina River, we had asked our Archangel'sk agent to seek an exemption for us. At the fairway buoy our VHF call to Port Control on channel 16 was met with a prompt, cooperative and informed response. A surprise and a relief. Satisfied with our expertise Port Control allowed us to enter the river without a pilot. Their working channel is VHF 14.

A series of broad and narrow sounds leads into the river proper. The buoys here are widely separated and may be difficult to see. Port Control monitored our progress and provided regular instructions about course alterations, together with the range and bearing to each of the buoys ahead. With very good radar vectoring, the trip across the wide and shallow sounds and into the narrow river was straightforward. From there, the tortuous 30 mile journey upstream to Archangel'sk is a delight, passing through forest interspersed with decrepit little villages, commercial wharves, abandoned factories and enormous log rafts.

<u>Caution</u>: the North Dvina River ebbs at up to 4 knots. The journey up-river will be very slow unless you use the tide.

Trawlers on the Dvina River

ARCHANGEL'SK

from previous page

The trip up river took us through forest, godown villages, industrial estates and log rafts. Endless crossover leads, back transits and unidentifiable navigation marks. After Poland, Lithuania and Latvia the parade of crumbling, deserted factories and rusty, purposeful vessels of all sizes and shapes was not unfamiliar and quite lovely. The contrast with Scandinavian neatness and chocolate box photogenicity is absurd. Now it is warm (24 degrees in the cabin), calm and sunny, with bumble bees, birdsong, flowers and rich smells (clearly we have grown used to those in Tainui's cabin).

Archangel'sk Yacht Club is a collection of small boats in a tiny estuary in town. Some purposeful quarter tonners; ambitious, coarse-welded steel 22 footers; indescribable plywood creations; a huge and very desirable two storey timber houseboat, and two small, rusty steamers. Cheerful sailors stop by to chat. We seem to be something of a talking point.

JOHN : PASHA

Notable mention must be made also of my second, invaluable internet contact. Paul (Pasha) Novojeeloff also responded to my crew seeker website post. An IT expert in Moscow, Pasha became infected with enthusiasm for Tainui's journey, even though he would not be free to spend more than a short time aboard. He rose to various administrative challenges posed by our trip - chart acquisition, Russian VHF transmitter purchase, research on river depths and air clearance levels - with enthusiasm.

Maxine and Pasha got together in Moscow and established a firm friendship, before I had met either of them. Pasha joined Tainui for a fortnight in Archangel'sk with his friend Maxim and has since become one of Tainui's regular crew recidivists.

On the Belomor Canal Pasha brought to Tainui his much-valued IT skills, enthusiasm, curiosity, practical skills, boatmanship and fun. He can steer for hours in lumpy seas and does not get tired. He and Maxine made a good pair, although in bad weather their endless cockpit laughter and chatter in Cyrillic made it difficult for the skipper to vomit in peace down below.

How fortunate I have been to have had Maxine and Pasha on board. I know they will sail in Tainui again. They will always be welcome.

Pasha

ARCHANGEL'SK

Telephone coverage starts only well into the North Dvina delta so that while you are waiting at the fairway buoy for permission to enter the North Dvina River, you will not be able to contact your shipping agent.

Customs and immigration formalities are conducted at Economiya Wharf 64 42.43/040 31.2 and phone contact with your agent can be made here, on arrival.

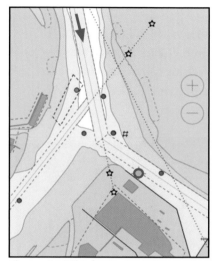
Ekonomiya Wharf

Approaching the customs wharf

Having completed formalities at Economiya it is another 2 hours up river to the city itself.

With about 350,000 inhabitants (2013), Archangel'sk lies 1,000 km north-east of Moscow. It has international flight connections and a rail line via Yaroslavl to Moscow. A good city for foreign crew changes.

The city was founded by decree of Ivan the Terrible in 1584, soon after which British and Dutch vessels had established active trade links. The Dutch have continued to trade actively here. In the 17th century up to 50 Dutch ships were visiting Archangel'sk annually. Furs and timber were the major trading commodity.

Despite being ice-bound in winter, Archangel'sk was Russia's major port until the founding of St Petersburg at the beginning of the 18th century. Now, with ice-breaker support, Archangel'sk is open for commercial shipping all year round. It is a major port for export of timber.

Our stay at Sailing Centre Nord was organised by Alex Galitsky. We tied comfortably to the outside apron of this quaint little boat club but with only 2.2 m of water at low tide we settled gently into soft mud. There are no facilities here but there is a large, idiosyncratic post-soviet hotel nearby, comfortable enough and with a restaurant of sorts. It is a short taxi ride across the bridge to the city.

ARCHANGEL'SK

JOHN

Sasha Laschenko stopped by again. A local construction engineer, Sasha sailed with Barry Woodhouse in Aenigma in 2000. Today he and his wife Anna have organised for us a tour of architectural sites in Archangel'sk. Tomorow we will get diesel, food, heaps of antifreeze concentrate and (most importantly) vodka. We hope to leave for the world-heritage listed Solovetskiy Islands on the top of the tide on Monday. It is a 24 hour trip across the White Sea. Back into the freeze but I am looking forward to it.

On board, the interpersonal dynamics are interesting. The boys, as we call them, are enthusiastic, wide-eyed, easygoing and adaptable. They are both IT experts from Moscow. Shaven-headed Maxim has a 35 foot yacht. He is quiet and loves his cognac. Pasha is less experienced but smart as paint and eager to learn. They have been invaluable contacts in Russia, organising charts, Russian VHF radios and the like.

Crew outside Archangel'sk Yacht Club

It shouldn't be too crowded on board, once we get going. Maxine and Pasha speak English but Max, the sailor, has almost none. So conversations are usually in loud Russian with much laughter and gesticulation meaningless to me, or in English, when Maxim is totally left out. It wouldn't work on a Hobart race but here, with goodwill, it is much fun.

Contact details

Sailing Centre Nord
social network contact:
http://vkontakte.ru/club3341028
phone: +7 818 223 3225

Shallow drafted vessels may be able to stay at Archangel'sk River Yacht club (club 'Vodnik'). This club has an active racing program for smaller yachts (quarter tonners) and for the last 30 years has held an annual regatta from Archangel'sk to Solovetskiy.

http://vk.com/club6054642

All engineering services are available in Archangel'sk, but there are few bespoke facilities for larger cruising yachts.

Much of historical Archangel'sk was destroyed during the Bolshevik revolution but there are interesting sites worth visiting. Of these, the outstanding outdoor Ethnographic Museum [www.korely.ru] is not to be missed.

Ethnographic museum

COOLANT PROBLEM SOLVED?? : JOHN

What a morning. Gorgeously warm and sunny, filled with purpose as we prepare for the next bit.

Pasha threw himself into our engine problem with quiet confidence. He took out the one section of copper pipe in the external coolant circuit which I have not yet examined closely (but had every intention of doing!). It is an inaccessible length of thick-walled copper tubing with no sign of corrosion or damage but the only segment outside the engine capable of undetected leak. Lo and behold, he found a tiny pinhole which may be the cause of all our problems. If that is the case, the loss would be very difficult to detect because of the piping anatomy.

Anyway, splendid Pasha cleaned, acid-washed and soldered the suspicious section and covered it with a length of clamped coolant hose. All this was done to a wonderful recording of Rachmaninov's Vespers, which the boys hummed along to. Maxine was off having a manicure. I sat in the cockpit, sipping coffee and enjoying the rare pleasure allowing someone competent to do the work.

Across the river the golden domes of Archangel'sk Cathedral glowed in the sun and the carillon pealed for Sunday service. With Rachmaninov at full volume and good coffee I felt very mellow, as Ian would say.

Now the system has been reassembled and we are ready for a beer. The final test will not come until we have motored for 8 hours. If the system still leaks, I will be no more disappointed than on each of the last 4 occasions when we supposedly found and fixed the problem.

Archangel'sk Marina Nord

SOLOVETSKIY ISLANDS

JOHN : SOLOVETSKIY : JOHN, 11-12 JUNE

I will not forget this place.

We arrived at 2 am after a very uncomfortable reach in 25-30kt northerly winds. Alex Galitsky had warned us about the seas off the northern coast of the island and he was not wrong. Poor Max was incapacitated by seasickness, this author renewed his acquaintance with his long-cherished personal bucket on several occasions, while Maxine and Pasha, loathsome persons both, were totally immune and sang songs, chatted cheerfully and ate. We had the staysail and 2 reefs in the main. Tying in the second reef I filled both seaboots with the iciest White Sea water, while sleet and hailstones abraded my face.

In smooth water we crept into the harbour and ogled at the huge monastic installation at the head. We tied up at a vacant spot on the commercial jetty and collapsed into bed. Our plans for 12 uninterrupted hours were rudely interrupted at 7.30, when the wharf security guard told us we had to move immediately to another wharf. We set off, shivering and half asleep.

30 metres to the left of our inbound track we took the ground, as they say. A hard, jarring event of the kind that skippers hate. There was a 1 metre patch protected by a cardinal mark which was not there (65 01.67/035 41.11). We got off unaided, fortunately, and proceeded to the new berth and tied up. Again we collapsed into bed.

30 minutes later the port captain arrived and told us that berthing at this wharf was prohibited, and that we must anchor off. Out of bed again, we did his bidding. So here we are, and I am off to bed. At least the weather has improved, my mood likewise.

After moving Tainui 4 times at the behest of the port authorities we seem finally to have found a permanent spot, rafted alongside a working tug in the outer harbour. After an acceptable omlette with cheese and Russian spam (luncheon meat or, as Ian calls it, "eyelids, lips and arseholes") we all collapsed into our own private comas.

Tainui came alive again at 7 pm. All of us except Max (still sick after that terrible trip here) set off exploring the monastery.

This quiet, brooding place stands behind quite unbelievable masonry ramparts. Orginally the centre of a huge monastic state in the 15th century, its history was severly tainted when Stalin established one of the first gulag prisons here in 1923. The hardships suffered by the prisoners were almost unimaginable. I stood spellbound in St Nikolaus Cathedral as the rich bass voices of monks in harmony sang evening service.

SOLOVETSKIY ISLANDS

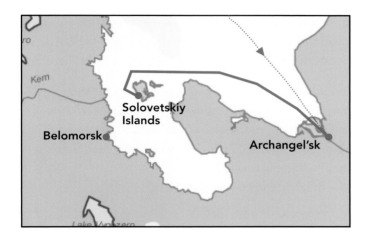

SOLOVETSKIY APPROACH

wpt   65 01.4/035 38.4

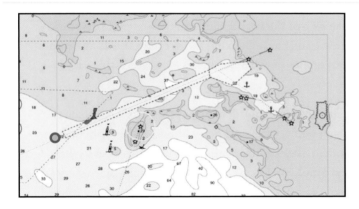

SOLOVETSKIY WHARF

wpt   65 01.8/035 41.4

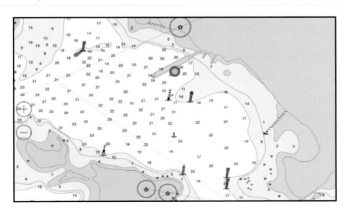

SOLOVETSKIY ISLANDS

SOLOVETSKIY : JOHN

Today it is sunny and Max is recovering slowly. I think cognac deficiency and gastritis are contributing to his malaise. Omeprazole, Aludrox and Kwells have been added to his rehydration solution, in anticipation of today's trip down to Belomorsk, 35 miles SW of here.

No sailor passing should miss the opportunity to visit this enchanting place. My brief, obvious advice to yachts entering Solovetskiy Harbour is to follow the leads and back leads closely on final entrance. There is a shoal patch (1m) to the west of the channel which should have a cardinal mark on it but doesn't. We grounded hard on this because of my inattention. In protected waters after the shouting and tumult die I get lazy.
That is how we ran aground on the Statue of Liberty in New York Harbour!
Now there's a confession.

SOLOVETSKIY ARRIVAL : PASHA

We came to the Solovetskiy Islands and entering Blagopoluchnaya (Happy or Well-being) Bay. It's 3 AM, but as light as a cloudy day. Visibility is limited only by the fog. Gale is left behind. Sea is still rough on the northern side of the island, but here the water is smooth as a mirror, and there is no wind at all. Narrow and curved channel with rocky shoals along the edges is also behind. And great walls and domes of the Solovetskiy Monastery, this sacred place Russia, are slowly rising from the fog.

Oh, these walls could tell a lot. About builders, who hand-laid huge stones in the 14th century. About the spiritual leaders of the Russian people, who lived here. About the heroism of monks who defended the monastery against attack of Norwegian and English fleet in the 18th century. About human injustice and cruelty in the 20th century, when the monastery was turned into a political prison and place of the massacre of people wanting to be truly free. We have to see it all and hear, but not today.

Now we want just to sleep. The passage was not easy. We departed from Arkhangel'sk on evening according tide, then engine troubleshooting took half a night, then the gale did not give us good sleeping. So quickly going to free space at the high concrete wharf. All around is quiet, no person, no sound, only the silent stones of the monastery are watching us.

Finally going to bed. Certainly not: After half an hour I woke to the sound of screams from the wharf. There was local guard. He had slept our arrival and mooring, and now has developed rigorous activity. Started with threats and promises the arrival of commercial vessel, to which this place belong, and finished whining that he is responsible for this place and he would be fired if his boss see us. OK, we understood that there will not be able to sleep peacefully. Going elsewhere.

continued next page

From the mouth of the North Dvina River it is about 135 miles across the White Sea to Belomorsk, with the Solovetskiy Islands lying conveniently en route.

After departure from Archangel'sk into the White Sea, in theory you leave Russian territory 12 miles off the mouth of the North Dvina River, but this doesn't seem to pose significant bureaucratic problems. Having finalised departure formalities, it remains for you to obtain permission to depart from the Archangel'sk port captain, and to notify the Belomorsk captain of your ETA at the mouth of the Belomor Canal. Your Archangel'sk shipping agent will organise this for you. His liaison with the captain of the canal in Belomorsk is most important - you must not arrive unexpected.

These jewels lie in the western half of the White Sea. The major attraction is the Saviour-Transfiguration Solovetskiy monastery, which has well-deserved World Heritage status. Founded in 1436, its imposing kremlin has massive ramparts enclosing various fine monastic buildings.

More information :

http://welcome.solovky.ru/new/
http://solovki-monastyr.ru/

SOLOVETSKIY ISLANDS

from previous page

I must say that the bay is quite shallow and rocky, Tainui's draft does not allow big choice of moorings. We have to go to another berth. There owner is declared immediately after docking with the same arguments - you can not stay here, commercial vessel is coming, mooring is prohibited for private vessels and so on. Striking contrast, such a magical place, and such a bureaucratic people. But we want to sleep, there is no way to argue and swear, so we are leaving to anchor.

Finally, all our problems were solved. We only had to sleep - and everything went fine. We finally found a place to tie up, hospitable people, sweet little hotel in an old wooden house, delicious cuisine, beautiful views and, of course, the history of these places. But this is a topic for another story.

Regardless of your nationality, language and religion this is a place worthy of your visit. To avoid problems, you just need to pre-arrange a mooring with the help of your agent or friends, and nothing will prevent you to enjoy the beauty of northern nature and unique historic site.

Once the centre of a powerful Orthodox city state, Solovetskiy withstood repeated attacks on its physical integrity and independence until the monastery was closed down during the Bolshevik revolution. In 1923 its history entered a shameful period when, under Lenin's orders, the entire kremlin converted into a gulag, probably Russia's first. Inmates provided forced labour for the construction of the Belomor Canal and up to 100,000 men died during the 4 year construction period.

The prison was closed in 1939 and the kremlin housed a naval training school until 1957. In 1990, religious activities were reinstated and 2 years later UNESCO bestowed world heritage status on the site.

About 900 people live on the islands permanently. There is a small shop, an even smaller pharmacy, a rudimentary hospital and comfortable little bed sits. Rental bicycles are available. In summer there are air and sea connections (expensive) with Belomorsk, Kem, Archangel'sk and Moscow.

Finding dockage in the harbour is a haphazard business. We first tied up behind a fishing boat on the left hand side of the basin but were asked to move. Indeed it took three relocations before we and the harbour authorities were finally satisfied about our location.

Note that buoyage in the harbour may be incomplete. During our visit one cardinal mark was missing and we sustained a solid but fortunately harmless grounding.

SOLOVETSKIY ISLANDS

BELOMOR CANAL

INTO BELOMOR CANAL : JOHN, 13 JUNE

The approach channel into Belomorsk is well marked. We called port control at the fairway buoy and were astonished to be told that the sea lock was open and that we should enter directly, port side to. Amazed and delighted, we did as we were told.

In half an hour, we were in the canal, tied up in warm glassy calm. There was no excuse for sobriety.

When the port authorities came down to Tainui, formalities were minimal. Heavens, there had been enough of them in the preceeding 8 months! They knew all about us and just wanted confirmation that we had adequate charts and inland waterways VHF radio capacity.

Poor Max had had continuing abdominal pain and vomiting since our rough passage across to Solovetskiy and it was clear to all that he needed medical assessment - electrolytes and abdominal ultrasound, I thought. Pasha and I took him to Belomorsk Hospital where he was kept for observation. They questioned cholecystitis although I did not think he had a "surgical abdomen", as they say. Anyway, his holiday time was up and we took sad farewells and left him at the hospital, from where he will take the train back to Moscow.

The following day, we set off on our next first step. We seem to have had so many first steps!

Maxim

Pasha

BELOMORSK

64 30.6/034 48.5
km 1333

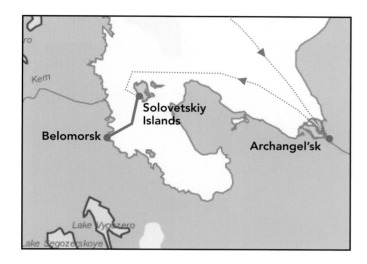

It is 35 miles down to Belomorsk from the Solovetskiy group and there are numerous small islands to avoid en route. As previously noted, paper charts are needed for this leg. The final approach to Belomorsk is reasonably straightforward.
Note that some lateral and cardinal marks may be missing however, so that careful navigation is important to avoid shoals outside the channel.

Approaching the Belomor entrance lock

BELOMOR CANAL

BELOMOR CANAL : JOHN, 14-16 JUNE

We are all alone here, creeping over glassy water between mysterious, dark and densely forested shores. Such are the healing powers of nature given half a chance - the sub-arctic coniferous here looks absolutely virgin. This is taiga - evergreen boreal forest.

The Stalin White Sea Canal, as it was originally named, represented a triumphant pinnacle of Stalin's First Five Year Plan. In the early 1930's it was just a giant construction site. It is almost impossible to imagine the noise, the chaos, the frantic activity here then. Nor the brutality suffered, the desperation, degradation and starvation experienced. 100,000 gulag workers built the canal in just a year and a half and between 10 and 25% of them died in the process. Anne Applebaum's book [Gulag: A History of the Soviet Camps, London: Penguin 2003] tells you more than you need to know about the horrors of the project. For hours at a time we sat in silence in the cockpit contemplating the cruelty, stupidity and folly of humankind.

BELOMOR CANAL

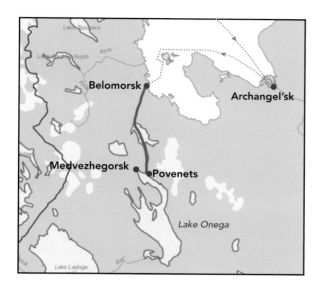

Belomorsk is the gateway to the inland waterways. Founded in 1938 to facilitate construction of the Belomor Canal, it has little to offer visiting yachts other than clearance into the inland waterways.

For further information – http://www.belomorsk-mo.ru/

The canal captain is Konstantin Timonin, who should have been forewarned of your arrival by your Archangel'sk shipping agent. His officials will require proof of adequate paper charts, crew competence in Russian language, marine accreditation, safety equipment and a VHF transmitter with Russian inland channels. We later met Captain Timonin and found him professional, competent and obliging.

One requirement - the need for a Russian inland waterways certificate of competence - may require resolution through sensitive negotiation. We had armloads of international licenses (RYA, ICC, CEVNI and two commercial masters tickets) but these were not acceptable. One of our crew had a time-expired Russian certificate of competence, which was accepted by the authorities.

Construction of the canal

BELOMOR CANAL

Inspection pier

First bridge after inspection pier

On passing through the sea lock at Belomorsk you will be instructed to lie alongside the concrete wharf before the bridge, just past km mark 1333. Here canal officials will visit to complete formalities. You are effectively trapped between the sea lock and the opening bridge at their pleasure, until these are completed. Our flares, certificates of competence, paper chart folios and Russian VHF radio were checked, but the process was not complicated.

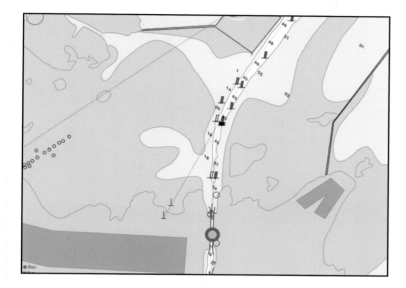

The canal is about 140 miles long, following a number of rivers and crossing 4 lakes. There are 19 locks - 12 ascending from Belomorsk and 7 descending to Lake Onega at the Povenets Ladder.

The minimum depth in the canal is just over 3.5 metres and the bottom usually (but not always) soft mud. Among the many islets and promontories along the way, there are many opportunities for peaceful anchorage. Ours, described on the following page, were secure, pretty and at convenient locations en route. Allow 3 days for a comfortable transit, assuming no enforced delays due to weather.

BELOMOR CANAL

OSTROVA NOSYREVA

wpt	64 06/34 10
km	1275

The anchorage here is behind two islands, good holding, bottom mixed sand and rock.

LOCK 9 SOUTH

wpt	63 10.5/034 52.4
km	1158

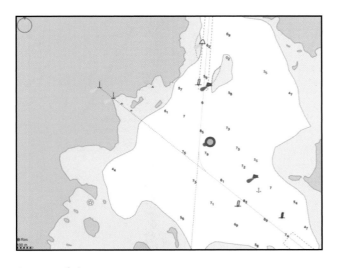

A peaceful spot.

LAKE ONEGA

MUSIC ON BOARD : MAXINE

The first sign of John's love for music was his ad on the internet crewing site, in which he listed a few of his favourite composers crew would be exposed to on board. Classical music was a big thing in Tainui. I didn't mind this at at all, as I have little idea about popular music.

In Tainui there is evidence everywhere that a music lover is in charge. Loudspeakers are installed in every cabin. John had more than 5000 pieces of music on his telephone.

After we set off from Tromsø on our first sail, John handed me his headphones and his iPhone before he went below for a power nap. I was left alone in the cockpit with Berlioz in my ears and the snowy Norwegian mountains all around me.

Every day John would ask us which music we wanted to listen to. Of course not wanting to listen to anything was not an option - then John would sulk, put on his headphones and listen anyway.

The best music gadget on board was the portable Bose speaker. Sailing and waltzing on deck in the evening sun on Lake Onega was just magical.

Lake Onega

LAKE ONEGA

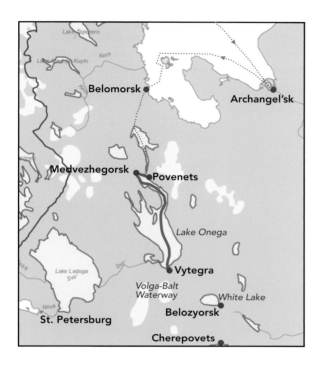

The second largest lake in Europe, Lake Onega contains over 1500 islands and is fed by some 50 rivers draining a catchment of 50,000 sq km.

It is approximately 130 miles from the Belomor Canal exit across Lake Onega, south to Vytegra and the entrance to the Volga-Balt canal system. 3 or 4 days should be allowed for the transit, including stops at Devils Nose and Kizhi. The shores are richly forested and anchorage can be found at a number of places along the eastern shore depending on wind direction (eg at wpt 61 58.9/ 035 40.9 – good holding in 28' of water). The waters are generally clean and clear, and we filled our tanks directly from the lake.

Lake Onega has a shallow and uneven bottom (30-120m) and a reputation for changeable weather with short, steep seas. When you reach the last White Sea locks (the 7 lock Povonets Ladder) you may wish to wait for favourable conditions for the 130 mile trip to Vytegra.

In bad weather it is recommended that vessels delay entry into the Povonets Ladder, as there is no immediate all-weather anchorage after the exit. There is good holding above the ladder at 62 52.7/034 51.4 before the first lock.

Below the ladder there is reasonable anchorage to be had immediately outside the last Belomorsk lock inside the seawall, in to about 30 feet of water 62 49.6/034 50.4
Caution - in places the bottom is foul.

There are extensive shoals immediately to the south of the Belomor Canal but the channel into the lake is well marked and lit. Local vessels cut between the islands to the west of the channel but we advise yachts planning a stopover in Medvezhegorsk to follow the marked route until the final south cardinal mark at wpt 62 45.9/034 53.1 before turning west and then back to the north. On Lake Onega there are no major hazards thereafter, except on approach to Kizhi.

LAKE ONEGA

POVENETS

This is a small hamlet. There is bus connection with Medvezhegorsk and Petrozavodsk, but almost no facilities. The bay is open to the south. From the Belomor Canal exit, shallow draft vessels can turn right immediately, with depths around 4 metres, to proceed north into Povonets Bay. There is a marked channel with transit leads on the shore ahead.

POVONETS SEAWALL ANCHORAGE

wpt   62 49.6/034 50.4
km   1115

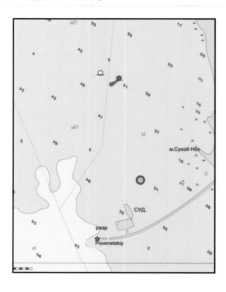

POVONETS VILLAGE WHARF

wpt   62 50.3/034 49.5

MEDVEZHEGORSK

We chose to bypass Povonets and backtrack 20 miles north to Medvezhegorsk because of the certainty of transport connections and basic facilities available there. The harbour is snug, easy of approach and provides secure anchorage.

The shortcut mentioned above is used by local vessels, but the shoals are not well charted or buoyed. It is safer to continue south in the marked channel from Povonetskiy Light before turning west and then north round the last cardinal mark mentioned above. Minimum depths on this route exceed 3.5 metres.

Note that at the time of writing Medvezhegorsk remains a closed port. The canal captain kindly granted us permission to enter and vessels wishing to stop here are advised to contact him before exiting the Belomorsk locks.

The port captain charged us 1,600 roubles per night, which to our mind was very much an unofficial if not arbitrary sum. In any event it was ridiculously high. Basic facilities and supplies are available. Fuel, food, alcohol, laundry - can be purchased in town. For crew changes there is a bus to Petrozavodsk, which has flight connections with Moscow and St Petersburg.

information: http://www.avtovokzaly.ru/avtobus/medvezhegorsk-petrozavodsk/

LAKE ONEGA

MEDVEZHEGORSK : JOHN, 16-19 JUNE

At the end of the Belomor Canal we came out of lock number 19 at 8 pm and cracked a bottle of chardonnic. Tired but happy.

From here the trip across Lake Onega to Vytegra is about 130 miles and this bit of water has a reputation for changeable weather with short steep seas. Although we are exhilarated at getting here we are tired and the wind is 20 knots right on the nose.

So we have crept into Medvezhegorsk to tipple and to sleep. Tied up at a disused shipping wharf we have the skeletal remains of huge soviet cranes hanging over us. We are the only living things in this tiny harbour. I embrace the feeling of isolation. A heavily tatooed chap with his chatty girlfriend and a labrador pup stopped by to see what and who we were. They wanted to see what the big white stick was, in the harbour. Tainui is the first yacht they had ever seen. The town itself is 5 km away and we will explore tomorrow. We will stay here until the weather improves. Sadly, our wonderful Pasha leaves us here and we have a few days to manage till Dirk arrives.

Before we collapsed into our bunks a huge thunderstorm passed over us. Fireworks but little wind. In any case this is a snug spot.

Medvezhegorsk images

LAKE ONEGA

A PROFOUNDLY MOVING PLACE : JOHN

Today Konstantin took us to visit the site of one of the region's blackest moments. In 1938 Stalin slaughtered more than 11,000 enemies of the state – political prisoners incarcerated on Solovetskiy Island in the 1930s. Why they were brought across to a lonely forest between Mevezhegorsk and Povenets to die, no one seems to know. But that is where they ended their miserable lives. I know there are many other such holy places around Europe and the world, but the power of this one overwhelmed me.

Lush pine woodland has been transformed into the saddest and most touching of memorials. In random fashion among the trees stand hundreds, perhaps thousands of posts and simple wooden crosses. Each is adorned with a photograph of one of the prisoners. Small beds of flowers are lovingly tendered by local people.

Installed and maintained by families of the deceased, these silent, scattered memorials to a shameful past spread endlessly into the forest in all directions. They bring tears to one's eyes. The power is in the absolute simplicity of it all. There are no grand headstones, no broad sweeping approach drive, no architecture. Those would be otiose.

SANDARMOKH MEMORIAL SITE

This open air memorial to the deaths of gulag workers who constructed Stalin's Belomor Canal is a 20 minute taxi ride from town and should not be missed.

information: http://en.wikipedia.org/wiki/Sandarmokh

KIZHI

A detour to visit this world heritage-listed monastery at Kizhi is highly recommended. Careful navigation is required through the islands and shoals leading to the site but the route is well-marked.Both the NW and SE channels have minimum depths in excess of 3 metres.

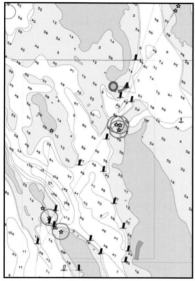

Kizhi approach

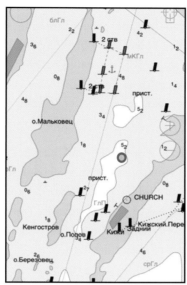

Kizhi wharf

LAKE ONEGA

ON GETTING OLD : JOHN, 20 JUNE

We anchored last night behind an island in a gorgeous calm spot, on the eastern shore of Lake Onega. Cuckoos called from the forest and the breeze was warm.

My battle with gravity and general senescence is relentless. Nouns depart, synovium disintegrates, hair gets thinner. Today is my birthday and I did not need reminding of the process. But I was. I will tell you how I celebrated it. Over calm seas we sailed south down the lake to the mouth of the Vytegra River. For my birthday I cooked pancakes on the way, took my obligatory power nap then unblocked a toilet. Meanwhile Maxine filled the tanks with pristine Onega lake water.

Then it was time for a celebratory tipple. The only alcohol we had on board was a bottle of cognac poor Max left behind when we took him to hospital in Belomorsk. That'd go very well with orange Tang, I thought. Stupid old man. I found a canister of the orange powder mix (ca 1996) and we drank to the success of Tainui's voyage. The mix was a bit gluggy, and after we were half way through I realised that I had used Metamucil, not Tang, with the cognac. Very stupid old man, indeed. Young readers take note.

The south end of Lake Onega is visited by a few yachts each year, all of them either coming from, or going to St Petersburg. But Vytegra is the beginning of the route east to the Volga. Altogether another story. No cruising yachts come this way. We are at the beginning of the real journey.

Pancakes while filling the water tanks

DEVILS' NOSE

wpt	61 40.9/036 00.9

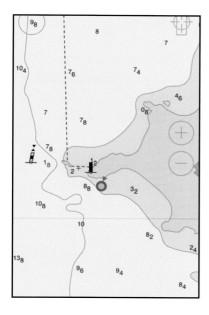

The 1,200 petroglyphs on the eastern shore of Lake Onega date back to 4th–2nd millennia BC. Discovered in 1848, they spread along a 20 km area of coastline in the vicinity of Besov Nos. The rock engravings depict animals, boats and various geometrical designs.

In calm weather you can anchor to the south of the headland. There are petroglyphs here, just above the waterline near the centre of the headland, a short dinghy ride away.

OTHER SIGHTS

Notable among the many other historical monuments scattered around the lake is the 14th century Svyat-Uspensky monastery on Cape Murom, on the eastern shore of the lake.

VYTEGRA TO WHITE LAKE

VYTEGRA : JOHN, 21–23 JUNE

At the southern end of Lake Onega we join the Volga-Balt canal system. To the west lie St Petersburg and the Baltic Sea, while on the eastern shore the Vytegra River leads to locks through White Lake and south east to the Volga.

Excellent transit leads take us though shoals into a narrow, lovely river in company with impossibly long, 5,000 ton ships. 5 miles later we burst out of the forest into Vytegra's small, busy and colourful roadhead. There are huge piles of freshly milled pine logs on both sides and the resinous smells are heady. Cranes, barges, tugs and odd-looking small vessels adorn the shores. No McDonalds, no neon lights, no marinas, no yacht masts.

Now Tainui is tied up about 500 m short of the first lock, next to two huge floating cranes. This is all a bit overwhelming. In the best possible way. Full bottles of melatonin and Prozac languish unopened in my toiletry bag and I am sleeping well. Not speedy, just engaged and productive. It is Maxine's birthday.

The crane owner and Maxine are in the middle of a protracted negotiation, of the kind which reaffirms once again how impossible this trip would be without a sailor who is a lawyer, who speaks Russian, who knows the way to achieve appropriate ends with Russian officials, and who is infinitely patient.

The crane people have two worries - indemnity, which we have offered to provide them with, and a general concern that they will be changing the measured length of Tainui when the mast is on deck and then we will not have correct measurement papers. I mean, really!

I have assembled the cross frames to support the mast while endless negotiations continue in Cyrillic. Once again I have to relinquish control over proceedings. I am learning to do this with grace, and I retire to a small therapeutic cognac. The dialogue is fascinating to watch and listen to, and Maxine's negotiating skills are masterful. Russians soon learn that they are talking with a professional, not a bimbo, and I love the way their demeanour changes as they do so.

And the next day....

Sipping coffee in the cockpit this morning I feel like a drugged patient in a hospital bed, the morning after having had a leg amputated. I keep looking in disbelief for the missing limb. Our mast lies inelegantly in three robust cross braces above the deck, dripping with stays, shrouds and miscellaneous lines. It is comfortable and so are we, although things just don't feel quite right.

APPROACH TO VYTEGRA RIVER

wpt   61 06.7 / 036 15.2

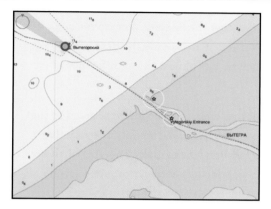

Permission to proceed from the fairway buoy must be obtained from Vytegra Port Authority (VHF channel 5). The river mouth is well buoyed and lit, with good transit leads. Expect dredging activity on both sides of the channel. There is a steady stream of commercial vessels and the river is tortuous and narrow, so that constant vigilance is necessary.

It is some 7 miles upstream to Vytegra and the journey is pleasant. Reeded shores intersperse with thick deciduous forest which come as a welcome surprise after the expanse of Lake Onega.

VYTEGRA

wpt   61 01.2/036 25.2
km   880 km

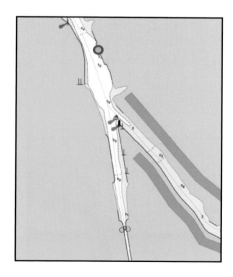

Vytegra (pop 10,000) is a pretty river port, with a continuous stream of commercial traffic passing between Lake Onega and the Volga. 6 locks ascend from here to the highest point on the entire waterway. Yachts can lie comfortably alongside concrete wharves on the northern

VYTEGRA TO WHITE LAKE

VYTEGRA, 22 JUNE : MAXINE

This is perhaps the most important date in modern Russian history. On that day in 1941, Nazi Germany invaded Russia. For Russians it was on this day that the Second World War began. As it happens, June 22nd is also my birthday. Whenever Russians ask me the date of my birthday, they usually fall silent. then ask me solemnly whether I know the significance of 22 June.

But ever since our trip through Russia, in my mind another event will be forever linked to that date. Because on 22 June, in Vytegra, our mast was lowered. Sod's law meant of course that this exhausting event would take place on my birthday. John was the lucky one - his birthday had been two days earlier and we celebrated that with wonderful weather, gorgeous sailing, pancakes and lots of cognac cocktails. I would have no such celebration and, to make matters worse, my partner Dirk was not going to be with me (his visa had not arrived in time).

We knew that the mast would be taken out by an industrial crane. The question was not whether the boat would be damaged but how much the damage was going to be. Then there was so much preparatory work that needed doing. Well, mostly by John. My job was making sure that everyone involved knew exactly what needed doing and when, and to make sure that all those men listened.

On the big day, John woke me early with coffee and a sandwich (which he proceeded to eat himself when I wasn't quick enough) and quasi-casually mentioned that he had not slept the whole night. Stress levels were high and we had not even started.

Suffice to say it was a long and worrying day indeed. My phone rang incessantly with well-wishers, many of whom I had to fob off until the next day. But in the end the mast was horizontally cradled above the deck. Evening was party time. Tired but endlessly relieved that the operation had been successful, we retired to the only decent restaurant in Vytegra. It had not yet been issued with an alcohol license but because it was my birthday the staff kindly went shopping for me to get us a bottle of wine.

That was a day we won't forget.

side of the river, before a shallow, blind channel which leads off to the town centre on the left. The first of the Vytegra locks can be seen just beyond this channel. Mosquitoes are a problem on the riverfront. The town, a short taxi ride away, has banks (Sberbank, Ul. Lenina 78), supermarkets (eg at Arkhangelski Trakt 4), fuel outlets and a couple of reasonable restaurants. Other than general provisioning however, there are no facilities for yachts. General engineering work and basic mechanical repairs can probably be organised. For vessels with height clearance in excess of 14 metres, this is the place to remove your mast (see insert).

There is no airport in the vicinity. There are bus services to Cheropovets and Vologda, not recommended for changes of crew. The bus rides are long.

General information:

http://vytegra.munrus.ru/in/md/main

Restaurant contact details
www.watergaterestaurant.ru
www.wardenclyffehotel.ru/restaurant/

VYTEGRA TO WHITE LAKE

VYTEGRA CONT. : JOHN

I had hoped Vladimir Putin would finish building higher bridges on the Volga-Balt Canal in anticipation of our passage but it was not to be. So down came our 20m mast and we now motor for 2,000 miles to Rostov-on-Don with our mast protruding fore and aft. I will need to drive carefully.

Yesterday was long, tiring and worrying, although the whole process went smoothly in the end. Anatoly drove Crane Number 83, a floating behemoth more than capable of lifting our whole boat. The iron slug above the hook weighed more than a ton and I had been concerned that Anatoly and Crane Number 83 might lack the necessary surgical delicacy. The crane clutch was an impetuous piece of machinery and the mast moved in 3 foot snatches. Wake from passing shipping had us rolling at very inopportune times. But we managed.

Today we are doing bugger all. Captain's orders. Tomorrow we're off into the first lock, en route Cherepovits to collect Maxine's adored man for the next bit. Soon we will join the Volga River and I am excited.

I have contact details for Anatoly and Crane Number 83, for those who follow us in future years.

Into the Vytegra locks

VYTEGRA TO WHITE LAKE

VOLGA-BALT WATERWAY : JOHN

It is a long climb from Vytegra. The locks here are industrial in size and purpose. The feeling of private privilege we felt in the Belomorsk Canal has gone, replaced by a realisation that we are now only a tiny, irritating part of a huge commercial process. One that has been going on for millenia.

The locks are very efficiently run. VHF instructions are clear (if incomprehensible) and concise (if incomprehensible). We share locks with huge vessels. At the top we join the parade of ships carrying lumber, gas and other bulk loads between St Petersburg and the Volga.

We follow Marshall Zhukov out of the last lock, into the basin where ghostly ships lie at anchor, waiting for their turn to descend.

I find myself jumping for my camera each time a ship passes, wide-eyed while knowing that I am not Cartier-Bresson or Adams. Indeed, the photos take themselves.

Early on, we are surrounded by hills covered with deciduous forest and fields of lupins, but the channel then becomes narrow, muddy and claustrophobic. The word Conradian comes to mind.

Our second day was hot and still. Tainui was repeatedly attacked by marauding bands of march flies. Anyone watching Tainui would have thought we were members of Tourettes Anonymous. Our conversations are interspersed with sudden flings of limbs and shouted expletives.

The caramel river is peaceful but we were glad when those flies went home at dusk. We anchored outside the channel and listened to evening birdsong. An occasional freighter passed but otherwise we were quite alone.

From Vytegra you ascend through 6 locks to the highest point in the entire Volga journey, some 1,000 ft above sea level. At the top of the Vytegra ladder a large pond accommodates the scores of commercial vessels waiting to descend to Lake Onega en route St Petersburg.

You are now on the busy commercial route connecting the Baltic and St Petersburg with Volga ports, the Caspian and Black Seas, in constant and at times disturbingly close company with the bulk carriers, double barges, tankers and tugs which ply the waters day and night. Timber, petroleum products, general cargo, ferrous metals, granite and grain comprise most of the goods transported along this vital highway.

For sailors this shipping is a source of constant interest and a delight to the eye. Ship masters slide their huge behemoths in and out of the locks with remarkable skill and often only inches of clearance. The whole exercise is choreographed seamlessly by lock keepers and vessel dispatchers, whose tolerance, patience and respect for our little vessel was flattering and reassuring.

From the top of the Vytegra ladder it is a two day journey along River Kovzha to White Lake. The canal is narrow, muddy and tortuous, with pretty, forested shores and occasional villages. Careful lookout is needed for floating logs in the water. Depths drop rapidly on each side and a stern anchor will be needed to keep you outside the channel without taking the ground at night. We christened this waterway "March Fly Canal" for eponymous reasons. The beastly flies depart at dusk, only to be replaced by clouds of mosquitoes.

The holding basin above Vytegra Ladder

KOVZHA ANCHORAGE

wpt	60 23/037 07
km	782

We found a tight but secure spot outside red buoy "66" (just beyond buoy "45") on the left hand side of the river. A stern anchor is necessary here.

WHITE LAKE

At the eastern end of the Kovzha River (our "March Fly Canal") the route takes you through a broad reach of marshland with low reeded islands, something of a relief after the claustrophobic and muddy canal. Be careful here, because some of those islands are floating! There are ample channel markers, sometimes in duplicate or triplicate, and they may tend to confuse.

White Lake is ovoid and shallow (average depth 5m). The NW-SE transit is about 45 km, with lit buoys every km or so. The lake has a reputation for storms and nasty seas, and a canal (Belozersky Canal) was constructed behind the southern shore to allow safe passage around it for shoal draft boats. This canal is no longer in general use.

BELOZYORSK TO CHEREPOVETS

JOHN : BELOZYORSK

It is a relief to be out of that two day long meandering muddy stream. March Fly Canal, as we call it. During the brief window between march fly bedtime and the arrival of nocturnal mosquitoes however, there is a time to be treasured. Last night's swim and carbonara pasta made it truly memorable.

A short, well-marked passage through marshes and floating islands leads from March Fly Channel to White Lake. Suddenly the pesky flies and mosquitoes are gone, although in only 15 feet of water we are hardly at sea. I think this could be a dreadful bit of water in strong winds, but we are blessed. Again.

After a shallow approach we tied up in the snug, narrow canal at Belozyorsk. As usual, it is not an approved port on our list but our excuse for stopping here - urgent need of fuel (ie vodka) - was accepted by the port captain, with Vladimir's help. Konstantin will be starting to realise that this is Tainui's way!

Belozyorsk is a pretty town. A Two Move town. We measure our ports by the number of times we are asked to re-anchor, change moorings or, in this case, run aground by believing the depths told us by the harbour authorities. A grumpy-looking thunderstorm is on the way but nothing can touch us here.

It is warm and sunny. Folk stop to ogle at our pristine, boat show vessel. We have just crossed 40 miles of White Lake - ovoid, calm, flat, 12 feet deep and truly white - and we feel as though we have rounded the Horn.

BELOZYORSK : 25 JUNE

approach wpt 60 02.7/037 46.8

On the south-eastern shore of White Lake, this is another port closed to foreign vessels. In good weather it is a very pleasant stopover. With help from Vladimir Ivankiv we obtained permission to break our trip at this small, underdeveloped lakeside town. The approach is shallow (2.8 m) and wide open to the north. Entry would be dangerous with any significant breeze from that quarter.

There is a boat basin to the right after a swing bridge. The bridge keeper will open the bridge if you sound your horn. The port authorities gave us permission to lie alongside the passenger jetty, on the left hand side of the channel immediately after the bridge. There is a comfortable little hotel right on the water who allowed us to shower, but it cannot provide registration for foreigners wishing to spend the night there.

Fuel can be obtained by the taxi/jerrycan method and there is a well-stocked supermarket in the town.

Contact details

Hotel "Rechnoy Vokzal'
Вологодская обл., Белозерск г., ул. Набережная, 80
+7 (81756) 2-62-62

MAXINE'S BAD HAIR DAY : JOHN

It has been difficult. There is too much salt in the bloody mary, the march flies are too aggressive, the toilet paper is too sandpapery, in Belozyorsk they don't sell the right cheese, the music's too loud (Janacek Sinfonietta too loud? – for heavens' sake!), the VHF charger isn't working properly – there seems no end to it.

She deals with each new march fly in gladiatorial fashion. Her shouted Dutch expletives sound like physio sessions in a TB ward. She seems unable to learn the languid Australian wave, which is just as effective and far less emotionally draining.

I cluck, fuss and coddle. I do my best to appease. I even pretend to like the grits she offers me for breakfast. Nothing works. Then, bless her heart, Maxine apologises for being such a pain. So she should, I think. But I graciously accept her apology and we move on out of White Lake.

A stately church ruin stands sentinel over the entrance to the White Lake-Cherepovets waterway. Once past the cable ferry we are again alone in our little world. The march flies are few and die bravely for Maxine's peace of mind. It is warm and there is the gentlest SE breeze. I think it is great and she reluctantly accepts that the world is a moderately acceptable place.

Madam mellowed later, but punishment is always necessary and she was banished to the foredeck with her bloody mary to sit in the sun and learn contrition. Alone in the cockpit I put Andsnes' D960 on very loud and float away.

Maxine, who adores Shostakovich, Berg and Golijov, has this bizarre problem with piano music. By any composer, played by anybody. Yet she likes harpsichord, spinet and every other keyboard. I do not understand this. Her man Dirk plays the piano and is a music lover with less infuriating prejudices. I am looking forward to some rational conversation with him about Cziffra, Lipatti and other vital subjects when we arrive in Cherepovets tomorrow. Until then I steal moments of late Beethoven or Schumann like a naughty boy in a lolly shop, when herself is banished to the foredeck or asleep in her cabin with her earplugs in.

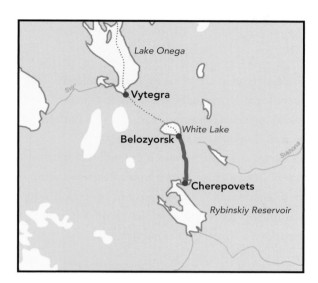

Allow 2 days for this section of the route, which follows the Sheksna River between White Lake and Rybinskiy Reservoir.

Flooded Krokhino church, Sheksna rivermouth

BELOZYORSK TO CHEREPOVETS

FEMALE SAILORS : MAXINE

Of course, I knew that sailing in Russia was not developed at all. What I had not realised though was a female sailor is an unknown concept for most ordinary Russians, in whose minds boating is strictly for men only. My previous experience sailing in Russia was limited to a regatta on Lake Baikal and a bit of to-ing and fro-ing on a reservoir north-west of Moscow. It was not much and it did not prepare me for the confrontations I would face on this journey just because I was a woman. In the south of Russia, things were better because sailing was more developed and there were enough good female sailors to be accepted as something natural. In the north of Russia however, where sailing is almost unheard of, I found it much more difficult to establish my authority and competence. Three occasions stand out.

In Vytegra, I had to go climb to the top of the mast before the crane workmen accepted that I was capable of any more than just making coffee. That act established my authority.

In one of the Volga-Don locks, a lock-keeper thought that there were no males on board and remarked on the fact over the radio. I asked him whether he thought that mattered. He giggled and did not know how to reply.

In the Sea of Azov, negotiating our way into Kerch, I had to provide the port authorities with crew details by radio. When I told them there were two people on board, the skipper and the first mate, they then asked who I was! They did apologise though, when I gave them an earful.

That being said, these episodes were only a minor irritation, never a real problem. Once we got south into sailing territory most people we dealt with were sailors. Even if they were male they were emancipated.

KIRILLO-BELOZERSKY MUSEUM-RESERVE

wpt	59 52/038 15
km	683

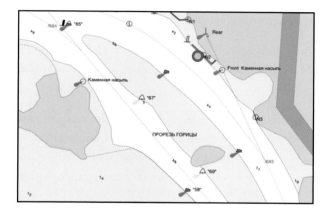

There are more than 60 buildings on this extraordinary 20 hectare site, including two 14th century monasteries, a 16th century convent and an early 18th century wooden church.

Ask for permission to lie alongside one of the tourist wharves. It is shallow outside the channel but it may be possible to anchor off. From the jetties it is a 10km taxi ride to the main centre.

http://www.kirmuseum.ru/en/

TURTSEVO

wpt	59 33.5/038.27.5
km mark	between 635-634

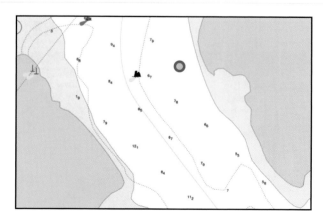

Secure anchorage can be found 3 km before Turstsevo inside white buoy #143.

There is one duplex lock just before Cherepovets at 59 14.62/038 29.8, allowing control of flow in the Sheksna River. The locking process here is smooth and fast.

CHEROPOVETS : JOHN, 27–30 JUNE

We're tied up at the tiny yacht club and all is peaceful. I don't think a foreign yacht has ever been here. The yard manager, a genial old bloke, took our lines and chatted amiably with Maxine in Cyrillic while I celebrated another gentle arrival with a small ale.

According to Wiki, this steel manufacturing city is one of the world's most polluted. We must be lucky then, because the air is clear and the water looks clean (I don't know what cadmium looks like though).

Dutch Maxine's Belgian friend Lieve's Russian husband's Russian brother Sasha came to meet us and took us in search of our greatest need, a Japanese meal. The splendid man found us a good Japanese restaurant in the Russian equivalent of Westfield Plaza. Stalin never ate at a restaurant like this. Maxine certainly has connections – as we ate, she mentioned that she had a discount card for this restaurant but had left it in Moscow!

Sasha told us that Cheropovets, like so many places we have visited, is a city in decline. Our local contacts in towns like Medvezhegorsk have tended to blame Gorbachev and perestroika, whereas here Sasha says the GFC is the problem. As we drive through town, it doesn't look like a dying city to me. There is a sense of energy and wealth here which was quite absent in the towns we have visited earlier.

Dirk arrives in an hour and Max is all agog. I am looking forward to some time alone on the boat to get stuck into the multitude of small jobs which accumulate relentlessly. – dismantle and repair the deck wash pump, which has severe prostate trouble; top up the batteries; repair a damaged rubbing strake; transfer the last of the diesel into the port tank; change the engine oil and filters; plan navigation for the next leg; straighten and reinforce the mast cross-braces; learn Russian, etc, etc. That will take a good two days, after which Max and Dirk will be back from their luxury hotel and we can depart.

CHEREPOVETS

wpt	59 06.8/037 52.7
km	537.5

 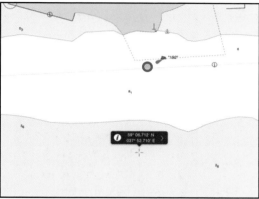

With a population of 320,000, this large industrial centre sits astride the Sheksna River at its outflow into Rybinskiy Reservoir. Cherepovets' steel works are among the largest in NW Russia and it is a major regional centre for trade, transportation and construction. It has the dubious distinction of being the 2nd most heavily polluted city in Russia.

There is a boat club past the bridge on the right hand side of the river, servicing small power boats and half a dozen harbour racers.

Approach to the boat club from the river is easy. Do not turn right until the entrance is abeam however, just past right hand hand (red) buoy #"192", because of shoals. upstream. Minimum depth on approach is 4.5 metres. Tie up alongside the concrete wharf in depths of 5 metres. You may have to move occasionally to allow fuelling of other boats. Shore power, water and tanker fuel are available. From here it is a short taxi ride into town. All provisions are available, with air connections with Moscow but no yacht services.

Contact details

Cherepovets Y/C
tel: +79212502081
manager - Nikolai

BELOZYORSK TO CHEREPOVETS

JOHN : NEW CREW

Dirk is the love of Maxine's life. As we approached Cherepovets she had become increasingly excited and, dare I say it, distracted. Her partner Dirk joined Tanui in Cherepovets for the journey to Nizhniy Novgorod. He is not a sailor and came to Tainui with some reluctance, although Maxine has been hoping this trip might just be his sailing epiphany. Sadly that was not to be, although Dirk did at least agree to join us.

Dirk is a ridiculously tall fellow. He brought pedantic analysis of English grammar to new lows in Tainui. The split infinitive, the noun clause and the gerund became matters of intense cockpit debate and, at times, violence. To be expected I suppose, from a lawyer , a Dutchman and an English public school alumnus. In Tainui Dirk folded himself like an umbrella into "the downstairs", as he calls it, where he livened the saloon with his dry wit and charm.

He is by any measure an eccentric chap, marching to his own tuneless tune. He is current holder of Tainui's Best Flakey Boy award (initiated by Ian so many years ago) and has commenced the lengthy assessment process for associate membership of the Society for the Preservation of the Subjunctive in the English Language. He will always be welcome back on board (Tainui might lose Maxine otherwise!).

WORK DAY : JOHN

Maxine and Dirk have cloistered themselves in a hotel for a couple of days. Tainui is suddenly quite a lot larger, not that Max takes up more than her allotted space on board. Indeed quite the contrary. But still, the boat is bigger. And I can make a mess without fear of being disturbed.

First a full engine service. Like refuelling, this is a job I have never learned to do without making a mess. Our old Ford diesel loves the attention though. Especially after the difficult access jobs - new oils for the injector pump and gearbox.

Next I adjust and tighten the mast supports on deck. A clown roared past us yesterday and the whole edifice lurched aft about a foot because my stays were not tight enough. This time, with the help of the anchor winch, all are bar tight and I only hope I don't banana the deck.

I don't hoover the boat often because our vacuum cleaner is stowed in one of the world's most inaccessible places. But getting it out was the next job. Maxine has been complaining about her lack of access to the cleaner and it now lives under the dining table.

Our decks are a bit of a mess up forward after some very muddy anchorages, so I then turn to the deck wash pump which, as I have said, has a prostate problem. I am still at that job, and the cabin sole is covered with a wealth of tools. It is time to stop for a palate-cleansing ale. I can leave the mess because I am all alone.

Cherepovets marina

TAINUI IS BLESSED : JOHN

Last night Sasha turned up with a vast array of beers, home brew spirits, wines for Maxine and a sumptuous feast for 10. He brought with him a Russian Orthodox priest with a long white beard, and a Georgian bloke.

The priest stood in the cockpit and asked us all to be silent, then began a lengthy bass baritone blessing of Tainui and all who sail in her. I was very touched. Then the endless round of obligatory toasts began, each washed down with this spicy, unrecognisable spirit of Sasha's.

We spoke in charade language and listened to music. As previously in Russia I found that Lonesome Valley, Taj Mahal and Ada Falcon did not impress. But when I put on Rachmaninoff's Easter Vespers their eyes lit up and there was silence. I have found this instant recognition of Russian music everywhere we have stopped.

Things got merrier and again I felt my Cyrillic inarticulacy a barrier to deeper conversation. I sent an urgent SMS to Maxine at her hotel and she came down to the boat soon after to interpret. As is usual with her however, she entered immediately into a long, animated and seemingly productive conversation with these blokes. In Russian of course (and yes Dirk, I know that Cyrillic is the script, not the language, but I like the word), so that I remained none the wiser about what was being said.

I retreated into my cup and was soon in my cups. An altogether memorable evening.

RYBINSKIY RESERVOIR

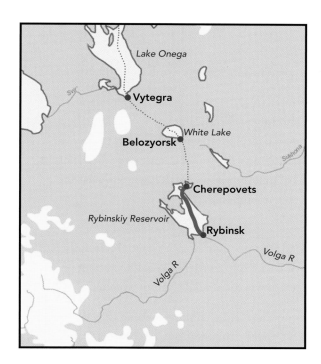

This section involves about 180 km of exposed travel across a shallow reservoir.

The Volga was dammed at Rybinsk in 1939. Filled by 1946 this hydroelectric reservoir became the largest man-made body of water on earth, requiring relocation of more than 100,000 people and the flooding of some 600 villages and small towns. It is the first of the 5 great reservoirs to be crossed during the 2,000 mile passage south to the Sea of Azov. The Volga, flowing north-east from its source north of Moscow, enters the south-eastern corner of the reservoir.

Depths are modest at best and, with reaches of 30 miles or more, short steep seas build rapidly with fresh winds. The shipping channel is well-buoyed and busy.

Allow 15 hours for the passage across to Rybinsk and do not depart if inclement weather threatens.

CHEREPOVETS TO RYBINSK

JOHN : A MISERABLE NIGHT AT SEA

We have just had a thoroughly miserable night.

We left Cherepovets with forecast 5 knot headwinds. The afternoon started well and fiveses were lengthy and voluble.

But the weather predictions were wrong. The worryingly shallow waters of Rybinsky Lake (5-10 m maximum) with 25 knots of wind on our port bow created very steep, short seas over a fetch of 40 miles. Poor Tainui without mast and steadying sails rolled abominably. The motion was made the worse because mastless, her centre of gravity was so much lower. At least the skies were clear and it was not cold. But just horrible nonetheless.

I was very worried about the mast and the three 6x1" cross frames I had made to support it. A couple of times I went forward for an icy douche, to beef up their support stays. Mercifully our Heath Robinson structure survived, although poor Dirk's dinner didn't. What a baptism of fire for him. Little Miss Perfect, immune to seasickness, just loved it all. Dreadful woman.

At 3 am, after 12 hours of this misery, we turned into the 15 mile channel leading into Ribena (Rybinsk) which brought us head into the seas. Our speed dropped from 4 knots to 1.9 and the constant pitching was very irritating and stultifyingly slow.

Finally we were able to drop anchor in the Rybinsk Roads in flat water, and collapsed into bed. Total loss - 1 jerry can of fuel, Dirk's dinner and my prestige as route planning manager.

After 4 hours of coma and in bright sun we entered the great Rybinsk lock, gateway to the Volga River. Today's fresh headwinds have veered 30 degrees. Had we deferred our departure from Cheropovets the winds would have been right on the nose for our crossing of Rybinsky Lake and I feel justified in deciding to cross the reservoir last night instead of today.

Dirk's seasickness, whose ground had been generously laid by our fiveses the evening before, vanished as we sidled along in the river's still waters. I have assured him that last night's adventure was not a normal sailing experience.

I advise those who follow to choose Rybinskiy Reservoir weather carefully, before setting out for the trip down to Rybinsk.

RYBINSK

The approach to Rybinsk is busy, well-buoyed and lit. From fairway buoy # "9" near km mark 415, fresh winds can generate short steep seas, making for painfully slow progress into protected water.

There is a small boat club (RSV Service) about 6 km before the lock entrance, at the north-western end of the island, at wpt 58° 07.2/ 038° 38.5. We did not visit this, but contact details are set out below for general reference.

Contact details

RSV Service
Tel.: +7 (4855) 295-665
Mob.: +7 (905) 131-15-62
email: rybinsk@rsv-yachts.ru
Address: 152978, г.Рыбинск, Ярославской области, пос. Судоверфь
http://www.rsv-servis.ru

YURSHINSKIY ISLAND

wpt	58 08.4/038 38.517
km	417

Vessels waiting for permission to enter Rybinsk lock can find safe anchorage with good holding on the pretty eastern shore of this island, about 1.5 miles before the lock entrance.

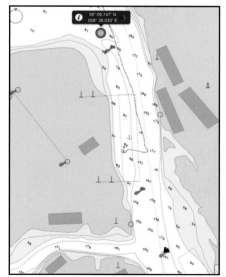

Approach to the anchorage

The first Volga lock

CHEREPOVETS TO RYBINSK

JOHN : THE VOLGA

The Rybinsk waterfront is mixed commercial and high rise residential. As the city recedes behind us we begin to realise that we are really here. In Russia, on the Volga River, and the first foreign-flagged yacht to follow this path in the last century.

It is about 60 miles down the Volga from Rybinsk to Yaroslavl, where we plan to spend a few days exploring this world heritage rated old city.

As for the Volga itself - well, after our unpleasant crossing from Cheropovets the river gave us a good excuse for relaxed and lazy motoring with some robust tippling. A beautiful, broad river here, with forested hills, towering onion-domed churches, tasteful dachas, busy commercial traffic and wealthy-looking towns. There are rich forests, steep hillsides, flat reaches with reedbeds and sandy beaches.

I still can't quite believe we're here.

Now it can be truly said that you are on the Volga. It is about 100 km from Rybinsk to Yaroslavl and anchorage opportunities are limited along the way. We did this leg in a long single day, arriving after dark and groping our way into YC Poplavok with the assistance of a local fishing boat. It would be better to stop overnight half way along this section, we believe.

RYBINSK TO YAROSLAVL

ARRIVING IN YAROSLAVL : JOHN, 4 JULY

After dark we groped our way through a maze of navigation lights into the city. Ever resourceful, Maxine called up a passing fishing boat, turned on her usual charm routine and asked for advice about places to stop for the night. The skipper slowed down, told us to follow him, which we did, into a creek and a peaceful little small vessel marina in the centre of town. Parkland and a million stars. Floodlit onion domes standing above the trees. Deep sleep.

We are all 3 of us captivated by this lovely town, which was founded by the Volga Vikings in around 1014. It is the first of a series of beautiful riverside cities and towns on what is called the Golden Ring - a broad sweep of the Volga around Moscow.

YAROSLAVL

wpt	57 37/039 55
km	522

This beautiful 11th century city is the first substantial town encountered along this section of the river. While Rybinsk does not offer facilities for yachts, Yaroslavl has berthing facilities right in the centre of town. Cruising yachts will certainly want to spend a few days here.

http://www.city-yar.ru/

Note that there are good air and rail connections between Yaroslavl and Moscow. We chose to commute by train from Nizhniy Novgorod further downstream, and I think Rybachiy Boat Club there provides more protection and security. The trip from Yaroslavl is shorter but only marginally so.

The yachting community in Yaroslavl comprises about 20 yachts - mainly quarter tonners and day sailers. There are 3 so-called marinas, although only two offer realistic possibilities for cruising yachts.

A kilometre south of the two bridges the Kotorosl River joins the Volga on its western side, just before km 522. The spectacular domes of the Cathedral of the Assumption provide an unmissable landmark.

Keep to the middle of the channel as you enter the river - the depths drop to about 4.3m and there are significant shoals on both sides.

Marina #1 (Poplavok Marina +7 4852 930288) - Immediately after entering the river turn north into a pretty creek. Do not do so however, until this creek is open ahead, and then favour the port side initially. Depths drop to about 2.4m. The bottom is soft mud and we do not think a grounding here would be problematic. Further into the creek the depths increase and the marina is obvious ahead, at the first corner.

The pens are deep and new, with only one problem - they are less than 30 feet long. The area is so well protected however, that we did not find this a problem even with 12' of mast projecting from our bows. Only use the pens on the south side of the finger wharf - those to the north are too shallow. At the time of our visit there was one yacht (Sandro's Carter 30) and a handful of power boats only.

MORE ON YAROSLAVL : JOHN

Tainui's berth in Yaroslavl could hardly be more central. The golden domes of the Cathedral of the Annunciation loom over her and their sonorous carillon rings loud every morning and evening.

Unfortunately though, there are big loudspeakers in the park next door which blare out a curious mixture of music all day - excerpts from Swan Lake, Star Wars and some techo noise that Maxine seems to know - played over and over. The third source of noise is the local restaurant at the end of our pier, which has Brazilian samba music, country and western songs and some more techno noise that Maxine seems to know. The overall effect is disconcerting. Dirk and Maxine don't seem troubled but it drives me crazy.

Poplavok marina

This marina has water (said not to be potable) and shore power. It is located right under the park with its world heritage churches looming above. The town is only 500m up the hill. It is the obvious choice for cruising yachts.

Cost 1,000 roubles per day, includes electricity (only our 2 pin socket worked) and water. No showers, laundry or wifi. There are two good restaurants attached to the marina and they will deliver food to your boat. Fuel is obtained only by the tedious jerry can/taxi method, made more awkward because you have to lug your jerrycans through guests dining at the restaurant to get to the jetty!

Poplavok marina would be an acceptable place to leave your vessel for a visit to Moscow, although Rybachiy YC in Nizhniy Novgorod is probably more secure. Moreover, Ribachiy boat pens are better and staff, all competent boat handlers, will look after your boat. In Yaroslavl you would need to make specific arrangements for boat care, there being no skilled marina staff on site.

contact details

Yacht Club "Poplavok"
Podzelenye Street, boat house (ул. Подзеленье, дебаркадер)
phone: 485 231 4343 (restaurant), 485 230 2854 (summer verandah)
http://www.rk-poplavok.ru
email: rk-poplavok@yandex.ru

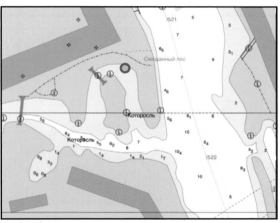

Poplavok Marina

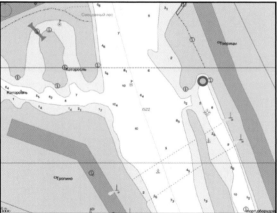

Marina No.3

Local yachtsman Sandro Gurchiani kindly took us for an afternoon cruise on his Carter 30, so we could gather some detailed information about berths and anchorages in Yaroslavl. Sandro is a friendly chap and a competent sailor. His local knowledge and his willingness to assist visiting sailors make him a useful contact.

email vdtalb@yaroslavl.ru

Marina #2 - Having turned off the Volga into the Kotorosl River referred to above, you can continue west for about 1 km in deep (6m) water, until another marina comes into view. Depths are good here but the marina sits beside a highway, further from the town centre. Power boats. Not recommended.

Marina #3

Marina #3 - Almost opposite the mouth of the Kotorosl River is Savinskiy Island, a long island on the east side of the Volga. Steer past the north end of the island in depths no less than 4m. To your right is an excellent anchorage on the eastern shore of the island. This is a very protected spot, with 6m water and good holding in soft mud. To your left is the third marina, next to the skeleton of an old ferry. Lie stern to with mooring buoys. A peaceful spot, but with very limited space available when we were there, and absolutely no facilities. You have to cross the Volga to get to town. Not recommended.

Marina #3

STUNNING ONION DOMES : JOHN

The Volga hereabouts is lined with onion-domed churches. To me, three things stand out about them - they are striking and very beautiful structures, they suit their setting perfectly and they display unexpectedly strong Islamic architectural influence.

Yaroslavl has many fine examples. Today we decided to visit the Church of St John the Baptist, noted for its fine frescoes and its 15 green onion domes. More domes than any other church in the vicinity, if not all Russia, they say.

We called a taxi. The driver, who to Dirk's irritation was morbidly obese (Dirk has a problem with obesity in others), had never heard of St John the Baptist or a church by that name. We pointed the spires out to him visually, and on google maps. But he refused to acknowledge the existence of such a place. He called his control officer who also had not heard of the church. Maxine's fluent Russian was not at fault, we knew. So we cancelled the cab and called another. Our second driver, a svelte young bloke, was also mystified by our destination. But he rose to the challenge and agreed to take us.

The church we had identified stands proud on a headland at the entrance to the Kotorosl River, opposite our marina. Finding it should not, we thought, have taken rocket science. When I showed the driver a photo of the church on my pocket camera he stopped the taxi and got out, took my camera with him and showed the picture to an old lady waiting at a bus stop. Armed with her instructions he drove on and we found what we thought was the object of our search. Along a dirt track in the trees on the shore of the Volga.

Our church was indeed grand and inspiring. But a couple of things were not quite right. Firstly, we could only count 14 onion domes, not the requisite 15. Secondly, it was barricaded and quite decrepit. Thirdly, there was no sign of an entrance or tourist facility. I was captivated by the combination of stately grandeur and decrepitude, but we knew it was not the right church.

To cut a long story short, with the aid of Maxine's iPad internet connection and our driver's infinite patience we found an address for the Church of St John the Baptist, which turned out to be in an industrial estate 3 miles from our 14 dome mistake. And this church had 15 domes and magnificent frescoes. The pictures speak better than my words.

Yaroslavl is a world heritage site and for good reason. In addition to the Cathedral of the Assumption there are many other beautiful churches worth exploring. The Kremlin in the centre of town contains numerous fine museums.

Our favourite by far was the church of St John the Baptist in Tolchkova, with its extraordinary collection of 16th century murals. Finding this lovely church was an adventure in its own right (see left). The address is Second Zakotoroslnaya Embankment #69.

Church of St John the Baptist

SPLIT INFINITIVES : JOHN

We left Yaroslavl at about 8pm. The evening is warm, calm. The river is almost a mile wide and is a serious waterway. We have a steady 1 knot current with us. Pleasing because we keep engine revs down to 1300 rpm to minimise coolant loss.

I should say something about Dirk. At the moment he is steering and clearly enjoying himself although he would deny it stridently. When he joined Tainui Dirk was anxious about all our cabalistic nautical jiggery-pokey. In Cherepovets I put him on the helm and he agreed reluctantly to try steering but insisted that he would only drive in a straight line and was not prepared to turn the wheel. That is for mariners, he would say.

Now he navigates, checking off the numbered buoys on the chart while humming tunelessly to himself. He has mastered the clove hitch and insisted I dig out my old sextant for a lesson on spherical trigonometry. He is ridiculously tall but has managed to jack-knife his angular frame into Tainui's unforgiving interstices with - well, with a semblance of efficiency if not grace.

Little Miss Perfect is very relieved that Dirk hasn't mutinied and fled, although he does go on about staying "just until the next train station". They are a delightful, odd-ball couple who make Tainui a happy ship. Conversation and laughter flow easily.

Dirk is intrigued by my sister's small but powerful International Society for the Preservation of the Subjunctive (membership currently 3) and may well qualify for junior associate trainee status in time. I am thinking about that.

Even Maxine, argumentative pedant that she is, has started attacking this tired and overworked skipper's rare grammatical solecisms with a triumphant "ney, ney John, split infinitive!" when I ask her to quickly take in a stern spring.

It is all very wearing.

The leg from Yaroslavl to Kostroma is about 77km.
The shores are generally wooded and pleasant.

KOSTROMA

wpt	57 46.7/040 48.2
km	591-2

Kostroma http://www.gradkostroma.ru/ was founded in the 12th century. It lies at the junction of the Volga and Kostroma Rivers and its city architecture expresses a successful mercantile history dating back to the 16th century. Kostroma's outstanding attraction is St Ipatiy Monastery [http://ipatievsky-monastery.ru/] built by Boris Godunov in 1650, on the site of a 14th century monastic institution. Godunov, a Tatar, had became Tsar on the demise of Ivan the Terrible's feeble-minded son Feodor, last ruler of the Rurik Dynasty.

With Godunov's death, Russia descended into a period of political and administrative chaos and lawlessness known as The Time of Troubles. Cossack unrest and wars with Sweden, Poland and Lithuania took place against a background of disastrous famines in 1600-04 which took some 2 million lives. (The famines are blamed on climate change caused by a large volcanic eruption in Peru).

Young Mikhail Romanov was brought up in St Ipatiy monastery. He was nominated Tsar in 1612 by a national military council assembled in Moscow, thus beginning the illustrious Romanov dynastic line. 300 years later the last Romanov, Nicholas the Second, attended the tercentenary

KOSTROMA AND THE NOUN CLAUSE : JOHN, 6 JULY

The marina at Kostroma is small, jet ski infested but friendly. We were welcomed warmly by Andrey and Anna, who had brought ice creams and 2 bottles of splendid isabella and raspberry wine. We settled into what has now become a Volga ritual - the arrival tipple. Decibels rose steadily as sincere but cheerful toasts followed one another rapidly. Incomprehensible Cyrillic is de rigueur, of course.

Much too late we extracted ourselves and went ashore to explore Kostroma's grand central square, restock Tainui's drinks cupboard and eat.

At a busy restaurant our conversation naturally turned to the noun clause. Dirk is hell- bent on provisional admission into the Society for Preservation of the Subjunctive but on this occasion he did not improve on his prospects. Later, rather touchingly, he asked me whether the Subjunctive Society has an emergency help line.

The argument, which is what it became, was impassioned. Dirk was irritatingly single-minded and would not listen to reason. Maxine tried to help each of us in turn but her contributions were not helpful. Waitresses and other diners at the restaurant began glancing anxiously towards our table but Dirk, whose youthful but quite misguided passion was the root cause of the attention we attracted, was not to be distracted. But at least he paid the bill.

The author of this post would like contribution from readers on the subject of the discussion. Dirk had said "Maxine is one of those rare women who get better with age". I suggested mildly that he should have said "Maxine is one of those rare women who gets better with age". Leaving aside the factual accuracy of the statement itself, which of these two sentences is correct? Is "one of those women" a noun clause?

Of course the question will be sent to the issues committee of the Society while, at the same time, Dirk's behaviour will be scrutinised by both the credentialling and the standards committees. But in the meantime an answer is needed.

Before we left Kostroma we visited the monastery of St Ipatiy - less than 10 domes but a walled haven of peaceful gardens, a grand 16th century chapel, monastic buildings and a Romanov palace. The devout queued to kiss the icon while we just sat in silence.

I like this sort of environment because it gives me relief from Miss Perfect's taxing disagreement with everything I say, and Dirk's stodgy pursuit of the only right answer to unanswerable questions.

Romanov celebrations in Kostroma in 1913. Within 4 years he had abdicated after the Russian Revolution and was executed along with his family in 1918.

Just before Kostroma there is room to anchor with good holding along the left hand side of the river in the vicinity of white channel buoy #"87". The waypoint below locates this anchorage.

Facilities for yachts in Kostroma itself are meagre at best. There is a small boat club on the left bank of the river, where it is possible for yachts to tie up at the end of the long floating pontoon, if space is available. This club is on the first wharf beyond the mouth of the Kostroma River, on the northern side of the Volga.

wpt	57 46/04054.8
km	599

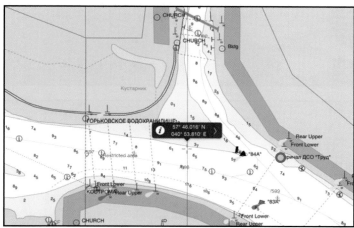

Kostroma Boat Club

YC contact: Andrey Apepenov 8-9038971155

There is a good hotel on a floating barge adjacent to the club (www.ostrovskij-prichal.ru, be sure to book ahead) From the club it is a short walk to the centre of town with its grand central square, pleasing neoclassical architecture and the extraordinary St Ipatiy's monastery, a jewel which is not to be missed. Kostroma has good transport connections with Moscow.

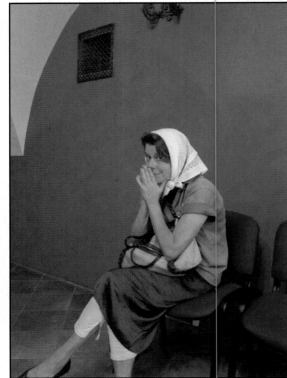

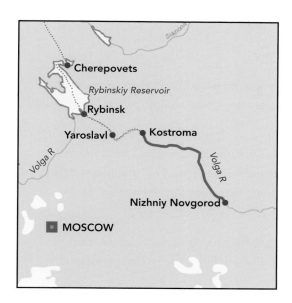

253 km, spread over 3 days.

PLYOS

Plyos [http://plyos-adm.ru/] was founded early in the 12th century and is mentioned in the Primary Chronicles. The village was popularised at the end of the 19th century by the Russian landscape artist Isaac Levitan, when it became a colourful and idiosyncratic artists' retreat. Plyos is now a popular tourist attraction in its own right. There is only one wharf and if you wish to stop here you will need to queue alongside tour boats, jet skis and power boats. We chose to move on.

KINESHMA

Sprawling along the river this industrial city, birthplace of Alexander Borodin, has little to offer yachts other than wonderful views of abandoned soviet factories slowly being subsumed by riverside vegetation.

KOSTROMA TO NIZHNIY NOVGOROD

A MEETING OF SEAMEN : JOHN, 7 JULY

Today is a day of national celebration for all mariners on Russia's inland waterways. Maxine tells me that VHF communication in Cyrillic between commercial shipping includes fraternal greetings and expressions of goodwill.

Near Kineshma we passed "Credo" a smart, home-built Russian sailing boat from Kazan, bound for Yaroslavl. Shortly after we had passed they called us up on VHF and asked if they could return and lie alongside us for a celebratory toast to the day. After a nanosecond's consideration we acceded to their request.

The cheerful group of sailors brought on board with them a bottle of rum, glasses made of real glass, and fresh oranges spiced with cinnamon. There followed one of those occasions which make cruising worthwhile.

The easy and immediate intimacy between folk with so much common ground, doing the same stupid things saw that rum disappear in barely 5 toasts. With much back slapping we bid each other farewell and went on our way, never to meet again but friends forever.

KRASNYE POZHNI

wpt	57 28.5/041 11.3.
km	695

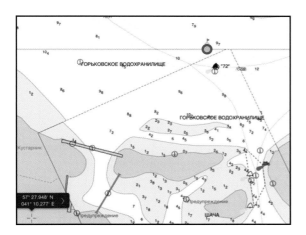

Just before Krasnye Pozhni, anchorage can be had on the inside of the river bend, in the region of fairway buoys "73", "72" and "71"depending on wind direction. The holding is good in about 8 m of water outside the channel.

UBEZHISHSCHE YURKINO

wpt	57 01.7/043 08.8
km	807

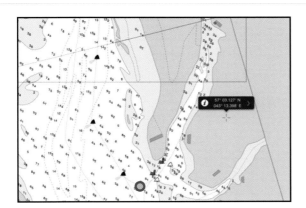

This deep inlet on the north-eastern side of the river looks easier and more inviting than it is. At the entrance to the wooded harbour the paper and electronic charts both misrepresent the depths and shoals. Moreover, only two of the charted buoys were in evidence when we visited.

Contrary to the charts, the deepest water after the red (port) can and the starboard cone - no less than 6.5 m - lies quite close to the right hand shore. Depths of less than 2 m extend out from the western side. At the head of the inlet peaceful anchorage can be found in the vicinity of wpt 57 03/043 12.

From Yurkino it is 45 km to Gorodets.

THE CHART WAS WRONG : JOHN, 8 JULY

Thunderheads loomed over us when, in fading light, we crept into a likely looking inlet for the night. Black night was upon us when we realised that the second set of channel markers was missing and the charted depth of 5 m was wrong. Drawing 2.2 m, Tainui had at times only 12" under her keel. We zigzagged along chasing the channel by depth sounder. I was reminded of our worrying approaches both to the Cayenne and Paramaribo Rivers in another life, where the channel is kept open by churning propellers of fishing boats (and us).

Finally we found deep water and secure anchorage. For those who follow, we anchored in thick mud at 57 deg 03' /043 deg 12'.

This morning Maxine swam gracefully in the tannin coloured waters while Dirk and I cleansed our palates with a brew. I was shamed eventually into a dip but Dirk, for whom hygeine has an idiosyncratic definition, read Private Eye in the cockpit. Our trip back out this morning was simple - depths did not drop below 6 m on the opposite side of the inlet, where our charts showed 1 m shoal. Nature rewrites cartography again.

An hour down the Volga we had severe overheating of the engine. There was no observable external coolant loss, the salt water circulation was normal and oil level and colour were normal. An hour's enforced idleness in the channel and 7 litres of coolant later, we set off again. This time, at only 1,200 rpm and with the radiator cap loose. I have decided to replace the capillary tube stack in the heat exchanger when we get to Nizhny Novgorod, even though it has pressure tested normal on several occasions.

Now we are motoring gently across a wide lake. There is a huge thunderstorm behind us but we are brave and determined. The engine temperature is normal and the spires of Gorodets stand above the horizon ahead in remarkable mirage. Dirk has asked that any argument about fata morgana and other atmospheric phenomena be left until dinner this evening.

GORODETS

Gorodets is an ancient fortress town, founded in 1153. Sadly, most of its fine church and monastic architecture was destroyed during the Bolshevik revolution.

Gorodets locks have an easy, all weather approach and their entrance lies inside a well-protected mole harbour. Here we were asked to pay the fees for the entire Volga-Don system – 19,000 roubles ($600) – but the lock keeper rather uncharacteristically suggested that we might prefer to postpone payment of this fee until we reached Nizhniy Novgorod.

There are 2 locks separated by a large ship basin. Beyond the second of these, it is possible to tie up at a tourist wharf on the left hand side of the river, to visit the historic old town and, in particular, Krayevedchekiy museum (Lenin Street 11). This is by no means a secure or comfortable spot to leave your boat.

Beyond the Gorodets locks comes a surprise and a delight – a steady 2.5 knot favourable current. The 57 km trip down to to Nizhniy is a fast one.

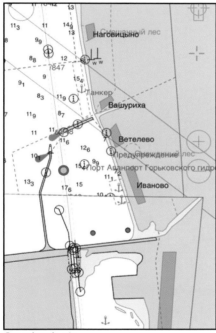

Gorodets basin

WHAT THE VOLGA DOES TO A YACHT : JOHN

Tainui is not looking her best. There is no doubt about that. In Baltic ports like Christiansand and Kiel she would stand out a bit beside those rows upon rows of pristine Eurovision Song Contest caravans (I will not mention their names - Bavaria, Jeanneau and Beneteau). But here in Russia's inland waterways, as in Newfoundland and Labrador, she is completely at home. And so are we.

NIZHNIY NOVGOROD

There is an opening bridge before Nizhniy – closed between 5 and 11pm and between 6 and 10.30 am. Anchorage can be had before the bridge, outside the channel behind a small island on the starboard side of the bridge approach. Turn off the river at km 900, after starboard buoy "128", taking care with depths close to the tip of the island.

wpt	56 21.5/043 54.4
km	900

There is fast current flow behind the island but holding is good in soft mud. Anchor close in to the shore, in the vicinity of wpt 56 21.4/ 043 53.8

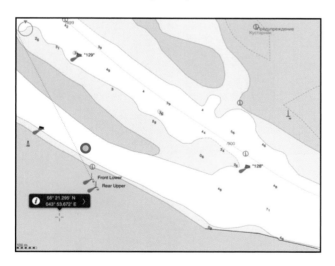

This bustling city lies at the confluence of the and the Volga and Oka rivers. An imposing fortress stands on a high bluff at the river junction. It is an historic city, well worth exploring. Many of its grand and grandiose churches (including the extraordinary Synaxis Church) were commissioned and built in the 17th century by the Stroganov family. An influential merchant dynasty, the Stroganovs were originally Pomor settlers from the White Sea coast. They were Russia's Medicis, with enduring interest in, and support for the arts. They provided substantial financial support for Peter the Great during the Russia's Great Northern War with Sweden (1700-1721).

AT LAST A REST FOR TAINUI : JOHN, 9 JULY

We passed through the open road bridge at 6 am. Old Gorky lay ahead, looking pretty wonderful, I must say. In the mist, at the junction of the Volga and Oka Rivers, a bold fortress stands on the headland.

Noble domes and neoclassical merchant buildings, the river busy with commercial traffic, beyond the shoreline a busy cityscape. It is quite exciting.

We motored gently downstream, the shores lined with huge noisy factories. Past the first two marinas, filled with small motorboats. Rounding a wooded island, Tainui crept across a 2.5 m shoal into a calm, narrow channel and anchored off Rybachiy Yacht Club until a berth was made available for us. The water is deep and our hosts friendly.

To me this feels like a milestone, but as Dirk said, every night since he arrived has been a milestone. We have doubled all our lines in anticipation of a week-long visit to Moscow. The yard manager assures us that the winds will be light. We are the first yacht the marina has seen other than a catamaran from Moscow a couple of years ago.

A planning meeting ensued. As chair I had great difficulty maintaining order. Dirk, in particular, was difficult to manage. Such are the trials of leadership.

Stroganoff's Synaxis Church

Nizhniy is a convenient place to leave your boat safely, if you wish to visit Moscow (4 hours by train). It is a 60 km ferry trip from here back up river to Gorodets, if you didn't stop there on the way through. In 1932 the city was renamed Gorky (after the author Maxim Gorky) but reverted to its old name in 1990. It was closed to foreigners in Soviet times because of numerous military industries in the area. Andrey Sakharov was exiled here from 1980 to 1986.

Volga-Oka confluence

Nizhniy river junction headland

KOSTROMA TO NIZHNIY NOVGOROD

THE GREAT FAIR AT NIZHNIY : JOHN

The bustling city of Nizhniy lies at the confluence of the and the Volga and Oka rivers. An imposing fortress stands on a high bluff at the river junction. It is an historic city, well worth exploring. Many of its grand and grandiose churches (including the extraordinary Synaxis Church) were commissioned and built in the 17th century by the Stroganov family. An influential merchant dynasty, the Stroganovs were originally Pomor settlers from the White Sea coast. They were Russia's Medicis, with enduring interest in, and support for the arts. They provided substantial financial support for Peter the Great during the Russia's Great Northern War with Sweden (1700-1721).

In 1932 the city was renamed Gorky (after the author Maxim Gorky) but reverted to its old name in 1990. It was closed to foreigners in Soviet times because of numerous military industries in the area. Andrey Sakharov was exiled here from 1980 to 1986.

Strategically located at the junction of trade routes between Siberia, the Baltic, the Caspian and the Far East, Nizhniy Novgorod has been a major trade entrepot since the middle ages. By the 19th century its annual trade fair, moved downstream from Makarieff, had become the largest in the world. For 2 months each year the population of Nizhniy increased by 250,000 people and the Volga and Oka riverbanks were crowded with vessels of all kinds. Tea, brought overland from China, was the major trade currency, but furs, Ural iron, salted Caspian fish, glassware, pottery, Persian cashmere, gold and silk were all on offer. The Nizhniy fair was finally closed in 1929.

Great Fair waterfront

Beyond the Oka confluence there are 3 yacht yacht clubs on the right hand side of the river, behind a series of low islands. Telephoning ahead, we found space at Rybachiy Motor Boat Club (RYC), the 3rd of these.

To reach RYC, turn off the river to starboard 2 km after the overhead cableway, just before km 915 (see wpt below). The minimum depth on approach to the estuary is just less than 3m. Inside, the water is deeper. The club is poorly signposted but it can be recognised by the blue houseboat. We were met and guided to a berth by marina attendants.

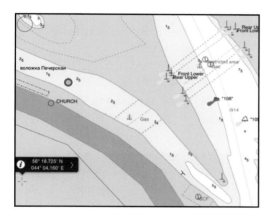

RYC, a 10 minute taxi ride from town, can be recommended. It is a safe place to leave your yacht if you wish to visit Moscow. Cost: 1000R per night. It offers showers, a sauna and (if you are lucky) a hotel room in the small, floating hotel. There is no laundry service and no wifi. The club's best asset is Dima, the young marina attendant, whom we invited to sail with us for a fortnight with his girlfriend Gerda. Dima will take good care of your boat if you leave it to visit Moscow.

Contact details

YC "Rybachiy", Ul Grebnogo Kanala 10,
http://parohodoff.ru/lodochnaya-stancia-yacht-club-rybachiy-nizhniy-novgorod.html
Director is Alexey. Tel: 8-9087556743

Marina approach coordinates:

wpt 56 18.6/044.06.1
km 915

RYC Nizhniy

ANOTHER CHANGE OF CREW : JOHN

Maxine's old friend Lieve joined Tainui for the trip from Nizhniy to Kazan. She brought much needed elegance and formality to a vessel deep in vulgarity and slipshod manners. Quiet and unflappable, Lieve became buoy spotter and track master extraordinaire. But there is one really weird thing about Lieve – she doesn't take drugs. By drugs I don't just mean the important, pleasurable ones, but also coffee, tea, eggs (!!), meat, tomato sauce, tinned foods and processed cheeses. We hope she will eventually win her battle with this extraordinary sobriety.

If ever your are in Moscow, by the way, you could have no better tour guide then Lieve. Historian, music lover and committed Muscovite, she made very good company in Tainui. And, being Flemish, she cleans the boat fastidiously and often.

A TYPICAL EVENING ON THE VOLGA : JOHN, 19 JULY

Back from Moscow to ready the boat for the next bit, I needed to refuel. I asked Dima, working on an adjacent boat, if he could call me a taxi for the tedious jerrycan transfer routine. 10 minutes later he came on board, took the jerrycans and did two trips to a local service station for me, refusing my offer to at least assist him.

Last night Dima came by and asked if his girlfriend Gerda could come to see Tainui. To cut a long story short, there followed a wonderful evening in company with these two 25 year olds. They arrived, of course, bearing whisky and juices of various sorts, together with a copy of volume 5 of the Waterways charts inscribed and dedicated to Tainui.

Gerda, a poet and music lover, has excellent English. She talked about Pushkin, her other love besides Dima. We listened to Taj Mahal and Rachmaninov while musing about life's infinite possibilities. She told me about her childhood and their hopes and aspirations together.

And today, Dima has insisted on driving me into Nizhniy to pick up Maxine and Lieve. He had started work at 6 am and I suspect he started early so he could take the time off for chauffeuring this old fart.

I ended the evening with Heifetz playing the Tchaikovsky fiddle concerto. I must say, he beats the Joshua Bell performance I heard at the Moscow Conservatoire despite the wonderful setting of the latter.

Like so many other young Russians I have met, these two wonderful people (Gerda and Dima, not Heifetz and Bell) will succeed, whatever they do.

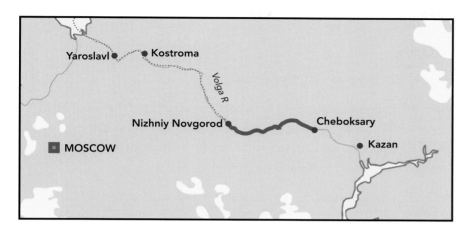

In this 270 km stretch you encounter some lovely countryside. Initially the Volga follows a fairly narrow and serpiginous course from Nizhniy Novgorod with high, forested shores. But halfway along this section of the river the scene changes and you enter a series of lakes and reservoirs with wide horizons and a layered landscape of rolling hills, fields, villages and woodlands. The channel across these lakes is narrow but well-marked.

MAKARIEFF

wpt	56 04.9/045 03.7
km	995

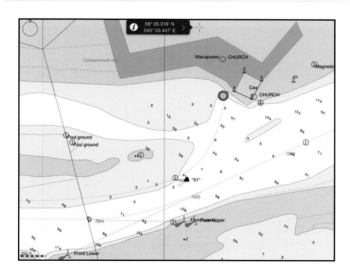

The kremlin walls of this imposing 15th century monastery leap boldly into view as you round a bend in the river near km 992.

Turn left after km 995 and steer straight to the floating pontoon below the kremlin walls. The pontoon is privately owned and restricted to commercial tourist vessels. We were given permission to lie alongside by the security guard however, with payment of a small gratuity.

further details - http://makariev.wix.com/monastir

NIZHNIY TO CHEBOKSARY

TIME DILATES : JOHN

5 am and an impossibly beautiful sunrise over glassy water.

Alone in the cockpit with my first morning coffee I have been thinking about the enormity of this voyage. We are approaching Kazan, meeting place of Orthodox and Islamic cultures and something of a milestone for dear old Tainui. But ahead of her are another thousand miles until she reaches Istanbul.

I wouldn't have missed all this for the world, but crikey, what an undertaking. The Volga just goes on and on. Time dilates and a hypnotic sameness threatens to stop individual days defining themselves.

Except yesterday, for example, when around a river bend there loomed Makarieff Monastery. Totally unexpected, its huge ramparts and massed golden onion domes glistened in the afternoon light. We stopped to visit the peaceful cloistered gardens and dark, brooding chapels. Unforgettable.

So, are the days really all the same? Of course not. An experience like Makarieff seems to come our way every few days, reminding us why we're here, demarcating the endless miles far more effectively than any clock or calendar. As if we should need reminding!

Time to strip off for a swim before I wake the girls and put on their coffee.

Makarieff images

NIZHNIY TO CHEBOKSARY

THE WRONG RIVER : JOHN

Astute followers of our Yellowbrick track may have noticed some interesting movement of Tainui this morning.

I have been stressing to Lieve and Maxine the importance of fastidious recording of our position as we pass each numbered buoy. Overkill perhaps, I said, but you never know when you might suddenly need to know exactly where you are.

Well, we left last night's anchorage after a refreshing swim. Calm, with clear skies. fortunately I was at the helm.

The Volga takes a sharp left hand turn off a moderate sized lake. About half a mile after that, beyond a low bluff, another river does a similar turn to the left. I was daydreaming, entranced by the light on the forest and missed the Volga turnoff. The channel was marked but became both narrow and shallow. Reeded sandbars were close on each side. The depth plummeted to 2.5 metres. I must be off line, I thought. It didn't occur to me to check back on the chart.

We entered the second, wrong river. When I noticed that the buoys were now laid in the opposite way - red cans to port and white nuns to starboard - the penny still didn't drop. Only when it became obvious that the 5,000 ton freighters we have been passing hourly for the last month couldn't possibly manage the tight turns in Wrong River did it dawn on me that I/we were in the wrong place. It came to nothing, in the circumstances. We backtracked and were soon on the Volga once again. But for one who has tended to pride himself on his navigation, what an embarrassment this was. More importantly, what if we had been approaching a dangerous shore in thick weather, tired and seasick, and a similar lapse had occurred? I shudder to think.

I suppose you need these sudden jolts back into reality from time to time. They serve to remind us of the narrow line between lazy travel and shipwreck. Your confidence steadily increases as you sail successfully. I think it was Hiscock who said that every yacht cruising the world will eventually wreck because of this dangerous hubris. My sailing life has been punctuated by such sudden reminders of my fallibility. I can remember each and every one of them and sometimes they visit me in my sleep. I get cautious for a while, then the cycle repeats itself.

Head bowed in humility, I apologised to Maxine and Lieve before pouring myself a beer.

FOKINO

wpt	56 10.8/045 52.3
km	1059

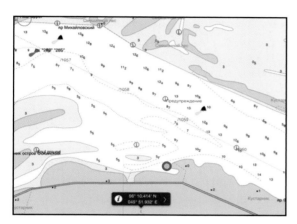

Comfortable anchorage can be found on the right hand shore here, with some protection from winds blowing up or down the river.

CHEBOKSARY

wpt	56 09.4/047 15.4
km	1171

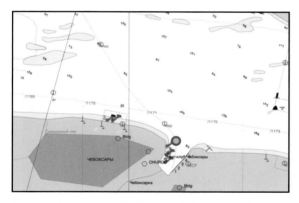 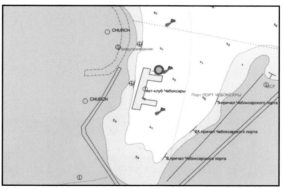

Situated on the right bank of the river, the town is new, having been rebuilt when old Old Cheboksary (1465 CE) was flooded by increased reservoir levels. The waterfront is lined with high, sloping concrete bund walls. There is not much of interest for visiting yachts, but this is a useful stop for provisioning

A boat harbour on the right hand side of the river before the town basin is tiny, crowded and probably too shallow. There is however a new, small marina at the commercial ship basin in the centre of town. By Russian standards it is expensive (2,500 rub per night) but the marina is secure and it offers good, if basic facilities. Shops and restaurants are a short walk away. The approach, from km 1171, is easy.

NIZHNIY TO CHEBOKSARY

CHEBOKSARY : JOHN, 22 JULY

The Volga follows a fairly narrow and serpiginous course from Nizhniy Novgorod with high forested shores. But today the scene has changed. We are now passing through a series of lakes and reservoirs with wide horizons and a layered landscape of rolling hills, fields, villages and woodlands. The channel across these lakes is narrow but well- marked.

We arrived in Cheboksary in the early evening and tied up in the basin in the centre of town. At the little marina they said we were the first foreign vessel they had ever seen. The town is new, having been rebuilt when old Cheboksary was flooded after the reservoir levels were raised by the locks about 5 miles ahead. The evening light was lovely.

Maxine had insisted we stop here because we had to replenish our wine stocks. Lieve is teetotal but easygoing. While I was happy to continue on relying on our vast vodka stocks, I have been known to take a glass of wine occasionally and was pleased to see some Chilean Chardonnay added to our drinks cupboard. In any case, you just don't argue with Maxine.

I was also keen to eat a Japanese meal, so after re-provisioning we repaired to the waterside restaurant. There's Japanese and Japanese - I will say no more. But a cheerful evening was indeed had, spiced with our increasingly sincere and garrulous toasts to one another. I even forgot the humiliation of my egregious navigation this morning.

The minimum depth in the town basin 5 m. Tie up on the northern side of the outermost of the floating finger wharves on the western shore of the basin, in depths of 3.4m. The basin is open to the north and there is considerable fetch across the river. In strong northerly winds this may make the berth uncomfortable, if not untenable. Wake from passing ships can be considerable and you may wish to use a kedge to hold off the finger wharf.

Small boat facility before Cheboksary

contact details

boat club: Y/C 'Vega" Moskovskoe embankment 11
+7 8352 585543
Cheboksary generally: - http://www.gcheb.cap.ru/

A PLEA : SOME CREW

Dear Hygiene & Cosmetics,

Tainui is a beautiful yacht, full stop. She is doing everything that keeps her in good shape. And she is in a very good shape. She is still strong, has all her wits about her and can sail just as far as her younger sisters. But her internal strength cannot fully compensate for her unkempt appearance. Unfortunately, poor Tainui usually gets neglected by the two of you.

Yes, this is a plea, Hygiene and Cosmetics, to both of you to pay more attention to her. Because the old girl suffers because you make her feel ugly. She'll love having shiny galley sinks, empty of mountains of discarded coffee granules. She'll applaud the use of detergent more often so the dirty dishes won't rub off on her. She hates itching caused by crisps spilled by some crew on her cockpit sole, and the irritating effect of red wine spilled by others. Or the lingering smell of tobacco in her midnight-blue upholstery. The Hoover is one of her most prized possessions, just waiting for you, Hygiene, to show up. Please Hygiene, get your act together! You can never be replaced by "some crew".

And you, Cosmetics, at least you will finally come by this winter to give the old girl her long overdue facelift. Her topsides are immaculate again. Let's hope that Hygiene follows suit. After all, old age must be beautified at all times. I want both of you to be proud!

Best regards, "some crew"

CHEBOKSARY TO KAZAN

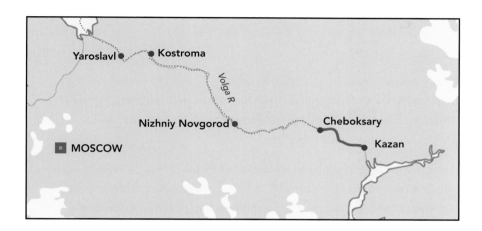

This 136 km leg takes you through hilly, pretty country which is intermittently forested and farmed. It may conveniently be broken into 2 sections, with layover at the stunning monastic site of Sviyazhsk.

SVIYAZHSK

wpt	55 47.4/048 46.2
km	1291

This is not to be missed.

There is a shallow passage leading direct to Sviyazhsk from the river but locals strongly warned us against attempting this route. It is much safer to continue along the Volga to km 1291 (at wpt above) near the transit leads on the southern shore, before turning back west, hard in against the land. At starboard hand buoy "4", you can steer straight for Sviyazhsk island.

Anchorage off the tourist wharf provides good holding in clean sand. Approximate anchorage coordinates are 55 46.3/048 40.3. Unfortunately, the Sviyazhsk anchorage is just outside the limits of both the iSailor and Navionics charts.

You are not permitted to lie alongside the wharf itself but there is a 20m long niche at the northern end of the wharf where, with permission, you may tie up alongside in 5m water over clean sand.

SVIYAZHSK : JOHN, 25 JULY

Yesterday was long and tiring, with rain and squalls. The first bleak weather we have had since Belomorsk Canal.

This morning I got up at 5 to watch sunrise over the monastery. Tainui is anchored meekly in the lee of Sviyazhsk Monastery. It is a beautiful, cold, clear morning with drifting fog banks. The onion domes loom silent, imperious with a full moon and mist on the water adding needless extra theatre. The full moon seems excessive.

In this abstemious vessel, happy hour last night was extended by the skipper's indulgence (starting time noon, closing time 10 pm) because 20 km before we passed the halfway mark in our Russian journey. Inexplicably clumsy, one of us spilled a bag of crisps in the cockpit. There is no need to mention the two glasses of red wine which might have been kicked over during the same session. So this morning I lifted the teak grates to sweep up the mess while the girls sat by, sipped coffee and gave useless advice.

The best thing about having Dutch people on board is that, carefully managed, their deep-rooted anal compulsiveness can be exploited usefully. And so it was this morning. Lieve (she's actually Flemish, not Dutch, but hey) felt she had no choice but to take control of the cleaning process. With the grates up, an intense, noisy and endless process of Flemish surgical sterilisation has begun. Wisely I retreated below.

Over the last couple of months Tainui has been slowly transforming herself from an ocean-going vessel into a sort of Romany caravan. Her decks are strewn with hoses, coolant and fuel drums, clotheslines, fenders, carpets, and sails. The chart table looks like a display table at a garage sale. I have found it quite impossible to avoid the transfiguration and I have given up. But now we have a spotless cockpit and the skipper is happy.

Now we're off to explore Sviyazhsk Monastery. At 9 we moved alongside to meet our friends from "Credo", the yacht we had met midstream on the Volga a week ago. They had driven from Kazan to meet us and show us the monastic site. An old man offered to watch Tainui for us while we explored.

Sviyahzhsk is a remarkable collection of buildings dating back to 1600, with that familiar history of Bolshevik sacking, gulag prison, psychiatric hospital and now, finally, treasured archive. We have noticed how many monastic towers we have seen are garbed in scaffolding. It is clear that Russia is spending time and money restoring these priceless sites. Today our guide was an architect whose pride in this island was touching. The pictures say it all.

CHEBOKSARY TO KAZAN

KAZAN : JOHN, 26 JULY

Kazan, largest port on the river system, sits at the confluence of the Volga and Kama Rivers, which ends its thousand mile journey from Siberia here. Protecting these vital trade routes, Kazan has always been a garrison town. Originally Tatar, it was taken by Ivan the Terrible on his third attempt, with huge loss of life.

More prosaically, Kazan will always occupy a special place in our hearts. Not only is it a safe place to park a yacht, but we have been met with so much warmth and generosity by wonderful friends here that it is difficult to leave.

Not long after we had passed under the Trans-Siberian Railway Bridge, "Credo" came out to meet us in the river near the Disneyland domes of the Church of All Religions and guided us in to the snug marina run by Oleg Tyurin. The impressive faux gothic Trans-Siberian railway station is 300 m away.

Willing hands helped us tie up and then there followed a lengthy party on Tainui and Credo both, with music and dancing, noisy but incomprehensible conversation, shashlik, salads and many, many toasts.

Such lovely people - Credo's owner Sasha and his endless supply of cognac; Andrey, who designed and built Credo; Andrey's quiet, astute music-loving daughter Masha; Tatiana with her sharp wit and beautiful smile, quiet Artyom and gorgeous little Egor; Damir the architect who guided us tirelessly at Sviyazhsk and then later through the Kazan kremlin; and of course Oleg.

It was Oleg who took our laundry home to wash, spent a whole day organising our provisioning and drove us across Kazan to find us our engine supplies. An easygoing, quiet but attentive bloke who circumnavigated in 1998 from Kazan, Oleg has an impish smile and a sailor's zest for life. What a gem of a fellow.

In Kazan we are bidding fond farewells to Lieve, our champion helmsperson and char, who has settled so well into our shipboard routine. She is replaced by Gerda and Dima, who drove down from Nizhniy Novgorod to spend a week on the Volga with us. They have been tucked into the aft cabin.

Kazan, birthplace of Chaliapin and Nureyev, is a rich architectural mish-mash dominated by its World Heritage kremlin. Onion domes now share the skyline with minarets and the Tatar and Islamic influence is everywhere apparent. Oleg reports that Fyodor Chaliapin and Maxim Gorky were boyhood friends here. They both applied to join the church choir but Chaliapin was rejected because his voice was not good enough (he went on to become the world's greatest bass baritone!). Such is life.

I understand that much of old Kazan was destroyed during the Stalinist years but there is an active reconstruction program well under way.

KAZAN

http://kzn.ru/

wpt	55 47/049 01.4
km	1307

If there were any doubt, the appearance of the extraordinary Church of All Religions on the left hand side of the river will confirm your arrival. In architectural terms this bizarre church defies categorisation. It stands bold on the left bank of the Volga Staroye Arakchino at km 1303. You can't miss it. Like it or not, you cannot help but to be impressed by it. Designed by the artist Ildar Khanov, who was born in this village, construction began in 1994. Close approach by boat is not possible because of shoals. By train it is 3 stops back upstream from Kazan.

Church of All Religions

The ancient city of Kazan sits near the confluence of the Volga and its largest tributary, the Kama River, which flows down from Siberian territory to the northeast. In Kazan there is a colourful fusion of Orthodox and Islamic cultures, both architectural, social and ethnic. Ivan the Terrible fought long and bitterly to secure the town, whose strategic, military and commercial importance cannot be overstated.

With a population of 1,200,000, Kazan is the capital of the republic Tatarstan, and is commonly referred to as the 3rd capital of Russia (after Moscow and St Petersburg). It is 800km from Moscow, with good air and rail connections for crew changes.

Arrival at Kazan represents something of a milestone for yachts on the Volga-Don route. You are now over half way to the Sea of Azov and for the first time it becomes possible to imagine the entire route ahead laid out in one's minds eye.

CREW CHANGE - THE CHILDREN : JOHN

Lieve returned home to Moscow from Kazan, leaving behind a cleaner, tidier and emptier ship. As is almost always the case with crew change, we were sorry to see her go.

In small boats you get used to one another or you don't survive together. You learn to tolerate foibles and respect privacies. I can only think of 3 crewpersons (and Lieve was most definitely not one of them) in 40 years whose departures have not saddened me a bit. Be it an ocean race or a languid cruise, the shared sailing experience is unique and you do not want to let it go.

Gerda and Dima arrived the following day. We met this wonderful young couple in Nizhniy Novgorod (see post "Typical Evening on the Volga"). "The Children", as we called them, drove down from Nizhniy Novgorod to join Tainui in Kazan. They stayed with us for a fortnight, until Saratov, and they fitted into shipboard life quite seamlessly. Their wide-eyed pleasure was a delight to behold. They are welcome to rejoin Tainui at any time.

Dima steered and navigated with skill, for hours (no, days) at a time. He is a natural boatman and has an assured future on Russia's inland waterways. Just do it, Dima!

Gerda's eyes sparkle. She has an infectious laugh and is a great cook. I hope she will help us put together our cruising guide to the Volga.

There are two marinas in Kazan, but the 100 year old Lokomotiv YC is the obvious choice for visiting yachts. It lies in a secure, all-weather pond off the north side of the river.

The approach channel from the above position is shallow (at times under 3m) but inside the pond the depths exceed 4 m. There is secure dockage, a fuelling wharf and a small cafe on site but apart from shore power and water, for the moment there is little else. It is a 30 minute walk to town, past the imposing Trans-Siberian Railway terminal.

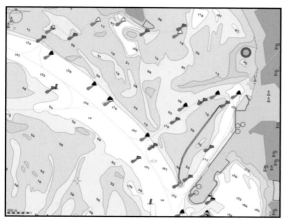 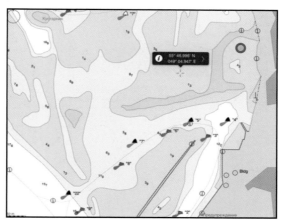

Contact details

Kazan, peninsula Lokomotiv 1
+7 (843) 297-72-40
Director: Oleg Tyurin

Oleg is a sailor who has circumnavigated. He speaks only a few words of English but more than makes up for this with his interest, friendliness, generosity and expertise with practical matters. He kindly insisted on doing our huge pile of laundry at his own house.

Our good friends from yacht "Credo" (Sasha and Andre) - were also wonderful hosts. They have agreed to have their contact details listed in this guide and, like Oleg, will be pivotal contacts for cruising yachts visiting Kazan in future years.

CHEBOKSARY TO KAZAN

SOME THOUGHTS : GERDA

I'm 24 and I always work a lot and have many things to do. It was completely impossible to leave my busy world even for two days. But all my worries and thoughts had been broken by my heart screaming: "YOU HAVE TO DO IT!!". So I took a bag, sunglasses and exciting expectations and left the apartment.

I've never traveled in Russia on yacht, especially with foreigners! So everything about this trip was new for me. I will always remember that steep wooden stair, that tiny kitchen (where I was constantly attacked by salt because of pitching), our cozy cabin and special morning coffee from the Captain. When we were sitting on the deck all together talking about everything I felt myself home. It was so strange and wonderfull, we used several languages for speaking but always could easily understood each other's feelings without speaking at all. We laughed so much during our two weeks together. We enjoyed landscapes and made it in different ways. John saw another new country, Maxine - new places, me and Dima - the whole new life... When something like this suddenly happens with you you know that it will change you.

One peaceful morning John have said: "Shut up, drink your coffee and enjoy the life!". And You know he was damn right! It seemed like time disappeared and everything in my life just had no matter at that moment. All my worries dissolved in consuming morning serenity... You can't describe it. You can feel it.!

Day after day my inspiration was growing. I felt myself free and happy! I was enjoying everything happening! And when the time to say goodbye had come I was a bit lost. And of course I want to come back to Tainui, John and Maxine again! To see that infinity night sky with thousands stars sparkling on the water mirror.. To hear magic flute... To feel that freedom...

(sorry for mistakes)

Among Kazan's many attractions for visitors, the following deserve special mention:

Kazan Kremlin - listed by the Unesco. Meeting of the Sunni Islam and Russian orthodoxy.

Kazan Mother of God icon - much revered by Orthodox Christians, the icon was returned to Kazan with much ceremony by Pope Paul 2 and is now enshrined in the Church of the Elevation of the Holy Cross (Big Red Street No 5).

<u>Peter & Paul Cathedral</u> Naryshkin baroque on M. Dzhalil Street 24,
http://eng.kazan.eparhia.ru/monastyri/churches/peterpaul/
Built to commemorate a visit to Kazan by Peter the Great in 1722, this church is a visual delight, with unusual architecture and grandiloquent facades.

An interesting historical review of Orthodoxy in Kazan may be found at
http://kazan.eparhia.ru/www/english/index.htm

THE VOLGA GETS BIG : JOHN

Departure from Kazan was difficult. Partly because our dockside farewells were protracted, and partly because we had to wait an hour while a mafioso gin palace refuelled before we could top up our tanks at the fuelling jetty. This huge motor yacht took on 2 tonnes of diesel, which it burns at around 600 litres an hour. The skipper was incredulous when I told them we could motor for nearly 6 days on that amount. Their total time between tank fills - 10 hours!

Wonderful Sasha brought Credo out to see us off. A huge jar of my favourite pickles was handed to us by Andrey. After we had waved our final farewells, Credo turned back and we set course into the Volga.

We are at last travelling south again. After the Kama confluence the Volga gets seriously wide. With a fresh beam wind and rain squalls we rolled our way down towards historic Bolgar. After our long eastern leg we turned right into the Kuybishevsky Reservoir. With a fresh SE breeze and a 7 mile fetch the seas were choppy, but the ever present current helped us along.

Darkness having fallen it was a relief to enter Karelskaya refuge, a snug little spot where we anchored in 3.5 metres of glassy water.

Today it is windy and wet. We delayed our departure with pancakes, alternator service, battery water top-up and fine tuning of the mast supports. Not until 2 pm, when all excuses had been exhausted, did we raise the anchor and motor out into the murk. In point of fact the wind eased and backed to the NE during the afternoon, so that we had a quite comfortable trip down the right bank of the Volga towards Bolgar.

Bolgar is a pilgrimage town for Tatar people in search of their roots. They were Central Asians who preceded the Mongols in this region. Half of them moved to central Europe (Bulgaria, no less) and converted to Christianity. The rest stayed, became integrated into Mongol society and ultimately adopted Islam. We had hoped to stop in Bolgar but the bleak weather was adequate disincentive.

The mean depth of the reservoir is 8 m, but outside marked channels the depths commonly drop below 3 m, especially in the northern part of the reservoir and on the eastern shore. Fresh weather can quickly create short, steep seas if the wind is from the S-SE.

After Ulyanovsk the marked route follows the western shore of the reservoir, but with easterly winds it may be more comfortable to keep to the eastern side, depths allowing.

There are numerous opportunities for anchorage along the way, of which those described below are but a few examples.

KAZAN TO TOLYATTI

The 360 km leg down the inland sea of Kuybyshev offers numerous possibilities for overnight anchorage.

KUYBYSHEV (SAMARA) RESERVOIR

A huge artificial lake, 320 miles long and 20 miles wide, Kuybyshev Reservoir extends from above the Volga-Kama confluence near Kazan south to Tolyatti. It is the largest reservoir in Europe and the third largest in the world, created with the construction of a barrage and hydroelectric station on the Volga near Tolyatti in 1956. Many villages and towns along the banks of the river had to be relocated to higher ground.

KIRELSKOE SHELTER

wpt	55 07.96/049 12.23
km	1390

This small port offers secure all-weather anchorage and has an easy, buoyed and lit approach. It is a convenient first night stop after you leave Kazan. Turn right at fairway buoy "85" and proceed along the south shore of the island. You can anchor anywhere, in soft mud. With strong easterly winds a lee may be found behind the western end of the island.

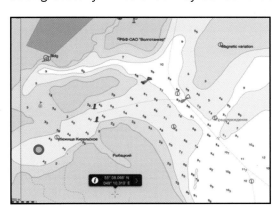

VOLGA BOATMEN : JOHN

Today's Volga boatmen drive huge double barges with great skill. Some are several hundred metres long (the barges, I mean), controlled by a single pushing tug at the stern. I could watch these blokes negotiating the locks and tight river bends for hours. Much more modest are the thousands of solitary fishermen at anchor in their flimsy inflatables, fishing for sterlet and other goodies along the whole length of the river.

For two days we have been motoring down Kuybyshev Reservoir, a huge inland sea some 300 miles long and up to 25 miles wide. Created when the Volga was dammed for a hydroelectric power generation at Tolyatti in 1956, the resulting interruption to normal river flow has been a mixed blessing, I understand. The ecology, marine life and even the weather of the Volga have been affected hugely and many riverside towns have had to be relocated. From a navigational point of view the river has been tamed. Gone are most of its shifting sandbanks, shallows and fast, unpredictable currents. The journey from the Baltic to the Caspian and Black Seas is now a reliable commercial route for some 4-5 months of each year. But check out the following picture - if that isn't algal bloom caused by low flow and phosphate runoff, I'm a monkey's uncle. Think what it is doing to oxygenation and the health of native fish stocks in the Volga.

We have had a steady 1 knot favourable current and modest (10 knot) headwinds. But the reservoir is shallow and with such a long fetch, steep little seas get up quickly. This must be an absolutely horrendous bit of water in a blow.

BOLGAR

Bolgar is said to have been the capital of Volga Bulgaria in the 9th century. As such, it is a pilgrimage town for Tatar people in search of their roots. The Tatars were central Asians who preceded, and battled strenuously with the Mongols in this region. Half of the surviving Tatars moved to central Europe (Bulgaria, no less) and converted to Christianity. The rest stayed, became integrated into Mongol society and ultimately adopted Islam.

For those wishing to explore the ruins, there is a buoyed channel for tourist ships, leading 8 km southeast from fairway buoy "79" to a wharf. We had hoped to stop in Bolgar but the bleak weather was adequate disincentive.

STARAYA MAINA

wpt	54 38.99/048 55.1
km	1470

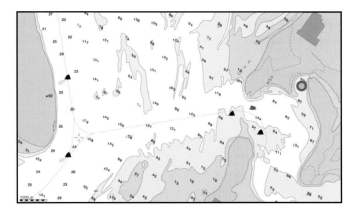

Staraya is a large bay on the eastern side of the reservoir. A channel leads left from the main channel (wpt above), before fairway buoy "61" at km 1470.

A secluded inlet on the north side of the entrance to Staraya Maina provides snug anchorage at 54 39/048 57.5. The bottom here is intermittently foul with waterlogged timber and we needed to reset our anchor twice. Once secure however, you will find that this spot offers good all-weather protection.

Fouled anchor - a not uncommon problem

NOT IN FRONT OF THE CHILDREN : JOHN, 28 JULY

Last night's anchorage was a deserted wooded bay at Staraya Mayna. Unlike yesterday's squally passage, today we have weather which is warm and calm. Maxine is having another bad hair day. Her main problem this time is my managerial and organisational failure. "How can I get home to see Dirk? How can I arrange for my friends to join Tainui? How can I arrange my summer when you refuse to give me any hint of a timetable, an itinerary, an overall plan?" She flounced and banged things in ways some readers (Dirk, are you there?) will recognise.

I tried to point out that here we were in the middle of Russia with no idea of what lies ahead, that the gas bottle has to be changed, the starboard alternator isn't charging and I have to find out why, the beeping of the solar panel alarm needs my undivided attention, but to no avail. Finally I retreated into Philbrick's book about the dreadful Charles Wilkes, which reassured me that there have been far worse skippers than me. My only consolation is that Chris and my daughters are not here - Maxine would then have all the ammunition she could ever need in this non-contretemps. I could only gesture towards Dima and Gerda and say rather lamely "Maxine, not in front of the children".

Maxine has read a draft of this post and warned me that if I publish it I will find out what a real bad hair day is like. Nevertheless I have decided to proceed, in the interest of press freedom and sweet revenge. Damn the consequences.

In the middle of the 30 km crossing of Kuybishevsky Reservoir we passed a Russian yacht from Tolyatti and stopped for the usual gam. It is perhaps the 3rd cruising yacht we have seen in the last 1,000 miles. These moments (the mid-sea meetings, not the bad hair day events) are to be treasured.

TURN ON THE TV SET : JOHN

True, Lenin was born here, but today Tainui is the big news. Do not miss Ulyanov'sk Prime Time TV tonight. We have had film crews on board all morning and Tainui will be the talk of the town.

Inside the big mole barrier is an all weather harbour. We tied up yesterday afternoon at a long, deserted wharf and settled into the by now familiar session of toasts, good cheer and assertions of eternal brotherhood with sailors from the tiny yacht club. It was Navy Day. Little children clambered over the boat and explored Tainui's secret interstices while we gravely accepted a Russian Navy Ensign, a Ulyanov'sk Yacht Club pennant, 4 smoked fish and a bottle of ethyene glycol-like home brew.

ULYANOV'SK

wpt	54 18.2/048 26.3
km	1530

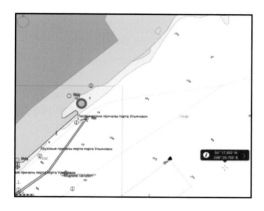

This is a moderate-sized town on the west bank of the reservoir. Formerly Simbirsk, this city was renamed in 1924 in honour of its most famous son - Vladmir Ilyich Ulyanov (Lenin).

Dating from the mid 17th century, Ulyanov'sk has retained almost none of its pre-revolutionary architecture. The childhood dwellings of both Lenin and author Ivan Goncharov (best known for his novel "Oblomov") survive however, and are popular tourist attractions.

There is a sturdy mole harbour on the right-hand shore of the Volga, after the second bridge, with deep, easy entrance. After entering, you will see the main harbour extending to your left. Directly ahead is a long concrete pier, for smaller tourist ships. We tied up here but were asked to move or pay the quite exorbitant commercial wharf dues. At the land end of this pier is the Ulyanovsk Yacht Club, in a pond swinging to the right. It is a tiny establishment, really no more than a cluster of converted shipping containers with only the most rudimentary of facilities. The enthusiasm and hospitality of members more than makes up for this. The pond is too shallow and too tight for deep-drafted vessels but YC officials will welcome you and find somewhere for you to tie up outside the pond.

Ulyanovsk YC

You should ask the club to phone ahead to arrange your berth at Tolyatti Yacht Club downstream.

KAZAN TO TOLYATTI

Ulyanov'sk is a Two Move Town (see Belyzorsk insert). Not long after we had tied up we were asked to move 50 metres along the wharf. We dutifully did so. An hour later we were told that we could not lie alongside this wharf without paying dues usually owed by large cruise ships.

We had to move again, to raft alongside a home-built power boat on the opposite side of the channel 4 metres away. I could not see the logic of this and refused. Maxine and the children had by now removed themselves to a watering hole in a converted shipping container (the yacht club) and I was alone.

There was no wind and I could have done this manoeuver alone without starting the engine. But as is so often the case in Russia I found myself surrounded by willing helpers shouting orders at one another, letting go mooring lines and pulling in all directions at once. Tainui was adrift before I noticed it. All went well in the end, but with any sort of breeze things might have gone awry.

I have not yet learned how to exert my authority in these situations. As skipper I expect people around me to wait expectantly for instructions. I like to speak in a quiet but authoritative way, without ambiguity, so that no one panics and everyone knows his or her job. That never works in Russia. And barking out orders seems to be a waste of time too. It all comes from their overweaning desire to help, to act preemptively and to take charge. It does not occur to them that we managed to get the boat here from Sydney without them, barely bruised.

After the 4 metre move had been completed and my crew had returned, I asked Maxine to tell the by now vodka-raddled crowd in the cockpit that instructions about mooring lines were mine and mine alone. There was much apologising, more toasts to brotherhood across the seas, and all was well. Until next time.

Tainui was the first foreign yacht the club had seen and we were treated like royalty. The evening ended in a candle-lit open shelter among the trees, where we ate shashlik, sipped tea and swore eternal brotherhood.

This morning the TV crews arrived and we were unable to depart until 2pm despite all our best efforts. Ulyanov'sk was a memorable stop for Tainui and, with obvious caveats, this harbour is to be recommended to future yachts.

And don't forget to turn on your TV sets tonight.

SO WHAT DO WE DO? : JOHN

Gerda and Dima have been with us since Nizhniy Novgorod and they are excellent companions. Maxine complains intermittently of what she calls Volga Fatigue (really, I think she is just missing her man) but is her usual cheerful, witty and efficient self. I tinker, read, and write stuff like this between power naps in my wonderful saloon berth.

We have settled into a comfortable routine. Of course the crew are now fully attuned to Tainui's demands. Maxine, for example, no longer complains about the absence of under-floor heating in the bathroom. Territorial claims over small spaces in the cockpit and below are made and respected. And there is always the foredeck, by turns a gaol cell, a remote mountain top and the meditation room. We respect one another's need for privacy, we move efficiently and do not fall over one another. Even Dirk, who was, and presumably still is about 9 feet tall, achieved some sort of harmony (well, at least an uneasy truce) with our cramped environment.

At anchor I am usually up at around 5.30 am for the first of my many coffees in the cockpit. I will never forget these Volga mornings, which are cool, still and often luminous. They give a real sense of the real power and timelessness of the river.

Maxine stumbles tousle-haired from the forecabin an hour later, struggling to find consciousness. Coffee, a plunge into the river and then her disgusting Russian grits breakfast usually do the trick.

We read in silence for another hour until the children emerge from their playpen (the aft cabin) bright-eyed, fully formed and beautiful.

As conversation warms up, all of it in Russian, I go below to give the engine its morning medications, then up comes the anchor. Breakfast follows (I am doing pancakes today) as we settle into our journey once again.

Dima does all the steering. He seems to love the buoy navigation, collision avoidance manoeuvers and route planning. I am not sure what the rest of us do, but what with eating, reading, laundering and just ogling there seems plenty to occupy us.

KRIUSHI BAY

wpt	54 07.37/48 33.17
km	1557

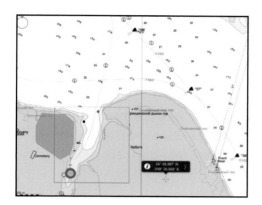

South of middle channel marker "38" this narrow bay is said to provide protection from all except northerly winds. Anchor to the south of the 3rd jetty, in 4m mud. Good holding. Local sailors recommended this as a good stop in fresh winds, although we did not explore the bay.

KAZAN TO TOLYATTI

THOUGHTS : DIMA

Прошел почти год с того момента как мы познакомились с Джоном. Произошло наше знакомство в яхт клубе в котором на тот момент я работал. Он остановился у нас на стоянку, на несколько дней .Джон оказался очень веселым и умным человеком ,у него очень молодая душа примерно лет 18 - ти Он пригласил меня и мою девушку к себе на яхту, мы долго общались. Предложил нам продолжить путешествие вместе с ним - мы согласились.

Это было незабываемое время, не променял бы его, даже на самый элитный курорт заграницей. Не знаю как это описать, но попробуйте представить: ночь, примерно около часа, вы лежите на палубе яхты, прекрасный свежей воздух, легкий ветерок и вокруг признаков цивилизации. Самое главное, вы нигде не увидите такого чистого неба. Казалось, что млечный путь повторяет изгибы судового хода...

Днем мы шли на яхте с маленькой скоростью, примерно 6-10 км/ч и можно было рассмотреть красоты окружающие нас. Погода часто менялась, но больше всего мне нравился вечер. Ветер стихал, становилось тихо и можно было услышать природу.

Я никогда не забуду время проведенное на яхте, спасибо тебе Тайнуй и конечно же Вам Джон!

It is now almost a year ago from the moment that we got to know John. We met him in the marina where I was then working. He stayed with us for a few days. John turned out to be a very cheerful and intelligent guy. He had a very young soul, about 18-20 years. He invited me and my girlfriend to his yacht where we talked and talked. He offered us to continue his journey with him – and we agreed.

It was an unforgettable time which I would never change, not even for the most elite resort abroad. I don't know how to describe it but try to imagine this: night, you're lying on the deck of the yacht, wonderful fresh air, slight breeze and few signs of civilization. Most important is that you won't find anywhere else such a clear sky. As if the Milky Way road repeats the meandering of the boat's road. During the day we sailed with a low speed of 6-10 km/h. We could gaze at the beauty of our surroundings. The weather changed frequently but most of all I loved the evenings. The wind died down, it became silent and you could listen to nature.

I will never forget the time we spent in the yacht. Thank you Tainui and thank you John.

SENGELAY REFUGE

wpt	53 58.06/048 48.5
km	1572

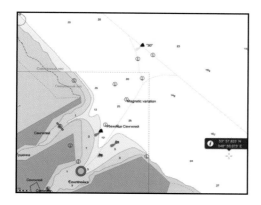

This little bay is entered southeast of fairway buoy "30" provides good holding in soft mud and is protected from all except east winds. There is an awkward old jetty on the northern shore with depths of 2.5 metres, which should be avoided.

TOLYATTI : JOHN, 30 JULY

Like every arrival, this one has come as a complete surprise to us. A power boat was waiting off the yacht club to guide us in, and many willing hands pulled eagerly but unpredictably on our shorelines. But we got in before massive storm clouds dumped their contents on us. I knew that Barry Woodhouse met with a force 12 squall just off Tolyatti and we were relieved to be tied up. As it turned out, there wasn't a lot of wind in this squall.

We were met by the usual press contingent, an efficient and helpful club manager and the vice president of the Russian Yachting Federation. Maxine says I will have to get used to this, but for now we have lost one one of the pleasures of cruising - anonymity.

Interviews completed, we repaired to the club premises, where an informal reception had been arranged in our honour.

We had met Vladimir and his tiny home-built timber yacht in Ulyanov'sk. Travelling south also, he had arranged to wait for us off the yacht club so we could meet up for a gam in Tolyatti. He accompanied us into the marina, and he and his crew joined our little party for the evening meal. More of Vladimir anon.

The yacht club makes Sydney's CYC look like a scout hall. I have not asked how it was funded. This is a major yachting centre and training of all olympic classes takes place in the large bay at the head of the locks. Overnight races are run throughout the summer. I cannot imagine a setting where local knowledge would be more important for race tacticians.

Showers, celebrations, sleep, handshakes, exchanges of fraternal goodwill and presentations of club T-shirts completed, we have just set off for the 4 mile trip to the dual locks in the barrage which contains the huge reservoir we have just crossed. Vladimir's little boat, waiting for us outside the marina, looks a picture.

Our next port is Samara, where I hope we can stop for a few days. I have to take the main alternator to an electrician to be tested. I think the diodes have blown. We are OK on our secondary alternator but running our fridge and other electrics is a big ask for its 55 ah output. If it croaks we always have our splendid Honda 1kW generator in reserve.

We are approaching what is known as The Big Bend. A cursory glance at a map will show why. Then our route turns SW towards the Volga-Don Canal, the Don and the Sea of Azov. But we still have 1,500 km to go before the mast goes up, the Chinese laundry comes in and Tainui becomes a sailing vessel once more. I can't wait for that.

TOLYATTI

wpt	53 27.1/049 20.9
km	1654

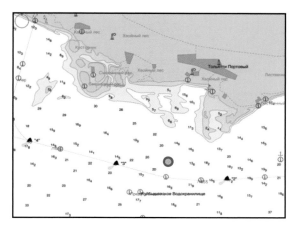 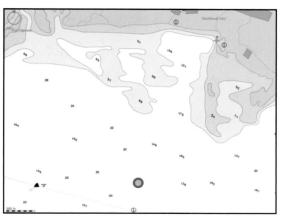

It comes as something of a relief to reach the southern end of huge, exposed Kuybyshev Reservoir. Tolyatti lies on the eastern shore, just before the locks and hydroelectric barrage which creates the reservoir. The approach waypoint above is located just beyond fairway buoy "3", and the imposing buildings of the yacht club are clearly visible ahead and to port.

Tolyatti reception committee

Tolyatti http://portal.tgl.ru/en/

Tolyatti is a large industrial town focusing on automotive and chemical industries. It is not a major tourist destination. Originally Stavropol, it was renamed in honour of the Italian communist leader Palmiro Togliatti when the Lada auto factory was founded in 1966, in cooperation with Fiat.

The club has two secure boat harbours to the right as you steer towards the clubhouse building. It is likely that you will be met at the entrance and guided in to your berth. Our spot was in the second harbour, close inshore. Minimum approach depth was 3.4 m.

Tolyatti Yacht Club comes as a real surprise. It is a large, modern and professionally run establishment with an active sailing school and a busy schedule of inshore and overnight yacht racing during the summer season. The club focuses on Olympic classes.

All facilities are available here and this is the first and only such installation you will encounter on the entire river system.

Tainui received a royal welcome. Dmitri Evgenevich Gulbitskiy, a club patron and a vice president of the Russian Yachting Federation, motored out with his son to meet us and guide us into the marina. The club's manager was both charming and helpful. To cap it all off, we were treated to an informal reception at the club's very fine restaurant.

http://yachtclub-tlt.ru/

TOLYATTI TO SARATOV

It is 515 km from Tolyatti to Saratov. In much of this section, hilly shores are close and the scenery is at times quite beautiful. A pleasant day sail beyond the Kuybyshev locks takes you around The Big Bend to Samara. Further south, Syzran, Balakovo and a number of other towns line the river, but in preference we sought out quiet anchorages en route Saratov.

SARATOV RESERVOIR

Construction of the dam near Balakhovo in 1958 created this 200 mile long hydroelectric reservoir. Both Samara and The Big Bend lie on the reservoir although Saratov itself lies beyond the dam. The western shore comprises low rolling hills, while to the east the vast Russian steppe extends for thousands of miles to Siberia, Mongolia and China.

THE BIG BEND

A cursory glance at the chart explains the origin of the term. The Volga takes a grand, 180 degree sweep around the Zhigulovskiye Mountains past Samara, flowing first to the east, then south and then back to the west. Rich in stories and culture, The Big Bend has an interesting history of piracy. Brigands in the mountains used to keep watch on the upstream side of the bend. When vessels were seen coming downstream the pirates would cross the neck of the bend overland and attack the unsuspecting ships when they came south round the corner.

NEW ORLEANS OF THE VOLGA : JOHN, 3 AUGUST

...or so Samara was called in the 18th century. The first performance of Shostakovitch's 7th symphony took place in Samara and Yuri Gargagarin recuperated here after he landed his space craft just up the road. We have been treated royally in Samara by Vladimir Antonov, ex-Aeroflot arctic pilot, and his ballet choreographer partner Tatiana.

Organising and synchronising crew has been difficult on this trip. To my great embarrassment I double booked Samara locals Vladimir and Tatiana as crew, against Gerda and Dima. When we arrived in Samara I had to tell Vladimir and Tatiana we could not accept them for the next leg down to Samarov. They were extremely gracious about this and their hospitality was undiminished. What kind people. What an idiot I am.

Our marina is a snug all weather spot about 30 minutes' walk from the centre of town. The only trouble is that taxis don't know where it is. Among the trees there are huge abandoned cranes above us, two Meteor hydrofoils sitting lonely on slips, endless deafening barking from the occupants of an adjacent dog gulag and rows of expensive, soulless motor boats. But we have WiFi, electricity and water on tap. Yesterday's rain has gone and the crew have turned to general and personal hygiene with a vengeance.

Samara doesn't get accolades in the travel guides but we like this place. The streets of mouldering classic buildings remind me a bit of Havana with soviet overlay. The town lies along the east bank of the Volga and embraces it.   An impressive art gallery concentrating on gloomy pre-impressionist works, a grand opera house, a large monastery and a huge brewery in neoclassical style attract the eye. To the west of the river is the nature reserve of the Szhigylovsky mountains, contained by the Big Bend. Pirates used to keep watch on the upstream side of the bend, and when vessels were seen approaching the pirates would go south across the neck of the bend and attack the unsuspecting ships when they came round the corner.

Among the numerous jetties and marinas, our obvious choice lay at the head of Samarskiy Inlet. The waypoint opposite marks the beginning of the approach to this old commercial facility. Staraya Gavan (Old Haven) is a new and very secluded marina which sits at the head of the inlet. This is the only marina we came across with wifi (and it is free, too!). At the time of writing the marina buildings are still under construction and there are no showers. Use of the toilets required pluck and gymnastic skill. It is a long walk into town and, as I have said, taxi drivers had difficulty finding the place.

After our press interview we lunched with Vladimir and Tatiana at at a riverside restaurant and watched navy paratroopers tumbling from planes into the river. Future cruisers might note that there is also a quite respectable Japanese restaurant in Samara.

SAMARA

wpt	53 10.37/050 03.37
km	1737

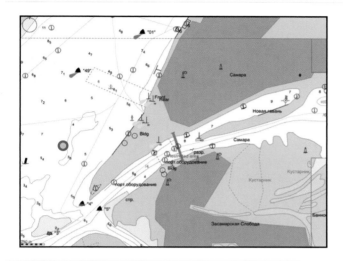

http://city.samara.ru/

Samara lies on the eastern shore of the river, on the outside elbow of The Big Bend. Cafes, restaurants and promenades line the long waterfront (said to be the longest embankment in Russia) and there is lively local river traffic. There is plenty to see and do in the centre of this pleasant town - the famous Zhiguli brewery (maker of Russia's best beer, they say), waterfront fish markets and an interesting art gallery.

TOLYATTI TO SARATOV

The old brewery

Vladimir and Tatiana

Among the numerous jetties and marinas, our obvious choice lay at the head of Samarskiy Inlet. The waypoint above marks the beginning of the approach to this old commercial facility.

Staraya Gavan (Old Haven) is a new and very secluded marina which sits at the head of the inlet. This is the only marina we came across with wifi (and it is free, too!). At the time of writing the marina buildings are still under construction and there are no showers. Use of the toilets requires pluck and gymnastic skill. It is a long walk into town and taxi drivers had difficulty finding the place.

Contact details

Molodogvardeyskiy spusk 2, Самара, ул. Молодогвардейский спуск 2
Tel: (846) 221 23 10, 221 23 98, 221 19 75, mobile +7 9376440066
e-mail: samara-boat@mail.ru
Website: стараягавань.рф or http://xn--80aaaaje7esahk2j4a.xn--p1ai/

Floating restaurant

JOHN AS SECOND FIDDLE : MAXINE

Poor John! A skipper with so many years of sailing experience, totally used to running his boat on his own with friends and family, managed to get this woman on board who was, and is not used to playing second fiddle, not used to translating every word being said, explaining every step being taken - someone who is more used to getting things done, conveying the results, then expecting them to be accepted without discussion.

John's usual crew had always been family and friends, of similar background and whose first language was English. It took me a while to realise that he had never sailed before with someone he found through a crewing website, someone whose first language was not English, whose background was not Australian or even Anglo-Saxon. He furthermore had never sailed with someone who could speak the local language in non-English speaking countries.

So John had to get used to someone from a culture he did not know, who instantly took over all negotiations regarding the boat and failed miserably to keep him updated at each step. Culture clashes one way or another happened all the time. These were not only between us, but between John and Russia, where a simple question to a local, which technically could be answered with a yes or no, would always be followed by an endless discussion. This would drive John absolutely desperate. Mooring off the boat with the assistance of locals would always make for great theatre, with lots of shouting and gesticulating. Poor John never got used to this loud way of life. In Saratov he retired to the foredeck to sulk. I again had only communicated to him a decision regarding the boat without explaining how I came to that decision. I apologised – again – and went on to doing exactly the same thing – again and again. I often found it easier to exclude him from the endless discussions leading to a decision. I really didn't want to have to translate and explain everything at the same time.

Looking back, it's perhaps just astonishing that the two of us managed so well together. But there was commitment, focus, infinite mutual trust and perhaps most important, a shared love for this unique journey.

PEREVOLOKI

wpt	53 12.6/049 13.8
km	1802

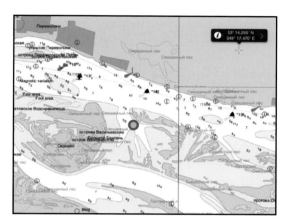 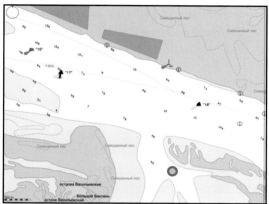

Before Perevoloki , acceptable anchorage can be found in an inlet on the left side of the river, in 5m water. This is just after black starboard cone buoy number "18". It took us two attempts to secure good holding.

BALAKHOVO POND

wpt	52 03.3/047 50.6
km	1999

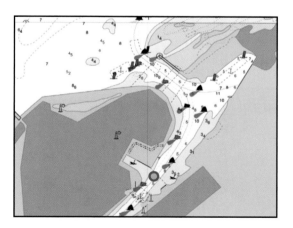

In good weather we sailed this well-marked section of Saratov Reservoir at night, in company with the usual succession of commercial ships. A dogleg channel, well lit and with good transit lights, leads from the reservoir to the locks. If you arrive after dark (as we did), a spacious pond leading off the left hand side of the channel provides comfortable anchorage for the night, with good holding, at waypoint 52 03.3/050 54. Beware though, that there are unlit piles on the left hand side of the pond, and a good lookout is necessary as you enter.

From here it is 75 miles to Saratov.

TOLYATTI TO SARATOV

MARX AND ENGELS : JOHN, 8 AUGUST

A couple of days ago we passed Marx and are now tucked into a little marina at Engels, opposite Saratov. Like many other places we have been, this is an old commercial ship basin, slowly dying. As in Samara, it is being taken over by the fast plastic boat industry. For now, the mix of old and new is touching.

For Tainui, this is where we are saying goodbye to Dima and Gerda, our splendid crew for the last fortnight. They will be missed.

Readers will know Engels as the home of Engels Trumpet Factory, now a major producer of tubes and piping. Engels seems still to be emerging from the tribulations of perestroika. Along the rutted dirt road from the marina are tiny stalls with meagre displays of fruit and vegetables. Clusters of picturesque timber dwellings sit among the trees and little old ladies with head scarves toil in small garden plots. Life does not seem easy for these folk.

But change is apparent and proceeding apace - smart cars are driven by blinged young things and on the water there are pristine gin palaces and jet skis. The grand bridge across to Saratov is raddled with concrete cancer but upgrading is under way.

Saratov boasts some fine old architecture and some dreadful new stuff, a warm and summery ambience and a splendid art gallery which should not be bypassed by visitors.

Traditional home of the Volga Germans who were sent packing during WW2, their influence is everywhere apparent. Long closed to foreigners because of its importance as an air base and centre of military manufacturing, Saratov is clearly coming alive.

We have fresh northerlies with a 200 open fetch down to Volgograd (Stalingrad). What a great spinnaker run today's passage would make!

Farewell to the children

USOVKA

wpt	51 46.5/046 33.2
km	2110

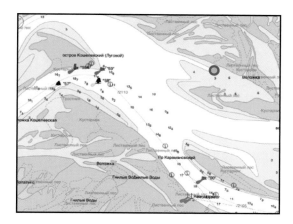

65 miles north of Saratov there is a maze of sandbars and islets in the vicinity of Usovka. These provide many opportunities for anchoring overnight. At 51 46.06/046 33 we found pretty surroundings, security and good holding in fresh NW winds.

SARATOV

approach wpt	51 29.8/046 01.5
km	2167

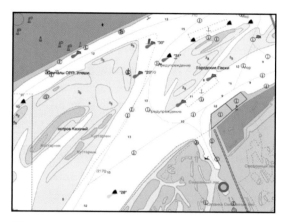

There are a number of marinas in Saratov. We chose Edelweiss, at the head of an inlet in the satellite town of Engels, on the eastern shore of the Volga. You should phone ahead to ensure a berth here.

The marina coordinates are 51 28.8/046 03.1.

Coming from north, turn left after the first bridge, in a broad sweep well beyond RHS buoy red "29". Give the red can "12" good clearance as shoals extend well south beyond it. The inlet itself has minimum depth of 4.6 m.

This snug inlet provides good all weather protection, although in fresh westerly gales a steep chop can make entry from the river difficult. Shore power, showers, restaurant and basic facilities are available. The only downside is the sometimes noisy music from the restaurant at night.

It is a 15 minute taxi ride into Saratov, which is a lively and cultured city. The high spot of our visit was the art gallery (Radisheva St 39 http://www.radmuseumart.ru/), whose superb collection deserves an entire day.

In the 17th century Catherine the Great (herself German) brought a great many Germans into Russia to increase the population workforce along this section of the Volga. Saratov was known as the home of the Volga Germans. In 1941, after 200 years in Saratov, almost half a million Volga Germans were stripped of their land and possessions and sent to labour camps in Siberia and elsewhere. A third of them did not survive. While most surviving Volga Germans either returned to Germany or migrated to Kazakhstan after the war. They left behind a city with rich cultural and architectural traditions.

Marina contact details

Marina Sazanki, City of Engels
(Проток Сазанки, город Энгельс, Саратовская область)
tel: 8 (845) 274-28-42.

The marina has no dedicated website, but mentioned in booking.com under "Edelveys Hotel"/ Engels city

WE NEED A GEOLOGIST : JOHN

This post is not about Russia, but I need to express my frustration with a crew issue. As we passed the diversion north to Bolgar, whose minarets were just visible through the rain, a fine stratified cliff lay on our starboard side. It prompted me to post this comment.

One of the things Tainui has often needed but sorely lacked is a geologist. We have had musicians, art directors, social scientists, economists, doctors, lawyers, tour guides, boat builders, playwrights, airline pilots but never, ever a geologist. If I had a dollar for every time we have marveled at a rock formation and wondered what it was and how it got there, I would be rich.

The pinnacles on the west coast of Campbell Island, the columnar basalt cliffs of Cape Raoul, those spectacular folds of marbled granite in Seno Pia Este, the extraordinary cliffs on the approach to Longyearbyen, the disappearing island south of Tonga, the grotesque volcanic oddities at Heimay, all of Loch Ness, not to mention the Gillen Landform in that greatest of oceans, the Central Australian Desert. In Tainui all of them spark curiosity and speculation but no answers. Over and over again we ask "where is our geologist?".

SAGGING, RUSSIA'S GREAT PROBLEM : JOHN

This is not about the effects of old age on a bloke's physiognomy but advice to readers about a wonderful opportunity to make money in Russia.

I had not realised the devastating impact of perestrioka on the lives of ordinary Russians. As Russia came to terms with its bankruptcy and opened itself up to free marketeering, standards of living plummeted, food queues grew, salaries went unpaid. But those ready to embrace the opportunities provided by private enterprise became wealthy very quickly. In her book Helen Womack describes the chaos of this process with clarity.

One thing Russia does not do well is roofing. Especially main roof beams. I do not know why this is. Wherever you look you see them sagging. You can even hear them groaning as they give up their battles with gravity. Like me.

There is real need here for an enterprising young bloke with carpentry and roofing skills. He would get rich fast and do Russia a great favour.

SARATOV TO VOLGOGRAD

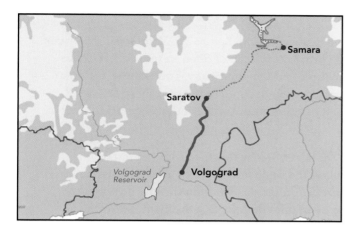

It is 360 km from Saratov down Volgogradskoye Reservoir to the locks at the Volzhskiy barrage before Volgograd.

VOLGOGRAD (VOLGOGRADSKOYE) RESERVOIR

Almost 300 miles long, this is the third largest of Russia's great reservoirs (after Kuybyshevsky and Rybinskiy.

The eastern shore is often shoal and generally the channel follows the western shore of the Volga between Saratov and Volzhskiy. The west coast is steep to, with low hills and cliffs fronting grassed steppe. There are remarkable horizontal sedimentary striations on the western cliffs, with numerous possibilities of anchorage in small bays and inlets.

Sagging, Russia's great problem

SARATOV TO VOLGOGRAD

MAXINE IS STUNG BY A BEE : JOHN, 9 AUGUST

It is 200 miles down the Volgadonskoye Reservoir from Saratov to Volgograd. The river is between 1 and 10 miles wide but the north-south fetch of open water is great, with uninterrupted sea horizons from the cockpit looking either way. The channel follows the western shore, which offers few inlets for refuge while to the east there are vast, impenetrable shoals. Depths vary from 8 to 20 metres and the southerly current runs at around half a knot.

 Sailors will appreciate that this is not the sort of place in which to be trying to travel against the wind. With a rising wind the sea conditions can rapidly become unmanageable, if not downright dangerous. Under sail, running downwind with the current in these conditions would have been pure delight. But in a boat like Tainui I doubt that anyone in his right mind would contemplate travelling in the opposite direction, either under sail or power. We had been warned not to leave Saratov yesterday because of forecast 20-25 knot northerly breezes gusting to 35 knots, but I decided that it would be better to roll uncomfortably but fast downwind rather than risk any future possibility of south in the breeze. So off we set. And it has not been unpleasant at all.

Rolling, treeless hills to the west remind me of Eden-Monaro. The channel is deep and it follows the shore closely. We are often only 15 metres offshore beside high sedimentary cliffs. To the east there are vast shoals but no sign of land. The commercial traffic is steady and at one point we were passed close by 5 southbound vessels, aligned bow to stern. Timber, oil, cement and grain seem to be the main cargoes. In balmy weather and softening breeze we pressed on till midnight when we crept into secure anchorage at Galka Inlet under GPS. I quite like night passages on these reservoirs although Saratov locals have warned us against travelling after dark. Tainui is of course a dry ship, but some of the commercial ships are not. Apparently the flow of vodka on their bridge decks can make their courses and speeds erratic. So far we have only seen exemplary IALA ship handling.

Our anchorage at Galka was free of march flies and mosquitoes. When we got in at midnight last night we rejoiced. But this morning Tainui was besieged by buzzing bees. Utterly harmless of course, but Maxine immediately launched into her Tourette Syndrome routine. Not surprisingly the bees were offended by this, and after her swim this morning they took revenge. Maxine was stung on the foot. Her response was impressively theatrical. Medical confidentiality would prevent me showing any photos of the lesion, even if it were visible, but I can show you the assailant, which poor little thing paid with its life for a single, brave and understandable act.

GALKA

wpt	50 22.6/045 48.6
km	2,334

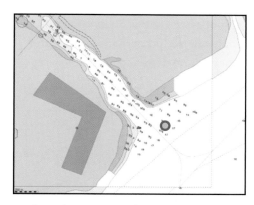

Midway between safe water buoys "64" and "65" on the western shore of the Volga, this peaceful little inlet is a convenient overnight stop between Saratov and Volzhskiy. It provides comfortable anchorage in all but fresh SE winds, with good holding, pretty surroundings and swimming.

The entrance is not easy to locate at night but the terrain is quite high and a radar approach is straightforward. At the entrance, watch out for the solitary port hand mark which is not lit.

From Galka it is 195 km down to Volzhskiy. In good weather you could do this leg nonstop. There are numerous anchoring possibilities along the western shore, if shorter legs are preferred, and we chose Rodnikiy Inlet.

TAINUI GETS BOARDED : JOHN, 10 AUGUST

This was not the sort of expensive and frightening bullying I had been warned to expect from officialdom on the southern Volga. The officer was reserved but respectful. He even showed us his ID badge. Maxine started weaving her magic while I put on the kettle. Soon it was all laughter and good cheer. He said "I have no idea what to do with you but perhaps you'd better show me some official-looking papers". I did so, he was satisfied and departed with a big smile, a friendly wave and wishes of safe voyage.

MAN OVERBOARD : JOHN

One of the more testing jobs I have each day is choosing the title for the web post. In the Southern Ocean, where noteworthiness was at a premium, I was scraping the bottom of the barrel with "Dave Thinks it's Wednesday".

Today's choice was easy. We had left Galka inlet and I was enjoying an ale in the cockpit in celebration of something or other, while Maxine was hosing mud off the foredeck.Suddenly the hose nozzle burst from the hose and went over the side. Before I could put down my ale, Maxine had stripped off and dived in after it. With not so much as a "by your leave". Never mind the 25 knot following wind and the associated chop. It was left to me to disconnect the autopilot, find somewhere to put my glass of beer, execute a Williamson turn, prepare the boarding ladder, heave to upwind and manage the controlled drift down to her. It was a textbook man overboard recovery. If proof is needed, the GPS track can be provided. Now I am finishing my ale while the deck continues its ablutions. And Maxine? - well I'm not sure about her, but that nozzle was a vital piece of equipment on Tainui.

SARATOV TO VOLGOGRAD

END OF A RESERVOIR : JOHN, 12 AUGUST

Our arrival in Volzshkiy is something of a milestone in Tainui's journey. It is the end of a long trip down the 500 km long Volgogradskiy Reservoir and almost the end of our Volga journey. From here we have just 35 kms of lock and canal waterway down through Stalingrad before turning west for 600 km through the great Volga-Don Canal and into the River Don.

We have been warmly greeted by enthusiastic members of the Volgograd yachting community and last night we were guests of honour at their annual regatta presentation ceremony.

Tainui is such a complete novelty here. Gifts of watermelon, rockmelons, grapes and bottles of vodka have been pressed on us by these lovely, hospitable people. Most of the yachts are micro cruiser racers and their crew examine Tainui with wide eyes. We feel very privileged and humbled by their warmth and generosity.

By day we are fanned by gentle northerlies and swimming over the side is de rigeur. The nights are still and balmy. It is impossible to imagine this place in winter, when the ice is a metre thick and temperatures drop to minus 30 Celsius. The sailors here are fanatical about ice yachting and we would love to try it.

There is a commercial inlet leading off to the left of the main harbour, to the south of which can be seen 3 small boat clubs (well, a row of converted shipping containers), whose finger wharves extend out from a sandy shore. There are no facilities. Behind the sandy beach is scrubland but not much else. It is a 30 minute drive through shabby industrial buildings to reach the town itself, where there are well-stocked supermarkets and general supply stores.

RODNIKIY INLET

wpt	49 17.75/044 58.3
km	2472

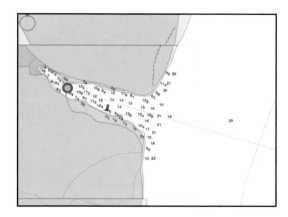

Another pretty anchorage. Although the coast is steep to, the safe approach is from buoy "18". We crept in on a black night and anchored in soft mud at wpt 49 17.5/044 56.8. As in Galka Inlet, there is an unlit red buoy on the southern side, this one about half way in.

Rodnikiy Inlet

SARATOV TO VOLGOGRAD

Our welcome to Volzhskiy

VOLZHSKIY

wpt	48 50.7/044 42.04
km	2528

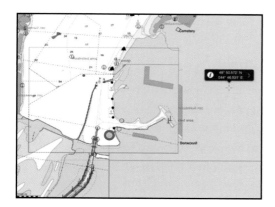

We found it a relief to reach end of this long body of water. The locks in Volzshkiy lie within a large mole harbour, whose entrance is wide and easy to identify. A downwind approach in fresh northerly wind is likely to be exciting, although manageable except in extreme conditions.

We arrived in Volzshkiy at the end of the annual yacht regatta and found ourselves honoured guests at the beachside presentation ceremony. Our reception was warm and touching. The president of the Yachting Federation of the Volgograd Region (Oleg Otchenashev) went far out of his way to assist us at every turn. We were happy to leave Tainui here for a week while we took R&R in Moscow and kindly Oleg insisted on driving us to Volgograd airport and to meet us on our return - a good 2 hour drive each way!

Things have certainly changed in Volzshkiy since perestroika, when the crew of Aenigma were held up at gunpoint and robbed.

Contact details

Oleg Otchenashev
email: otchenashev@icloud.com
Tel: +7 927 5264101

SARATOV TO VOLGOGRAD

THE DOTING FATHER : JOHN

After a break in Moscow, Maxine and I flew back down to Volzshkiy with a most precious cargo in tow. My two daughters have flattered and surprised me once again by agreeing to join Tainui for the last leg of her journey to the Sea of Azov. Neither of them sailors, they are great adventurers and have filled Tainui's saloon with life, laughter and light in Patagonia, Cuba and Scotland.

Jenny, my gorgeous elder daughter, is elegant, thoughtful, caring, articulate and deeply committed to bettering the world. She trucks no nonsense, our Jen. She has a wry, dry sense of humour. Like her sister Rosie, she is clever, very argumentative but this behaviour is tolerated by their loving father. Such a delight to have them both on board together. Jen navigated, steered and handled lock work on the Volga with quiet efficiency. Jen is currently looking after asylum seekers in Australia, with tireless passion.

Rosie is loquacious, smart, vivacious and very funny. Jenny's younger sister, she is a nascent film maker whose mind runs at a thousand miles an hour. She's very messy on the boat but highly entertaining and she cooks to die for. She is an actor, writer and secret graffiti person. She plays the oboe beautifully and her father (the skipper) wishes she'd do that more often. Wonderful Rosie sailed with Tainui from Stalingrad to Istanbul. Her protective big sister kept an eye on her during the first part of this journey.

Jen

Rosie

VOLGOGRAD

wpt	48 43.78/044 33.32
km	2545

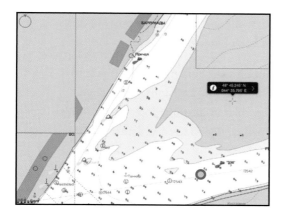

http://www.volgadmin.ru/ru/

After the locks it is a short trip down to Volgograd between sandy shores, with a 3 knot favourable current. Looming over the city skyline on the western side of the Volga is the grand statue Mother Russia, erected in memory of the horrors of the Battle of Stalingrad. A visit to the site cannot be missed. The city itself offers no convenient facilities for visiting yachts but Piligrim Yacht Club is a good spot for a sleep.

Stalingrad's epic history scarcely needs repeating here. In terms of loss of human life in WW2 the Battle of Stalingrad stands alone. While the precise number of casualties is not known, the gross figure is likely to have been around 1.3 million - the German Army lost more than 750,000 men killed, missing or wounded, with cold, starvation and typhus significant contributors to this astounding figure. Russia lost 478,741 men killed or missing, and 650,878 wounded.

SARATOV TO VOLGOGRAD

MOTHER RUSSIA : JOHN

This grand memorial to 1.4 million wasted lives looms over the factories lining 40 km of Volgograd waterfront. Standing in silhouette against the sunset Mother Russia is theatrical, overstated, profound and deeply moving. We walked in silence through the surrounding gardens, struggling to comprehend the events which took place here in 1942.

We had left Volzshkiy in light winds and clearing rain for the short trip downstream to Volgograd. In the big double locks the girls ogled while Maxine and John toasted safe passage through our last Volga sluice. There is strong current after the locks as the entire river system channels between narrow, golden sandbanks. Reedbeds and forest line the shores until the bleak factories of Volgograd come into view.

At Piligrin Boat Club we tied up beside a grand Jaroslavitz class motor vessel (ca 1938). I dream of owning one. When I am too old to sail (not, I hope, for 2 or 3 years yet) I would love to bring one of these skinny-ribbed, purposeful vessels back to Sydney for my twilight tinkering. Gun-metal grey, with bold Cyrillic script and old car tyres adorning the topsides, what a sight, powering up Sydney Harbour on a sunny Saturday afternoon!

We were greeted warmly by sailors we had met at the Volzshkiy regatta a couple of weeks ago. After a typically noisy Russian welcome with cockpit toasts, T-shirt exchanges and blessings to Mother Russia, sailing boats and the world in general we retired below for a splendid galley creation of Rosie's.

It is a short trip downstream from here to the entrance to the Volga-Don Canal. That is where the Black Sea commercial fleet divides, half going east down to Astrakhan and the Caspian Sea, the remainder powering up the Volga. It is only 100 miles from here to the Caspian and we have looked longingly at it on the charts, but we just do not have enough time. In Astrakhan the Volga delta is a wildlife heritage area but the Caspian Sea itself is big and not entirely welcoming (geographically or politically). In any case, autumn is not far away and time is of the essence. That excursion will have to wait for another day.

Civilian casualties in the Battle of Stalingrad are less certain, with estimates varying between 10,000 and 40,000. This relatively low figure was largely the result a mass civilian exodus from the city after the German air bombardment and the ferocity of the street fighting which followed. Russia took almost 100,000 German prisoners of war after the battle, less than 10% of whom returned to Germany after the war.

Marshal Zhukov, whose eponymous ship Tainui followed up the Vytegra locks, was the much-lauded architect of Russia's victory.

For obvious reasons Volgograd is now architecturally a relatively new and uninteresting city. But the Mother Russia memorial site more than makes up for that. Take a guide, it makes for a much more rewarding visit http://www.stalingrad-battle.ru/

To reach Piligrim Yacht Club, proceed to the waypoint above, before the bridge, before turning back upstream along the western shore into the side arm.

Caution - there are shoals in the vicinity of 48 44.76/044 34, more extensive than shown on the chart. The buoy on the western side of the shoals was absent and we grounded gently on the way back upstream to the yacht club. To avoid the shoals, continue south midstream to wpt 4 44.5/044 34.15 (at km 2544) before turning towards the western shore. Locals advised us to then keep close inshore (no more than 50m off) until approaching Piligrim YC. We did this and minimum depths were around 4 m.

The yacht club can be recognised easily by its light blue painted floating hotel. Do not attempt to enter the encosed area inside the finger wharves - it is too shallow. Tie up outside, on the floating hotel. The current here flows south at up to 3 knots so that an upstream approach is easy.

SARATOV TO VOLGOGRAD

AN IMPRESSION : ROSIE

Russia is a country we are all familiar with but what I came to realise upon arriving in Moscow was how little I really new about the diverse and dominating country that sprawls across the forehead of our globe. I would be lying if I said I wasn't nervous, this I have to say was mainly because of the hoops that required jumping though, and even over on occasion, to gain a visa to travel there, but every day I was surprised and excited by the friendliness and hospitality of the people we met.

Moscow is a capital city like most. It has plenty of beautiful grand buildings and a bustling metropolitan feel. It was full of historical museums and gravestones of Soviet Russia but I found my real education came when I left the capital and travelled down to meet the waiting Tainui.

We flew into Volgograd and were met by a minivan ready to take us to Volzhskiy. The driver was dry and cheeky and nattered away to Maxine while I plastered my face to the window soaking in what finally felt like everyday Russian life. The grand buildings of Moscow were replaced by hollowed out abandoned factories, the cosmopolitan girls in Gucci with old women in paisly dresses swaying down the street with a trail of stray dogs nipping at their heels. It felt so foreign and so wonderful, and for the first time in a long time I felt like a tourism pioneer, as if I was one of the lucky few to be let into this world.

The whole time motoring down the Volga we were treated as a fascinating novelty. The boat was poked and prodded, inspected by aspiring sailors and given the nod of approval from the cabin with a nip of Russia's finest. Inviting people on board seemed to be the highest honour and the gratitude and respect we received was warming. The most interesting thing I found when meeting Russian people was the complete lack of anger or resentment at their country's turbulent history. Although when questioned about the battle of Stalingrad people were of course sombre but there was also a sense of positivity and frankness when discussing the millions of deaths as if it is just the way of life. There is an overwhelming lack of self pity within the Russian peoples and it's hard not to be caught up in the flow of everyday life.

My favourite experience by far was in between two locks waiting to be herded through by the voices that barked out of the radio. We tied up to a wall where two men were fishing. They wandered over wine in hand to have a chat. They spoke no English and I no Russian but the conversation was beautiful. One was an ex gunner from the Russian army who told me of the horrors he saw, miming battle and looking to each other for encouragement they painted a harrowing picture but as soon as I started to feel weighed down by the sadness in their faces they shrugged and laughed and touched my face. They had never seen a foreigner before and told us to wait as they wandered into the scrub to a house. They returned with armfuls of vegetables, fresh basil, tomatoes, chillies, potatoes and more from their own garden. These men who clearly had very little pressed their laborious fruits onto me with pride and I felt so lucky to share the meeting with them. The image stuck in my mind is of us motoring away while the two men jumped and waved us off till we couldn't see them anymore.

The trip down the Volga was an amazing adventure and one which I count myself very lucky to have had. I fell in love with the country and the people and will return in the not too distant future.

Spasiba Bolshoe

The floating hotel at Piligrim Yacht Club

Contact details

Y/C Piligrim 48°45'47.56"N, 44°34'49.13"E
Adress: 16 Matevosyana Street, Volgograd
Tel: +7 (8442) 27-13-42, 8-904-436-36-77

Services: berthing, secure car parking, hotel, restaurant, café, sauna, billiards

Яхт-клуб "Пилигрим"
Координаты:
Широта: 48°45'47.56"N (48.763211)
Долгота: 44°34'49.13"E (44.580314)
Адрес лодочной станции: Волгоград, ул. Матевосяна, 16
Телефон: +7 (8442) 27-13-42, 8-904-436-36-77
Услуги: стоянка катеров и яхт, гостиница, охраняемая парковка автомобилей и прицепов, ресторан, кафе, сауна, бильярд.

VOLGA-DON CANAL

TURN RIGHT AT LENIN : JOHN, 27 AUGUST

From our Volgograd berth we sped 35 km down the Volga in warm sunshine with 2.5 knots of favourable current.

The beginning of the great Volga-Don Canal, marked as it is by an imposing statue of Lenin, cannot be missed. As the only portal between the Black and Caspian Seas it is a busy waterway and we were told to anchor off for 4 hours to wait for our turn in the queue. After obligatory swims the crew turned Tainui's cockpit into a beauty parlor while John dozed.

In the late afternoon we finally left this grand river, which has been part of our lives for quite a time and for thousands of miles. We understand why it is an object of such affection for Russians.

Passing under an impressive faux neoclassical archway, we entered the first lock in company with a bulk carrier and a tugboat. Moving through locks in close succession, you tend to travel with the same vessels, which become familiar friends. We pressed on into an inky black night under a zillion stars, passing huge ships at very close quarters in the narrow channel.

It is quite fun managing locks and channels in the dark and we had hoped to continue with our friends, but approaching Lock 2 the engine temperature suddenly skyrocketed and we limped alongside the lock entrance. The cause was found and fixed easily - a weed-clogged salt water inlet - but we lost our friends and our place in the queue and settled in for the night.

Everywhere we stop, Tainui and her crew cause wonder and delight. At Lock 7 for example, two local fishermen told us they had never before seen a foreigner, let alone a foreign yacht. They chatted interminably and were very curious. Clearly enamoured of Rosie, they pressed armloads of fresh garden vegetables on us (her) and marvelled at our very existence here in Cossack country.

Tainui's crew now works like a well-oiled machine. Rosie is the bespoke chef while Jenny is a full-time line handler. She lassoes impossibly high lock mooring hooks with grace and ease. Maxine manages the bureaucracy and radio work. She also shares general boat management with John, who sits back and feels proud, a bit old and very blessed.

LEAVING THE VOLGA

From Piligrim Yacht Club, strong current makes for a fast 30 km passage down to the beginning of the Volga-Don Canal. In the vicinity of the bridge below Piligrim, keep an eye out to port for the memorial to the thousands of soldiers who died during transportation across the Volga here to defend Stalingrad. The entrance to the Volga-Don Canal is easily identified by an imposing statue of Lenin, on the downstream side of the approach.

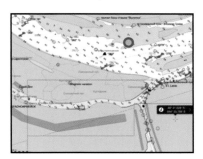  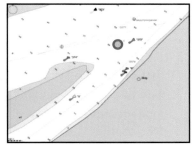

Commercial traffic here is busier than anywhere else upstream. We had to wait over 4 hours for a place in the lock queue and anchored at wpt 48 32.25/044 31.89, km 2573, about a mile before Lenin's statue. There is also anchorage closer to the lock entrance, in a pond on the right hand side. The lock-keeper told us we could tie up alongside a boat house here but the charted depths were a bit worrying and we did not enter this pond.

Caution: there is a significant discrepancy between the paper chart folio volume 8 part 1 (dated 2010) and electronic charts here. The paper chart does not show the large sand cay which sits between red buoys "376" and "374". It certainly exists! This was the only significant charting discrepancy we found in our entire trip.

The approach to the first lock begins at km 2577, leaving red buoy "372" to starboard. We wondered whether it might have been possible to cut the corner and enter the approach leaving buoy "379" to port, as per the paper chart, but according to the electronic charts the waters are shoal (2.4m at one point) and we chose to take the long way round.

VOLGA-DON CANAL

KEEPERS OF THE LOCKS : JOHN, 27 AUGUST

The locks themselves are a delight, embraced as they are by grand, sometimes grandiloquent architectural edifices - neoclassical arches, balustrades, columns and porticos. Testament both to Stalin's hubris and the vital commercial importance of the engineering system.

Management of the constant stream of commercial shipping on the inland waterways is a complex choreography, run with calm efficiency by the lock keepers and dispatchers.

Larger vessels need to be locked one at a time, often with only inches to spare on each side, and there is a limited number of roadsteads where those waiting their turn can be parked. The waterways are busy and it is difficult to imagine how they could cope with an influx of small pleasure craft like ours. As it is, we are an absolute novelty, hence the indulgence we are given.

The canals are often very narrow and ships in transit need to be spaced carefully. They pass one another smoothly in impossibly tight places, day and night. We usually anchor off the fairway at night and I never cease to marvel when one of these huge behemoths looms silently into view and glides past us. The whole business runs smoothly and we have not heard of logjams or accidents, although they must occur.

We cannot speak highly enough of the efficiency and calm professionalism of the lockkeepers and despatchers. They all know Tainui and they regularly call us up to see how we are going. At Lock 13 for example, the keeper said she had heard from Lock 12 that we needed to do some shopping. She advised us where to anchor once through the Lock 13 and arranged for a taxi to be be waiting for us on the shore to take us to the supermarket.

Setting out into Tsimlyansk Reservoir she called us to check that we had an anchor. When we said yes, we had 5 of them, she was bemused and reassured. And at the southern end of this long reservoir she was relieved that we had tied up in Volgadonsk without mishap.

The canal itself, winding through rich deciduous forest and reeded islets, is narrow, tortuous and very pretty. Vessels transit day and night, with passage choreographed by shipping dispatchers. Convoys of 5 or 6 vessels progress alternately east and west through the system. Clearly the canal is running to absolute capacity and there is relentless talk about building a second canal system or a parallel reduplication of the current canal.

VOLGA-DON CANAL

This 100 km long waterway connects the Volga and Don Rivers. The dream of a canal linking these 2 great rivers has been alive for over 500 years, with the first documented construction efforts undertaken by the Ottomans in the late sixteenth century. At the beginning of the eighteenth century Peter the Great constructed a 25 lock interconnection north of the present canal, but only a few hundred vessels completed this very difficult transit before the project was abandoned because of continuing, prohibitive financial problems.

Stalin built the present canal in 1952. 80,000 prisoners toiled in wretched conditions for 4 years to finish the job. Sergei Prokoviev's eponymous tone poem was written to honour the opening celebrations. The canal provides the vital link for commercial shipping passing between the Black Sea, the Caspian and the Baltic. Interestingly, most of the 11 million tonnes of cargo transported annually now passes from east to west, with more than half of that oil and petrochemical products exported from Caspian ports.

From east to west in the Volga-Don Canal there are 9 uphill locks with combined elevation of 90 metres. 4 downhill locks then descend 45 metres to Tsimlyansk Reservoir on the Don, with just 2 further downhill locks after the reservoir at Volgadonsk, descending to the Don River. The locks and canal system accommodate vessels of up to 5,000 tonnes, 140 m in length, 16.5 m beam and drawing 3.5 m.

VOLGA-DON CANAL

THE LITTLE ONES : JOHN

As I have said, the Volga-Don Canal is a busy commercial waterway. But we have found the lock-keepers helpful, friendly and efficient. We squeeze past huge tankers, bulk carriers and barges with sometimes only metres of clearance. At the entrance and exit from locks our movements are supervised with skill.

Today we have been travelling in company with a 60' lighthouse and buoy service vessel. The lock-keepers call us both "The Little Ones" and we are treated with maternal care and, dare I say it, affection. Huge bulk carriers are kept waiting while The Little Ones struggle to latch onto lock hooks which are sometimes only just to low enough for us to reach, doddle along at barely 6 knots and are late for their entries, or just aren't quite sure where to go.

We have just come out of Lock Number 9, which is our very last uphill lock for the entire journey. We have 12 or so more locks to go but, as they say, it is all downhill from here.

There are two good things about uphill locks. First, because you are entering a deep canyon, there is no wind, so that coming alongside without damaging the 3 metres of mast projecting forward from the bow is easy. Second, as you rise, a new landscape appears over the lock sides which comes as a surprise, whatever it turns out to be.

There is one problem with uphill locks. The floating hooks which rise on rails set into the lock sides may not come down low enough when the lock is empty, so that when you enter and tie up you can find that your bespoke hook is out of reach. Getting a line attached requires a skill which few, other than Jenny, have mastered.

VOLGA-DON CANAL

AND QUIET FLOWS...(WE HOPE) : JOHN, 28 AUGUST

Chris wrote to me expressing the hope that my crew would instil in me some much needed feminine sensibility. Now, after 3 days of constant bullying, the girls have managed to discover the warm, sensitive inner self I knew I always had.

Anchored below Stalin's magnificent Lock 13, the girls have gone shopping and I find myself splendidly alone on the boat and able to do important bloke's things without tedious workshops, planning meetings and debates about attitude, respect, consideration and the like. Wiring in new sockets for the multitude of chargers and adapters needed by our iPads, iPods, iPhones, VHF radios, and cameras requires none of that. Only logical thinking, problem-solving and occasional brute force. With Tristan and Isolde up loud it is such a joy.

For 3 days we have meandered between grassy shores, reed beds and islets along Stalin's pride, the Volga-Don Canal. The breeze has been gentle and warm. As background there are wide fields of wheat, low hills, arachnid power line towers and occasional drab villages and towns. Built by German prisoners of war in the late forties, this canal has become a vital commercial link between the Volga, the Caspian and the Black Seas. Huge oil tankers and bulk carriers glide smoothly along the narrow waterway all day and night, sometimes with only a metre or two to spare, giving us new meaning to the concept of close quarters navigation. It is surprising how blase you get after a day or two of this.

The gorgeous girls have gone ashore to cater for Rosie's lavish menus over the next few days, Jenny's fresh vegetable obsession, Maxine's white wine requirements and my shamefully modest needs. Ahead of Tainui lies the lock's splendid, intaglioed neoclassical arch and to port, an imposing monument to those who fought and died in The Great Patriotic War. Children are fishing on the shore and there is a gentle breeze. Things couldn't get much better.

We have ahead of us just a few kilometres of channel before we reach the River Don. From there it is 90 miles across the large, shallow Don Reservoir to Volgadonsk, whose local yacht club eagerly awaits Tainui's arrival. And from Volgadonsk we have another 125 miles of Don River before the Sea of Azov. The end is getting near and we have very mixed feelings about that.

We are hoping the Don flows quietly for us.

LOCK 11 ANCHORAGE

wpt	48 39.76/043 52.37
km	2662

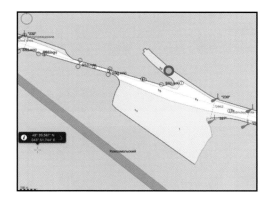

This is a bulletproof hideyhole on the right hand side of the canal, immediately before lock number 11. Anchor fore-and-aft in 3.5m water. Turning in the narrow inlet requires a good deal of backing and filling between the trees lining each side.

FATHERS' DAY ON THE DON : JOHN

Today is Fathers' Day and my present was the best low calorie cake known to father. My candles were Belomor Gulag cigarettes. I believe I was the only father in the entire world with this cake adornment. The children have played cards, Rosie has been cooking, Jenny has navigated and steered while I celebrated Fathers' Day. Maxine hasn't knocked over a drink for hours. All is well on board Tainui.

Just before our second last lock on the Don the poor old engine suffered its second catastrophic coolant loss. Fortunately we had just tied up and the diagnosis was quickly made - a ruptured copper coolant pipe installed by engineers in Norway against my better judgement. We missed our slot in the lock queue but the problem was quickly fixed - one of those permanent temporary repairs which adorn Tainui.

MORSKOY ANCHORAGE

wpt	48 33.7/043 25.8
km	2699

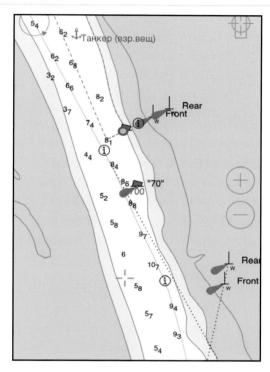

We anchored between buoys "70" and "71" at a lovely spot beside reeded islets on the east side of the river. The western shore comprises a series rolling grassy hills and bluffs, under which numerous ships lie at anchor (fore-and-aft) awaiting passage north into the canal system.

VOLGA-DON CANAL

JENNY : ON MY TIME IN RUSSIA

Half the people I told what I was doing were amazed. The other half thought I was crazy. This is generally what I think about my dad. Half the time I am in awe of his adventures, the other half I think he is completely and utterly mad. There are definitely pros of having an utterly mad adventurous father. Not only do you get the most amazing opportunities to see the world, you also get to see the world from the perspective of a small sailboat moving from place to place like a turtle with your home on your back, ready to visit any little nook or cranny you wish (given the depth of the water is more than 2.5 meters).

I often wonder how my father could have given birth to two such anxious and neurotic daughters. Given our neurosis my sister and I are not natural sailors. I probably hold the record of how many times you can ask in an hour "you sure we are not going to sink?" "but, do you promise?" Whilst I adore the romantic notion of sailing into the sunset this doesn't quite match the reality of projectile vomiting, fear of what lies beneath, beside or above and the constant realisation of how completely insignificant you really are in the whole scheme of things.

So after quite a hedonistic 2 month adventure around Europe I was wondering if I'd made the right choice to come join my dad, Max and my sister on a sailing adventure. The bureaucratic nightmare of entering Russia had almost been a deterrent as well as the anger and fear I felt around the recent introduction of the horrid anti-gay laws. Despite these deterrents I decided to push through and found myself in Moscow at a train station I didn't know the name of, waiting for my sister to pick me up with our friend Lieve.

Stepping into Russia was like entering another world. I had not previously realised what a vast empire it was. Its history was so present, from its stalinist architecture to its culture of suspicion symbolised by a love of mirrored glass which prevented the outside world from looking in. From the outside Russia appeared cold and I was uncertain of what things meant or how to read the signs (in social interactions and also quite literally - cyrillic script is quite difficult). I have travelled a lot to many different places but it was here that I felt more like a foreigner than anywhere else.

In high school I was an avid history nerd and had studied the Russian revolution with fascination and intrigue. My school friends and I had nicknames for each other - Trotsky and Lenin - we talked about which one we'd rather be and which one we'd rather have as our boyfriend. Russia for me had always been a place of mystery and revolution and to be honest in hindsight a place I had quite problematically romanticised.

continued next page

BALKA MECHETKA

wpt	48 11.0/043 06.0
km	2760

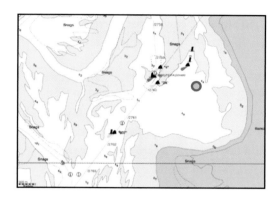

There is good holding in this rather exposed roadstead before the northern end of Tsimlyansk Reservoir. We found ourselves anchored in close company with many commercial ships waiting to proceed north to the Volga-Don canal locks. Local fishiing boats are active here and their trap floats not always easy to spot. This anchorage is unlikely to be tenable in fresh southerly winds. In a 25 knot easterly (offshore) breeze the 3km fetch was enough to give Tainui lively motion.

VOLGA-DON CANAL

from previous page

I was acutely aware that not only were we foreigners in this land but we were also foreigners on a sailboat sailing for fun (a concept foreign to many). I must admit a lot of the hard work was done before I got there. I was joining a trip that had already been through rivers and oceans, where the crew had become accustomed to navigating the culture and were familiar with how to ask and answer questions.

Regarding being on a boat I think what struck me most was how strange people thought we were but also how little on the outside they seemed to show it. I remember thinking how much I would have loved to speak Russian. I think a lot went over my head and I only saw a tiny piece of a much larger puzzle. I remember thinking how strange it was to have everyone just assume that I spoke Russian, and how surprised people were to find out that I didn't. Moments like this are incredibly healthy for native English speakers, who without a doubt have oodles of privilege bestowed undeservingly upon them from the mere fact of being born where they were born.

I have a lot of memories from sailing down the Volga river. Mostly I feel so privileged to have witnessed a part of the world that many do not get to see. For some people we came into contact with this was the first time they had ever met someone from outside the ex-Soviet Union. Travelling by boat down the rivers allowed a snippet of an insight into the everyday lives of people whose livelihood was the river.

Next time I visit Russia I would love to have learnt to speak Russian fluently so that I can speak to people about their lives, and hear what they think about the world and about a crew of people sailing a small boat through their waterways.

Late arrival at Volgadonsk

TSIMLYANSK RESERVOIR

The Don was dammed at Volgodonsk in 1948 and the reservoir was filled by 1953. It is reputed to be the most productive fishing reservoir in Russia. 320 km long and nearly 40 km wide, it is on average 8 m deep. This reservoir is filled by the Don, which enters at Kalach-na-Donu, near its north-eastern end.

The shores of the Tsimlyansk Reservoir are fertile, particularly on the northern side. Produce includes wheat, maize, alfalfa, fruit and grapes.

There are only 3 more locks downstream of the reservoir, the first of which was built in 1918 as a flood control barrage for the lower Don River.

In Volzshkiy we had been warned to treat this large sea with respect. Prevailing winds from the south-west sector quickly create steep little seas against which headway can be difficult if not impossible. So what else is new, we asked.

The south-eastern shore offers no safe refuge. Along much of the north-western side there are shoals which limit access to a weather shore in the event of strong north-westerly winds. Karnukhovskiy Bay is the major exception, although with the fresh easterly winds which prevailed during our transit we did not explore this. The south-eastern shore is generally steep to, and for much of our passage we tucked right in under its barren cliffs, in gusty winds but with smooth water. As was so often the case, we yearned for a mast and our big reaching genoa.

VOLGA-DON CANAL

VOLGODONSK : JOHN, 30 AUGUST

Like all of the reservoirs, Tsimlyansk is an imposing body of water. A wonderful place to sail, if you had a mast. But if there is any breeze, motoring in shallow waters with steep chop and no steadying sail is quite tedious.

The river below Lock 13 is quite beautiful, with rolling hills to the west and low green islets and reed beds on the eastern shore. We anchored, swam and wolfed down one of Rosie's splendid meals before retiring for the night. Such is the endless struggle of remote exploration.

Out on the reservoir we found secure anchorage the next evening at an open roadstead in company with a dozen northbound freighters and oil tankers waiting to enter the river system. The wind was rising and a 25-28 knot breeze was forecast for the following day.

A small fishing boat stopped by to give us fish as, with some trepidation, we set out for a slow bash south.

Our track was initially a bit exposed but later in the day we were able to tuck in below the windward cliffs on the eastern shore and we followed them all the way down to Volgodonsk. Cows came down to the water to drink and swim (udderstroke?).

Maxine did a memorable and spectacular backflip over the side while collecting a bucket of water. The moment lives only in memory but we have photographic proof of herself and bucket in the briny.

Tsimlyansk Reservoir, created by a barrage across the Don River at Volgodonsk, is the gateway to both the Don and the Volga Rivers. In any other part of the world you would expect to see little sailing boats everywhere but here there are none. Indeed, in the last week we have only seen one pleasure craft, a Russian motor boat on delivery from Yaroslavl down to Rostov-on-Don.

At dusk we reached the imposing Volgodonsk lighthouse, where Alexey Chirkin, the yacht club director, had kindly arranged for a local yacht to lead us in to the yacht club. It is a shallow final approach and despite guidance we ran aground twice (gently, in soft mud) as we crept into the snug creek. The paper and electronic charts are quite wrong about depths in the harbour and it is all much shallower than stated.

Sadly Jenny Wren, our expert if anxious navigator and helmsperson, leaves us shortly to start a new adventure in Jordan. Her dry humour and her gentle, contemplative demeanour will be missed by all, especially her adoring father.

We are now encountering a series of rather sad Lasts. Tsimlyansk was our final reservoir and now we have just 180 river km and 5 more locks before Rostov-on-Don. Looking back on this journey of ours we find there is too much to hold in mind at once. It has been an unimaginably rich and rewarding experience. Our overriding memory is of the warmth, generosity and friendliness of the wonderful people we have met along the way. Finding perspective will require space and time.

VOLGODONSK

wpt	47 33.6/042 09.4
km	2868

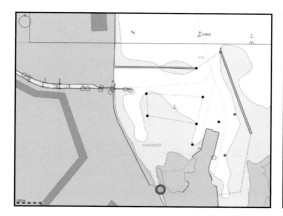 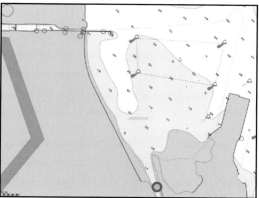

http://www.volgodonskgorod.ru/

Because of shoal water it is not possible to follow the rhumb line along the south-western shore straight to the harbour mouth. You need to take a long leg out to the vicinity of km 2865 before turning left and paralleling the shoreline for 4 km to the to the harbour entrance.

Once in flat water inside the breakwaters, you will see commercial facilities to the left, and the entrance to Volga-Don Canal lock number 14 on the right. The shallow creek leading to Volgodonsk Yacht Club is at the corner of the harbour between them.

Warning - the south-western corner of the harbour is very shallow and the charts are of no help. We were met at the entrance and guided in by a local yacht but despite this we ran aground 3 times. The bottom is soft mud, but frail little channels between the shoals had to be sought out with much blind groping about. Leaving (by ourselves) was even worse.

Once inside the narrow creek there are depths of 2.9 m of water and space to tie up at rather fragile floating pontoons, with the half dozen or so small day sailers. Shore power, showers and sauna are available and the club members are typically welcoming and hospitable. Facilities aside, the Volgodonsk Club is impressively marketed,with a dedicated website and leaflets.

The town of Volgodonsk is quite new and has little to offer cruising yachts apart from much needed sleep. Connections are good and crew changes could be made here.

Contact details

Marina: "Admiral Ushakov"
Portovaya st 12, Volgodonsk
phone: +7 903 460 0016; +7 903 328 7525; +7 920 890 3488
http://www.admiralushakov.ru
Director: Alexey Chirkin (Speaks English!)

While you are here it would be wise to telephone ahead to Avral YC in Rostov-on-Don, to arrange a berth at their marina. See Rostov section for contact details.

DON RIVER

QUIET DAY ON THE DON : JOHN

Our consensus view is that the Don is the most beautiful of rivers. Quiet and tortuous, lined with deciduous forest, it encourages languid silence on board. I am sure it has been doing so for its thousand year commercial history.

Anchored out of the stream last night I sipped medicinal tomato juice and watched the terns, egrets, ducklings and kingfishers doing avian things against the sunset. I contemplate the Cossack Dons - equestrians by the age of 3, fierce fighters, loyal Russians and staunch anti-Bolsheviks, they were sent back to face Stalin's retribution by agreement at Yalta after WW2. They suffered untold misery both in allied hands and on their return to the USSR.

Now, after 3,000 miles, we are waiting for our space in the third last lock. We hope to be in Rostov-on-Don by lunchtime tomorrow for Jenny's celebratory meal (she has graciously agreed to stay aboard after Volgodonsk to ensure we navigate carefully along the Don).

Should you decide to bypass Volgodonsk Yacht Club, you can anchor for the night on the right hand side of the lock approach continuing on into the lock the next morning. This enables you to avoid the shoals and inevitable groundings on approach to the club moorings.

From Volgodonsk there are just 3 more locks before you reach open waters flowing down to the sea - Nikolayevsky, Konstantinovsk and Kochetovsky - all of which have relatively small level changes. The last of these was constructed as early as 1919 and doubled in 2006. Below Kochetovsky lock, river depths for the 130 km stretch down to Rostov are maintained by regular dredging.

DON RIVER

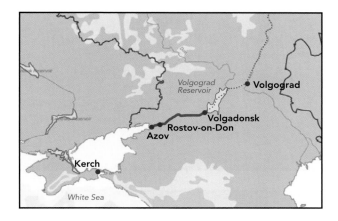

KAMYSHEVSKAYA ANCHORAGE

wpt	47 34.6/041 48.5
km	2904

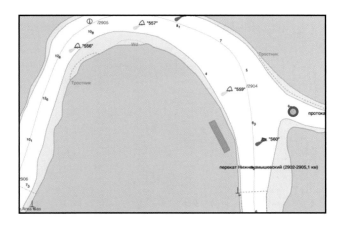

At a lovely bend in the river, we found good anchorage here at the mouth of a shallow estuary coming in from the north.

DON RIVER

KOCHETOVSKIY LOCK

wpt	47 34/040 53.5
km	3001.5

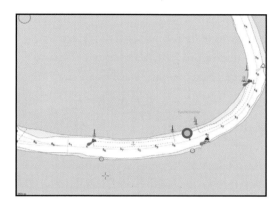

There is good anchorage at the commercial roadstead on the northern side of the river about a mile before this, the last of the locks in the entire waterway.

We felt a mixture of genuine sadness and heady excitement as the lock gate opened and we motored out of the canal and onto the river Don. From here it is just 130 km to Rostov-on-Don. The river is narrow and quite lovely until the first signs of Rostov begin to appear around successive bends.

DON RIVER

CAN'T BELIEVE WE'RE IN ROSTOV : JOHN, 3 SEPTEMBER

A rich sunrise this morning gave the Don a Monet look. Now a blustery west wind is bringing squalls up river.

We arrived in Rostov-on-Don at 6 last night. Another milestone in Tainui's journey. Here we say goodbye to gorgeous Jenny, get more beer for Rosie and refuel for the 30 km trip down to Azov where we put up the mast. It is only 35 km to the open sea from here and I must say I am ready for it.

Rostov is a wonderfully busy commercial port. Tankers and bulk carriers are anchored 3 abreast in the narrow river. Factories line the shores. Convoys of up to 6 vessels at a time depart for the journey up the Don to Volgograd and ports beyond. Purposeful workboats streaked with rust power back and forth across the river and the air is filled with industrial noise. There is much to watch.

We found 3 mooring facilities within the city limits. The first two, on the left hand side of the river, seemed deserted and probably only provided boat access to adjacent hotels and restaurants. The third - Avral YC - met our needs and can be recommended.

ROSTOV-ON-DON

http://www.rostov-gorod.ru/eng/

There is no mistaking the purpose of this city, with its huge and active commercial waterfront. The waterfront is exciting and while there is much of interest for those who love the sea and ships, Rostov offers little in the way of facilities for cruising yachts.

AVRAL YACHT CLUB

wpt	47 11.23/039 39.3
km	3141

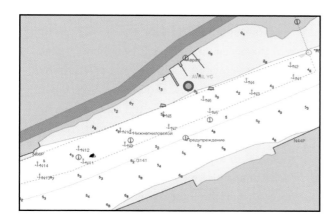

Avral YC has a small marina on the right bank (city side) of the river, before the final bridge and overhead cable across the Don. There are 3 finger wharves, with mooring stern line to buoy. There is also room for one vessel to lie alongside and we were fortunate in having access to this spot.

The club is 100 years old and its facilities (including a restaurant) are in the process of being upgraded. In addition to a small museum, there are shore power, laundry, showers and good security. Taxis can be ordered easily for the 20 minute trip to the centre of the city. Wake from passing vessels is a minor irritation. There is a continuous 1 knot current here, and much shipping activity to watch.

DON RIVER

ROSTOV : JOHN

After her beery farewell at Rostov's Library Restaurant (much recommended), Jen has flown off to Jordan for her next adventure. How sad to see her go. Back on board Tainui we have done nothing but sleep, read and eat. I am surprised by how tired the last few days have made us.

Avral Boat Club is small (9 yachts and the usual power boats) but welcoming and well-serviced. And it has the added advantage of being located by the big ship anchorage to the west of the city. I watch in awe as 7,000 ton ships creep in and anchor fore-and-aft just 50 metres apart. They are such good skippers, these blokes.

Lieve's friend Zinaida (yes, Lieve again!) and her daughter Anna took us out for a wonderful lunch on Rostov's left bank a grand, faux Spanish restaurant. She had sent a car to pick us up and would not allow me even to share in the cost of the occasion. Such is Russian hospitality. Now Rosie is ensconced in the aft cabin with her newly recovered computer and an enormous hard drive packed with movies. She had left her computer in Moscow and Lieve (Lieve, again!) had DHL'd it down to Zinaida here in Rostov. Maxine is networking, wheeling and dealing in the forward cabin while in the cockpit I watch the endless parade of ships creep past.

In contrast to Zinaida's hospitality, two events stand out in my mind. Both of them typically Russian, Maxine says. First, we were phoned by someone from Rostov TV who requested a television interview. We said yes, as we always do. But when the interviewer told us that we would have to pay 1,000 euros for the privilege, we declined only slightly politely. Second, the port officer told us we would have to pay 2,000 roubles (A$75) to help with his relocation expenses for his new posting in Siberia. We thought it politic not to refuse that one.

The club has a crane capable of lifting masts to around 18 metres. A couple of the local yachts use this regularly and others use local tugs with a masthead line to haul over for passage under the last, 18 metre bridge at wpt 47 11/039 38.3.

Contact details

http://www.yachtclubrostov.ru/
Director: Suzanna Gubanova
mobile: +7 918 581 1296
office: +7 863 303 0561
email: gubanova_s@rostov.aston.ru
email: yacht-club@rostov.aston.ru

OBUKHOVKA BOATYARD

wpt 47 09/039 27.2

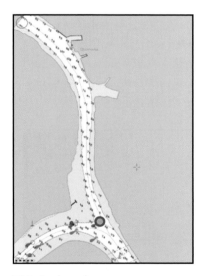

This is the place to get your mast up off the deck and back to its rightful place.

From Avral it is about 15 km down river to the Obukhovka estuary, which opens off the northern side of the channel. Turn right off into the estuary at red buoy at wpt 47 07.8/037 27.5. This waterway is deep, well-buoyed and lit. The shipyard is on the right hand side, at wpt 47 09/039 27.2, one of those modest affairs with apparently no facilities but in which almost anything can be done. And very professionally too. Ivan Parada took over his father's workshop and is both professional and obliging. We found him inexpensive, endlessly helpful and efficient.

There is 2.6 m alongside his wharf and the soft mud bottom is forgiving, if you take the ground. The wharf is a bit exposed in fresh south-westerlies but we found it comfortable up to about 20 knots.

DON RIVER

DOWN THE RIVER TO OBUKHOVKA : JOHN

Departure from Rostov was interrupted for an hour while Maxine and John dived over the side and groped in chilly water with the propeller, which had become fouled by a mooring line. In the water poor visibility and a 1 knot current added to this adventure. Luckily they were able to get a bow line back ashore before the current got to the boat, so that Tainui sat safely while in the water our core temperatures slowly dropped.

Away at last, we tippled our way 35 km downstream towards Azov at the mouth of the Don.

Just before Azov we turned north into a broad estuary and tied up at Obukhovka Shipyard, where the mast is finally to be set up once more. There, one of us spilled a glass of home brew beer from Rostov, provoking a major search for our cockpit sponge. That sponge is fat, brown and a much loved old thing. What stories it could tell, Rosie says. It lives in one of the cockpit lockers and, like a wise old woman, says nothing but absorbs everything. It knows John and Maxine particularly well.

At the moment we have fresh westerly winds and rain, which will make the mast exercise interesting tomorrow. Then we move down to Azov for the tedious departure formalities, the problems of which we have been forewarned about. We will need to engage a Ukrainian agent for our arrival in Kerch' (yes, the apostrophe is meant to be there), 200 miles across the shallow Sea of Azov. These westerlies would make for a slow and uncomfortable bash into the steep, short chop for which the sea is famous. But that worry is for another day.

Obukhovka

Note: Obukhovka is in a border zone and the authorities will need to know where you are. You must notify them on VHF ch 16, through Azov port traffic control or the Don dispatcher. Unaware of this obligation, we did not report in and were reprimanded.

Contact details

Obukhovka Boatyard
Director: Ivan Parada
Tel: +8 928 212 7658
http://yaxt-club-obuchovka.narod.ru/

Ivan Parada

Obukhovka celebrations

OUR MAST GOES UP : JOHN

Tainui's mast was lifted off the deck and swung across to cradles ashore both gently and efficiently by Ivan. This lovely bloke knows boats, cranes and the petty worries of a tired and elderly sailor. He and Andrey cossetted and coddled us and John wallowed in it. We marvelled at how much bigger Tainui had become without those cross frames and the confused stalactites of rigging paraphernalia.

After our anxious experience with Volga-Balt crane Number 83 in Vytegra we had been worried about getting the mast back up. But next day Ivan took control and everything went smoothly. Ridiculously so. After it was all done there was much celebration and a fine rendang curry - Rosie's of course.

Our only problem, a topping lift lost through the deck sheave, was dealt with expeditiously by Maxine. She clambered up the mast, sat rather cheekily at the top and fed a messenger down to me. Everything is now in its proper place and there remains only the mast wiring to be reconnected.

On day 3 at Obhukovka, Ivan brought us a batch of fresh farm eggs and a jar of the most excellent homemade apricot jam. He then drove us in to Rostov so we could visit passport control, fill a gas bottle and stock up at a supermarket. We got the gas and heaps of food but the passport control office did not want to know about us. Just go anywhere else but here, they seemed to say.

DON RIVER

HOW TO GET OUT OF RUSSIA : JOHN

This is a long post but I feel the need to set down some aspects of Russia's dark underbelly. They have loomed larger here than elsewhere, as we had been warned they would.

Our epic, 2 hour trip down river from Obukhova to Azov was a delight. We still cannot get used to the clear decks, the mast above us, shrouds and stays where they are supposed to be, and above all the gentle and proper motion of a balanced yacht.

In a short inlet in the commercial port of Azov we tied up at our bespoke wharf. The water was glassy. Boatmen shovelled gravel into flour sacks, friendly dogs waited patiently for food scraps, adolescents sat idly in boom box Ladas, old men stood immobile with fishing lines equally immobile, while an endless parade of ships passed sedately by our stern.

Gateway to the Don River, Azov is a small town whose entire purpose is directed towards the loading, unloading and service of commercial ships. Just my kind of place. But it has no experience with yachts and its bureaucracy seems quite unable to cope with us.

Maxine and I walked across to the port authority for the first of many meetings. After passing through the by now familiar barrage of wrong buildings, relocated departments, turnstiles, steel security doors and progressively more senior uniformed officers we were finally led up a crumbling, ill-lit staircase into the quiet and overheated office of someone with many stars on his epaulettes. A nice young bloke, he was at first confused and then bemused by us and our request to leave Russia. Maxine worked her magic tirelessly and he warmed to the novelty and challenge of finding a way to help.

You would have thought that Tainui required only a simple series of stamps and signed clearance papers. But no, it is not that easy. The problem is that we are not part of the usual process. Dealing with thousands of commercial ships every year is simple because the procedures are well-established. But there is no bureaucratic pathway for a phenomenon like us.

First we were told that we had to sail Tainui back to Rostov to the regional head office, for processing. We explained that there were bridges lower than our mast and that was not possible. Even if we were to drop the mast again, we could not clear Russia from Rostov because then we would have to come back down river and stop for 3 days at Obukhovka again, to repeat the mast installation exercise. We told him we had driven up to Rostov from Obukhovka yesterday and the passport office there said they could not help us. Finally they accepted the logic of this and began searching for other ways of sorting things out.

Port authority, customs, immigration and FSB (KGB) officials are all genuinely keen to help us. It is the maze of conflicting legislation, regulations and protocols which confound them. They are apologetic and, I think, slightly embarrassed by our difficulties.

Finally we were told to repair to the boat while they tried to find a way of sorting things out. What we needed most was some sort of official document from the KGB in Rostov, granting the Azov authorities here permission to process our clearance application. We were told we needed to write a letter to Rostov requesting this document. Fortunately a nice young immigration

AZOV

In Azov, there are no marinas or facilities for small vessels. We found a pleasant, unused wharf in an inlet on the south side of the river (wpt 47 07/039 25.4).

While port authorities were happy for us to stay there, immigration officials were not. We were unable to find out why that bit of river embankment was a cause for concern to the immigration people. The port owner was overruled and we moved as instructed. For 3 days we sat between cargo vessels unloading at a commercial wharf on the main river (wpt 47 07.2/039 24.7). Much river traffic. Of course there were no facilities, no shore power and no water.

Caution: Recent events in Crimea create uncertainty about the entire process about exit from Russia. It may be that clearance formalities will be transferred from Azov to Kerch in Crimea. You will need to clarify this prior to entering Russia.

In principle, yachts can only check in and out of Russia in those ports which have "passenger facilities", whatever that means. Azov is the logical port from which to clear out at the end of the trip because by then you will have passed under the last bridge and overhead cable, raised your mast at Obhukovka and readied yourself for sea. Huge shipping port that it is however, Azov is only a cargo port. Rostov, some 15 miles back up river, is the designated port from which to clear. That was where we were supposed to complete exit formalities. Our problem is that if we had cleared Russia at Rostov we could not then stop at the Obhukhovka boatyard, go ashore and reinstall our mast.

It took us a good deal of explanation before this difficulty was understood and accepted by the port authorities in Azov. Finally however, they acknowledged our dilemma and arranged to clear us out of Russia themselves. It took us 3 days and innumerable discussions to finalise this.

After some negotiation, both Customs and Immigration officials in Azov agreed to deal with us directly rather than through a shipping agent. Exit fees were 1,110 roubles.

officer who came down to the boat helped us draft our letter and undertook to see it dispatched to Rostov without delay.

Relieved, we settled back into a calm evening to enjoy Rosie's most splendid chicken satay. Then a uniformed official came down to the boat to tell us that we had to move 200 metres downstream and tie up for the night at a customs secure area, between 2 huge ships on the main river. So we motored out into the dark to locate our nominated spot in the blaze of port lighting, only to be told over the radio that we had to go back because there was a series of complicated shipping manoeuvers about to begin. We did so.

An hour later we were informed that now it was time for us to move. After all the folderol of the last few days I was both tired and fed up with this nonsense. Any sensible port traffic control office would have been happy to see us tucked securely out of the way where we were. But no, we had to move. Right away, at 11 pm. Not in the morning. So we did.

While Maxine began a 3 day exercise in debate, negotiation and form-filling, I did boat things and felt otiose. And we needed to get a Ukrainian courtesy flag, line up a Ukrainian shipping agent to handle our arrival in Kerch', service our engine, get that bloody diesel fuel and connect up all the mast wiring.

We have a weather window approaching and I want to leave Russia tomorrow for the 2 day trip across the Sea of Azov to Kerch'. Immigration still has not received authority from the KGB to process our exit applications. So we sit and wait.

At 3 am tonight we are putting Rosie on a plane to Ukraine so she can meet up with Beth, then both will join the boat in Yalta. Rosie's departure from a customs controlled zone but not as Tainui crew creates yet further difficulties for us (well, for Maxine).

As always, I am excluded from the endless Cyrillic conversations and negotiations. When I ask Maxine to translate she tells me to shut up and be patient. She is clearly enjoying all this nonsense but keeping me in the loop is an irritating and unnecessary complication, so she doesn't. By now I have come to trust her implicitly and I acquiesce. She assures me all is going to plan and I should attend to blokes' stuff on the boat while she flutters her eyelids at the nice young officials who litter out path.

We have one more authority to deal with - the Office of the Port Captain. We are off to see them shortly and we have no idea what sort of response we will receive [Note - Maxine has just been told that we also need clearance from the Azov veterinary and sanitation authorities. I think she will be able to dismiss that requirement successfully].

As usual, Maxine has worked wonders with the bureaucrats. She is assiduous and tireless. A gracious bully. In Azov she is now known, liked and respected by all of the authorities with which we have dealt. Maxine is a priceless asset in Tainui. The simple jobs - engine service, mast wiring and fuel transfer - have been left to me, while gorgeous Rosie has seen us all superbly catered for (Dirk, I know I end this sentence with a preposition).

On Wednesday, if all goes well, we will be on the open sea! Tainui is ready and so are we. We even have an old Ukrainian courtesy flag, donated by a kind deck officer on bulk carrier Volga-Balt 226. The flag is 15 square feet in size and I hope that impresses the Ukrainian authorities.

We recommend that you use a shipping agent to prepare your exit paperwork, if you can negotiate a reasonable fee for the service. Fortunately, the officials in Azov helped Maxine with our documents but she found it a complicated and tedious business.

Your exit documents can be downloaded from the IMO website (www.imo.org) Russian authorities feel that they do not have to provide you with the forms because they are international and your own responsibility. Also note that there are no simplified procedures for small pleasure craft

Finally, note that once you have been given clearance to depart Azov, you have to leave. There can be no anchoring downstream for a snooze or to wait for a weather window. You will be in a Russian border zone, hence closely monitored.

DON RIVER

JOHN : DO SVIDANIYA RUSSIA

Well, we're off. After 3 days of rigorous and tiring negotiation and 4 hours of paperwork on board this morning, we were given clearance to leave Russia by the Port Captain and officers from the departments of Immigration and Customs. Maxine is the hero of the day.

Now we are motoring down the Don in late afternoon sun with a light headwind and bright blue skies. The sea is just 5 km ahead.

We both feel quite flat, not least because we had so little sleep last night. Rosie left at 3.30 am and phoned us at 5.00 to announce that immigration at Rostov airport would not let her board her flight because her Russian visa expired yesterday. That was all sorted eventually, but sleep was the big loser.

This is neither the time to sum up, nor to give an overview of our rich, eventful summer. That must wait for another day.

Crew connections - it is a 30 minute taxi ride to Rostov-on-Don for flights to Moscow and elsewhere.

Port Authority

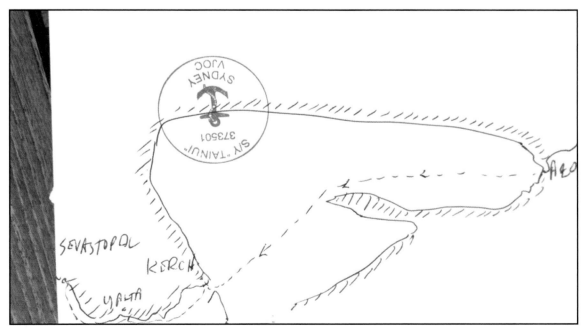

Skipper's hand-drawn route plan, a mandatory element of departure documents

SEA OF AZOV : JOHN

The short stretch of the Don below Azov is just as beautiful as the waterway above it.

Looking back at Azov as we motored down river I was sad to be saying goodbye to all those wonderful ships. Needless to say, we cracked a bottle of chardonnay at the river mouth and solemnly saluted the last buoy. There is a long and very narrow dredged channel extending 20 miles from there, out to sea. It is well- buoyed but not wider than 30 metres and at times less. The depths are 1 metre or less on each side. Ships pass only with difficulty.

It was in mid channel that our salt water inlet suddenly became blocked with weed. I pulled off to one side to clear the inlet pipes but we were kissing the bottom the moment we left the channel. Back in the channel we dropped anchor to get the coolant flowing again.

After I had dismantled the pipes Maxine announced that a large bulk carrier was approaching though the gloom of the dusk. She called it up to warn we were NUC (not under control) while down below I scrambled to clear the mess and remantle the hoses. Somehow we got the engine sorted and the anchor up within about 4 minutes, leaving just enough time to move to the side of the channel to allow the oncoming ship to pass.

By now we were seriously tired and we dropped anchor for the night about 20 miles offshore. Nearby a veritable city of ships sat at anchor, waiting to enter the Don. Never was sleep so welcome.

The 200 mile passage Azov to Kerch' in Ukraine is divided into two equal parts.The first leg of our crossing was a gentle square run with everything poled out, warm sun, good food and wine. An endless parade of ships passed us to starboard.

With a splendid sunset we dropped the pole, rounded the corner and turned south to Kerch. Under starry skies and with a freshening breeze, Tainui danced through phosphorescent seas with a bone in her teeth. We were faithfully steered by by our Aries wind vane, which had not really done any useful work for a very long time. All night we rushed south with a steady beam breeze. Dawn brought relief from the constant vigilance required by the huge volume of commercial traffic.

Finally we were granted permission to enter the port of Kerch', where we anchored awaiting instructions about what to do next.

Pasha, our newly appointed shipping agent, worked wonders for us. We were told where to tie up and an army of smiling, uniformed officers of various kinds were waiting for us. Cheerful formalities were soon over and we fell into bed.

After last night's ship dodging and this morning's radio shenanigans we are both buggered. To put it mildly.

SEA OF AZOV

After slow silting by the Don River, this has become the shallowest sea in the world, with average depths of only 13 metres. It can be a most unpleasant bit of water when the winds are strong. The 20 mile channel out from the Azov river mouth, narrow and very busy, requires regular dredging. There is a crowded commercial roadstead off the seaward end of it and in calm weather we anchored and fell into deepest coma there.

The shores offer little of interest for cruising yachts. On the Russian coast there are a number of commercial ports (Taganrog, Novorossiysk and Yeschk, for example) and it may be possible to clear out of Russia at one of them. These ports are all well off the rhumb line however, and by now you will be relishing the prospect of the 2 day uninterrupted passage down to the Strait of Kerch, thence out into the Black Sea. The western shore of the Sea of Azov is Ukrainian territory and not open to foreign yachts. Max, that's what our Kerch agent told me.

Your passage to Kerch will be monitored by coast guard stations, especially as you approach the strait. Kerch is little visited by yachts but it is a logical place to rest before you cruise either west to Crimea or south, across the Black Sea, to the Anatolian coast of Turkey.

Ukrainian immigration formalities in Kerch are not straightforward and a shipping agent there will ease your arrival. See www.tainui.org for details of our experiences there.

JOHN : UKRAINIAN POSTSCRIPT

Readers will know that September 14th is annual Kerch Day. Yesterday, despite wandering thunderstorms and intermittent rain there was a festive spirit in the town – tooting car horns, fun rides, concerts, WW2 re-enactments and streets full of strolling families. A suitable evening for Tainui's 2013 Awards Night.

It will come as no surprise that Maxine scooped the pool at the awards ceremony, running away with the coveted Tainui Special Merit Award (not once but twice!), in the categories of both Overall Competence and Navigation Excluding Transit Leads. The entire restaurant erupted into applause at the presentation itself and madam seemed genuinely tearful, delighted and deeply moved.

Fortuitously, a band appeared behind our table and dancing began. Then there were the Kerch Day fireworks as icing on the cake.

Maxine leaves for Moscow in 48 hours. Tainui will be a much bigger, lonelier and less efficient boat without her.

OVERVIEW OF THE RIVER SYSTEM

The Volga rises in the Valdai Hills between Moscow and St Petersburg, 228 metres above sea level, falling to nearly 30 metres below sea level at the Caspian delta. The Volga catchment is huge (up to 500,000 sq miles, depending on how you measure it), and it includes 10 of Russia's largest cities.

Four bio-regions are described:

TUNDRA

Circumpolar tundra is characterised by stunted plant life and permafrost caused by low average temperatures, limited sunlight and very short growing seasons. Tundra does not occur south of about 55 degrees north. The only tundra you will encounter between Norway and Azov is on the Kola Peninsula and, if things go according to plan, you should never get closer than 12 miles to this icy, featureless and generally inhospitable coast.

TAIGA

South of the tundra belt is the evergreen boreal forest known as taiga, comprising mixed coniferous forests of white spruce, hemlock, pine and larch. Taiga makes up 30% of the world's forest. To the north, large tracts of taiga line the shores of White Sea, the Belomor Canal and Lake Onega.

TEMPERATE FOREST

You will notice the gradual appearance of mixed deciduous species the further south you travel. Oak, Hornbeam, chestnut, laurel, holly and rhododendron intersperse with fir and silver birch. The complex temperate forest ecosystems in Russia are seriously endangered by deforestation and uncontrolled expansion of farming along the Volga. Less than 5% of them by area have been granted protective status.

STEPPE

Steppe (savannah) is a region of grassy plain and shrubs. The steppe you see along the eastern shore of the Volga south from Kazan extends for many thousands of miles east to Mongolia and is the largest in the world.

OVERVIEW OF THE RIVER SYSTEM

In geological terms, most of the Volga floodplain comprises a thick sedimentary layer which overlies Pre-Cambrian crystalline rock. Repeated glacial advances and retreats over 100,000 years have left complex imprints on the plain.

THE BELOMOR-BALTIC–VOLGA–DON RIVER SYSTEM

It is approximately 3,700 km from Belomorsk on the White Sea down to the Sea of Azov. Given the length of the system, it can be difficult to retain an overview of the entire route in one's mind. Detailed information about the various administrative and geographic sections may be found in the body of the guide. In summary however, the route can be divided as follows:

1. **The Belomor (Baltic) Canal** - This provides a now little-used link between the arctic waters of the White Sea and Lake Onega, passing through thick taiga forest. There are occasional settlements en route but the shores are generally wooded and undisturbed. Quiet anchorages abound. The system is about 225km long, with canal sections interlinked with lakes and sounds. It was completed in just 4 years by gulag workers toiling under exceptional hardship. It is estimated that 100,000 of them died.

2. **Lake Onega -** Lake Onega is the northern meeting place of Russia's network of shipping routes from, and to the White Sea, Baltic, Caspian and Black Seas.
   The White Sea (Belomor) Canal enters the northern end of the lake at Povonets. Passage via Lake Ladoga to St Petersburg commences on the western shore near Petrozavodsk while the huge Volga-Balt river system leading south-east to the Volga and Don rivers begins at at the south-eastern end of the lake at the Vytegra River.

3. **Vytegra, Kovzha and Shekshna Rivers**
   Vytegra River enters the S-E corner of Lake Onega, this gives locked access east via the Sheksna River up to Rybinskiy Reservoir.
   Kovzha River flows from the top of the Vytegra barrage into the western side of White Lake.
   Shekshna River flows from the eastern side of White Lake through to Rybinskiy Reservoir.

4. **Volga River**
   The Volga flows into Rybinskiy Reservoir from its headwaters near Tver and the hills north of Moscow. With its historic cities and towns, grand man-made reservoirs and lakes, the Volga courses east to Kazan before swinging south down to Volgograd.

5. **Volga-Don Canal** - Just below Volgograd, the Volga turns east for the final 100 miles of its great journey to the Caspian delta at Astrakhan. Here Stalin's pride, the Volga-Don Canal, takes off roughly westwards, connecting the lower reaches of the Volga with the Don.

6. **River Don** - Flows west from near Volgadonsk to Rostov-on-Don and the Sea of Azov.

OVERVIEW OF THE RIVER SYSTEM

THE GREAT VOLGA RESERVOIRS

In the late 1930s, Russia began an ambitious program of barrage construction across the Volga and Don Rivers. 60 years ago this project was complete, changing forever the face of the rivers. A series of interlinked waterways ended the dangerous, uncertain and tediously slow process of moving ships up and down the waterways. Finally, river navigation had become reliable, safe and predictable.

From north to south along the Volga and Don Rivers, the large reservoirs are shown here.

(Note that smaller catchments on the headwaters of the river between Moscow and Rybinsk are not discussed here).

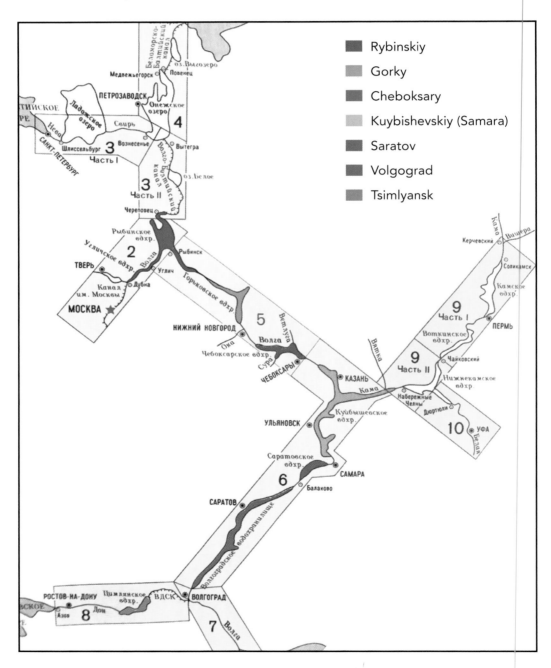

- Rybinskiy
- Gorky
- Cheboksary
- Kuybishevskiy (Samara)
- Saratov
- Volgograd
- Tsimlyansk

The oldest of these, Rybinskoye Reservoir, was at its time the largest man-made body of water on earth - 1,700 square miles were inundated from 1935-41 with the flooding of more than 600 villages. Its 345 mW power generation is now considered otiose. We had a miserable crossing of Rybinskoye and learned to respect these big reservoirs.

Kuybishevskiy (Samara) Reservoir covering 2,325 square miles, is the largest in Europe and third largest in the world. The basin was flooded in 1956-7 to provide hydroelectric power. We had generally good weather across this one but in any case we found refuge in various harbours and inlets on the western shore.

Gorkiy Reservoir is narrow and did not make an enormous impression on us.

Tsimlyansk Reservoir, the southernmost reservoir, is on the River Don. It has retained fish stock of commercial value.

Constructed primarily for power generation, the dams which created these great reservoirs incorporated bypass locks allowing shipping movement to continue. Between Belomorsk and Azov there are now some 56 locks, with many more in the Volga's tributaries and side arms. But the price has been high.

POLLUTION

Slowing of river flow combined with a proliferation of farming and factories along the shores has caused erosion and silting, phosphate run-off with algal blooming, and deforestation. Fish stocks have declined markedly. Of the 40 types of commercial fish in the Volga it has been the migratory species (whitefish and sturgeon) which have suffered most.

These problems have been superimposed on more general problems such as deforestation through uncontrolled logging, industrial and urban waste run-off, none of them properly regulated until recently.

By the mid-1990's, about 20 cubic kilometres (yes, that's kilometres!) of industrial and agricultural waste water were entering the Volga each year. More than half of this was untreated or inadequately treated [Komarov 1997, www.biodat.ru/doc/biodiv/part6b.htm].

Waterfront industry

OVERVIEW OF THE RIVER SYSTEM

Klement Tockner et al [Rivers of Europe, Academic Press 2009] list the following annual toxic discharges into Volga waters:

Nitrates	350,000 tonnes
Phenols	90,000 tonnes
Sulphates	521,000 tonnes
Chlorides	384,000 tonnes
Organic matter	87,000 tonnes

A further 26 million tonnes of mixed toxic substances are discharged each year into the atmosphere over the Volga catchment area.

While reduced surface water flow rates in the great reservoirs lowers clearance of toxic waste, the primary problem in the Volga catchment has been an enormous increase in industrial and farming activity on the shores of the reservoirs.

In the 1990's, Russia established a new Ministry of Ecology and Natural Resources. A raft of environmental legislation has since been passed and we can only hope that this will slow, if not stop and reverse the degradation of one of the nation's most priceless assets.

Algal bloom near Kineshma

RIVER FLOW, CURRENTS

More than half of total Volga water discharge is sourced from snow melt in spring. Winter flow by volume is less than 10% of the annual total, while summer and autumn flow rates are equal. Seasonal variations in river flow have been reduced appreciably with construction of the great reservoirs, but the total annual outflow volume (300 cu m per second per year) has not altered very much.

Flow rates, as opposed to flow volume, have changed greatly since the reservoirs were filled. Rates are maximal with the spring melt and also high beneath the winter ice. Reservoir morphology, wind force and direction, bottom contours and convective forces all contribute to very complex patterns of current.

Understandably, flow rates are greatest in the narrower waterways, especially further south along the Volga. We met south-flowing current in excess of 2 knots after the Gorodets locks and below Volzshkiy, although generally the rate was between 0.75 and 1.25 knots. At no time did we encounter adverse currents, although eddies in the reservoirs and persisting southerly winds do cause these.

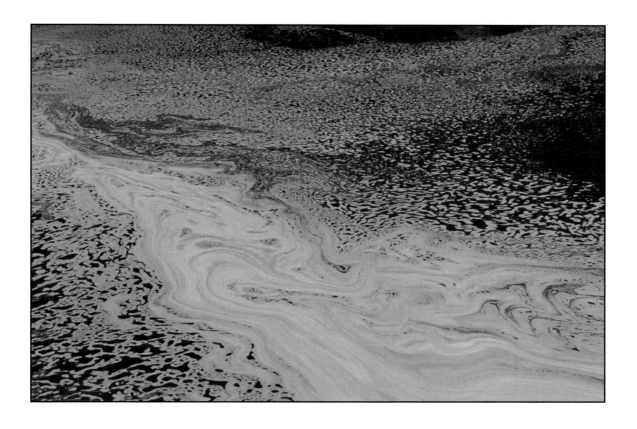

HISTORICAL NOTES

Nicholas Roerich 'Guests from Overseas'

The history of what is now European Russia is rich, complex and at times confusing. For 2 millenia, the Volga catchment has been washed by wave after wave of invaders, settlers and traders. A bewildering array of different ethnic and cultural peoples have come and gone. One after another, polities and kingdoms have flourished then faded away; political allegiances forged, exploited and broken. This brief list of the major players and some of the historical forces at play may be of interest to readers.

Known to the Greeks as the Rha, the Volga appears on Ptolemy's map of Europe in 100 CE. In commercial terms the river did not acquire importance until the early Middle Ages. By the 8th century the Vikings were using Volga trade routes regularly. The Icelandic Sagas describe a Viking journey south from Sweden to the Caspian by Ingvar the Far-Travelled in 1040, but there is no historical record of further travel by the Norsemen via the Volga to the Caspian after that. This has been attributed to the decline in availablilty of silver, from southern trading centres.

By 1200 most Varangian (Viking) trade between the Baltic and the south had been transferred to western routes down the Dnieper River to Kiev, where there was a fusion of Viking (Rus) and Slavic culture and ethnicity. By this time the upper reaches of the Volga had been settled by Slavic tribes, the central region secured by the Bulgars and the southern by Khazars (see below).

Under the Golden Horde and the Duchy of Moscow the Volga was exploited extensively as a trade route, but it was not until the fall of the southern khanates in the 16th century that the entire river came under Russian control.

FINNO-UGRIC PEOPLES

The Volga Finns (note these are not Finland Finns) and Permians were related ethno-linguistic groups living on the shores of the Volga from around the 9,000 BC. Their origins are buried in the sands of time but Finno-Ugric cultures survive across Arctic Norway, Finland and Siberia. The semi-nomadic Sami people for example, continue to herd and farm reindeer across large sections of the northern Eurasia. About 2 million Russians still speak Finno-Ugric languages and there is a resurgence of interest in sustaining their identity.

NEOLITHIC PEOPLES

5,000 years ago Indo-European peoples were hunting and fishing on the Volga. During the Bronze Age (2,000 - 1,000 BC) nomadism gave way to more permanent and sedentary communal living, with organised farming and more complex social organisation.

Around 1,000 BC the **Cimmerians** - an Aryan nomadic group - invaded, conquered and became established along the river. Their origins are unknown, but they dominated the Volga region for about 300 years until the appearance of the Scythians.

Scythians arrived from Central Asia around 700 BC. They were fine goldsmiths, warriors, archers and horsemen. As decribed by Herodotus, they were much to be feared in battle.

HISTORICAL NOTES

A LETTER ABOUT THE VIKINGS

Ahmad ibn-Fadlan, a 10th century employee of the Caliph of Baghdad, travelled as a member of the Caliph's embassy visiting the Volga Bulgars. He fell in with a band of Viking marauders in the middle reaches of the Volga and, in an oft-quoted letter, describes them in the following terms:

They are the filthiest race that God ever created. They do not wipe themselves after a stool, nor wash themselves thereafter, any more than if they were wild asses.

They come from their country in the North, anchor their ships in the Volga River, and build large wooden houses on its banks. In every such house there live ten or twenty, more or less. Each man has a couch, where he sits with the beautiful girls he has for sale. Here he is as likely as not to enjoy one of them while a friend looks on. At times several of them will be thus engaged, each in full view of the others. Now and then a merchant will come to a house to purchase a girl, and find her master thus embracing her, and not giving over until he has full had his will.

Every morning a girl comes and brings a tub of water, and places it before her master. In this he proceeds to wash his face and hands, and then his hair, combing it out over the vessel. Thereupon he blows his nose, and spits into the tub, and leaving no dirt behind, conveys it all into this water. When he has finished, the girl carries the tub to the man next to him, who does the same. Thus she continues carrying the tub from one to another until each man has blown his nose and spit into the tub, and washed his face and hair.

I was told that when their chiefs die, they consume them with fire. When I heard that one of their leaders had died, I wanted to see this myself. First they laid him in his grave, over which a roof was erected, for the space of ten days, until they had completed cutting and sowing his funeral clothes.

At the death of a rich man, they bring together his goods, and divide them into three parts. The first of these is for his family. The second is expended for the garments they make. And with the third they purchase strong drink, for the day when the girl resigns herself to death, and will be burned with her master.

When one of their chiefs dies, his family asks his girls and pages, "Which one of you will die with him?" One will answer: "I." From the moment he utters this word, he may not go back. Mostly, though, it is one of the girls who volunteers.

Regarding the man of whom I spoke, one girl answered "I will." She was then entrusted to two other girls, who kept watch over her and accompanied her everywhere she went. The people were preparing the dead man's funeral clothes, and this girl gave herself over to drinking and

continued next page ...

300 BC heralded the arrival of **Sarmatians** from Persia. They invaded and routed the Scythians, dominating the Volga basin for around 600 years. The Alans were the most influential of the Sarmatians and some historians believe that it was they rather than the Vikings who were the original Rus people. In present day Russia, Alan descendants are the Ossetians.

GERMANIC PEOPLES (3 CENTURY BC - 7 CENTURY CE)

Pre-Mediaeval times saw the spread of these so-called Teutons into the Volga basin. With names familiar to every schoolboy (Goths, Visigoths, Ostrogoths, Vandals, etc), this loose ethno-linguistic grouping of tribes had emerged in Europe by 500 BC. Wrongly blamed for the decline and fall of the Roman Empire, their origins are a matter of dispute.

In eastern Europe, Baltic Goths (3rd-4th century CE) and then central Asian Huns (400- 600 CE) controlled the Volga regions in succession. With the deaths of Attila and then his son Ellac, the Hun empire lost strength and cohesion, fading from history.

HISTORICAL NOTES

'A Letter about The Vikings' from previous page ...

singing, and was cheerful and gay.

When the day had come that the dead man and the girl were to be committed to the flames, I went to the river where his ship lay, but found it had already been drawn ashore. The dead man lay at a distance in his grave, from which they had not yet removed him. Next they brought a couch, placed it in the ship, and covered it with Greek cloth of gold, wadded and quilted, with pillows of the same material. An woman, whom they call the "Angel of Death," came and spread articles on the couch. It was she who was to slay the girl.

They drew the dead man out of the grave and clothed him. They carried him into the ship, seated him on the quilted covering, supported him with the pillows, and brought strong drinks, fruits, and herbs to place beside him. Finally they brought a cock and hen, slew them, and threw them in, too.

The girl meanwhile walked to and fro, entering one after another of the tents which they had there. The occupant of each tent lay with her, saying, "Tell your master I did this only for love of you."

It was now Friday afternoon, and they led the girl to an object they had constructed which looked like a door-frame. They lifted her and lowered her several times. Then they handed her a hen, whose head they had cut off. They gave her strong drink and admonished her to drink it quickly. After this, the girl seemed dazed. At this moment the men began to beat upon their shields, in order to drown out the noise of her cries, which might deter other girls from seeking death with their masters in the future.

They laid her down and seized her hands and feet. The old woman known as the Angel of Death knotted a rope around her neck and handed the ends to two men to pull. Then with a broad dagger she stabbed her between the ribs while the men strangled her. Thus she died.

The family of the dead men drew near, and taking a piece of wood, lit the ship. The ship was soon aflame, as was the couch, the man, the girl, and everything in it.

At my side one of the Northmen was talking with my interpreter. After their conversation I asked my interpreter what he had said. The Northman had said:

"You Arabs are stupid! You would take him who is the most revered and beloved among men, and cast him into the ground, to be devoured by creeping things and worms. We, on the other hand, burn him in a twinkling, so that he instantly, without a moment's delay, enters into Paradise."

THE VIKINGS (9TH-11TH CENTURY)

The Atlantic exploits of this bold and ferocious people are familiar to all. Less well-known however, are the extraordinary Viking journeys of discovery east and south into Russia, from Baltic waters down to the Black Sea, the Caspian, to Baghdad and beyond.

The Invitation of the Varangians by Viktor Vasnetsov: Rurik and his brothers Sineus and Truvor arrive at the lands of the Ilmen Slavs.

Originally from near what is now Stockholm, Swedish Vikings (Varangians) had established communities on Lake Ladoga (near present day St Petersburg) by the end of the 8th century CE. For more than 300 years their reach extended 4,000 km south to Constantinople and, via Muslim trading settlements on the southern shores of the Caspian, as far as Baghdad, joining the great Mediterranean and Central Asian trade routes. Vikings journeyed to the Black Sea also via the Dnieper River, to Slavic lands in the vicinity of present day Kiev.

The Vikings were known as "Rus" and It has been suggested that this is the origin of the name Russia, although there is still dispute among academics about this. There remains also vigorous dispute about the ethnicity of the Rus people and the interrelationship between Vikings (Varangians) and the Slavs, particularly in the lower Dnieper region. In Rus settlements around Kiev, Swedish Viking identity and ethnicity were slowly subsumed into predominantly Slavic culture.

Historical sources include archaeological finds (particularly coins) in the Volga watershed and the surprisingly detailed accounts of authors such as Persian geographer ibn Khordadbeh (820-912 CE).

HISTORICAL NOTES

Nicolas Roerich - Ready for the Campaign (The Varangian Sea)

It seems to have been trade rather than territorial expansion which motivated the Vikings. There are records of their having paid taxes for right of passage through territory controlled by local tribes down the Volga. Viking currency included honey, furs (beaver and black fox) and slaves. It has been suggested that in return they sought crucible steel, the forging of which was more skilfully practised in the Middle East.

Great seamen, the Vikings exploited the rivers and lakes wherever possible. Because so much portage was required between Lake Ladoga and the headwaters of the Volga and Dneiper Rivers, their wooden ships tended to be less than 14 m in length.

By the end of the 11th century, Viking influence along the Volga dwindled and they quietly disappeared from historical view.

There is a fascinating and detailed appraisal of Viking exploration in Russia in Melvyn Bragg's BBC 4 series "In Our Time".

THE SLAVS (6-12TH CENTURY)

This diverse Indo-European ethnic group developed in southern and central Europe. By the middle of the 6th century CE its influence extended across most of Europe, thence spreading north-east into Siberia, north to Scandinavia and east into Asia Minor. By the early Middle Ages various Slavic groups had populated the shores of the upper Volga.

Sergei Ivanov - The Rus trading slaves with the Khazars: Trade in the East Slavic Camp

THE KHAZARS (6TH-13TH CENTURIES)

As Slavic tribes settled the northern Volga and the Bulgars the central shores near Kazan, nomadic tribes of Turkic stock began to populate the lower Volga in the 6th century. Known as Khazars (Hazars), these tribes had migrated west from the polity of Khazaria, which lay to the north-west of the Caspian Sea. Many Jews had moved north to Khazaria, seeking refuge from Middle Eastern turmoil. By the 8th century, Khazar rulers (but not their subjects) had themselves formally adopted Judaism.

In the 9th century the Khazar Empire encompassed the northern shores of the Caspian, the lower Volga basin and most of what is now Ukraine. But with Viking incursion from the north and numerous Byzantine and Arab assaults on its southern borders, its authority and identity declined steadily until its overthrow by the Mongols in the 13th century.

Note that there is little evidence of connection between the Khazars (Hazars) and the Hazara in Afghanistan and Iran.

HISTORICAL NOTES

VOLGA BULGARIA (7TH -13TH CENTURIES)

In the early Middle Ages the Bulgars, a semi-nomadic Turkic people from Central Asia, established this khanate near the confluence of the Volga and Kama Rivers south of Kazan. Old Great Bulgaria, as it was called, flowered only briefly before it was partially subsumed into the Khazar Empire at the end of the 7th century.

The larger state of Volga Bulgaria retained its ethnic and cultural identity under the Khazars however, becoming Islamicised in the 9th century. Volga Bulgaria underwent a renaissance in the late 9th century as the power and scope of the Khazar Empire declined. Ultimately, Volga Bulgaria fell to the Mongols in their westward sweep under Genghis Khan in the 13th century.

GOLDEN HORDE (13TH-14TH CENTURIES)

In the 13th century, the Khazars and Bulgars were overrun by a mixed group of Mongols and Turkic peoples, who secured Volga territories south from Nizhniy Novgorod. "Golden Horde" is the name given to the western khanate of Genghiz Khan's great Mongol empire. By the 14th century it had become fully Islamicised. The Horde capital was Sarai, one of the largest cities in the mediaeval world, near modern day Volgograd.

The Golden Horde khanate was both violent and internally fraught, ultimately fragmenting into a number of Tatar Khanates, notably Kazan (central Volga), Astrakhan (Caspian) and Crimea (Black Sea). The first two of these fell to the Russians in the 16th century Russo-Kazan Wars, although the Crimean Khanate survived as an Ottoman vassal state until its annexure by Catherine the Great in the mid-18th century.

TATARS (13TH CENTURY - PRESENT)

Originally a loose nomadic federation of Gobi tribes, the Tatars (or Tartars) became part of Genghiz Khan's army. The Golden Horde khanate comprised both Mongol and Tatar ethnic and language groups. Later the name Tatar was used to refer collectively to populations in the Volga region, Astrakhan and Crimea.

From the Volga, Tatars spread west and north into present day Ukraine, Belorus and the Baltic states. The Volga Tatars were (and still are) located principally in and around Kazan and this region is now the Federal Republic of Tatarstan. In the city of Kazan, the ethnic, architectural, and cultural fusion of Tatar and Orthodox is everywhere apparent.

Genghiz Khan statue, Ulaan Bator

GRAND DUCHY OF MOSCOW (13TH - 16TH CENTURIES)

In what is now European Russia a number of Slavic principalities evolved in the early Middle Ages. The largest and most influential of these was the Grand Duchy of Moscow, which existed in uneasy cooperation with its Mongol rulers. By the 14th century the Duchy had become a major cultural centre and in the 16th century its princes finally routed the enfeebled and divided khanates of the Golden Horde.

At last divested of the Mongol Yoke, the Grand Duchy pursued consolidation of the other Slavic principalities, laying the groundwork for the establishment of a unified Russian state.

Of particular interest is the ferocious and bloody struggle by Muscovite Ivan the Terrible for annexation of the khanates of Kazan and Astrakhan by the Grand Duchy of Moscow. With his conquest of Kazan in 1522 (after 2 failed attempts), the Volga finally became Russian from its source to the Caspian. Worth remembering when you next gaze upon St Basil's Cathedral in Red Square.

Ivan the Terrible

Boris Godunov

HISTORICAL NOTES

Stanislaw Chlebowski - Tsar Peter I and his court

Alphonse Mucha - Abolition of serfdom in russia

THE POMORS (12TH-19TH CENTURY)

The Pomors were not an ethnic group but early Arctic explorers, settlers and traders. They had migrated north from Novgorod and established themselves initially along the western shores of the White Sea. From there they explored Russia's Arctic coast including the Kola peninsula, Spitsbergen and Novaya Zemlya, charting the Northern Sea Route between Arkhangelsk and Siberia, trading in fish and furs. The Pomors were hardy folk and superb seamen.

Pomor boats (koches) were usually 40-50 feet long. By the 16 century there were over 7,000 of them in the Barents Sea and surrounding waters. They were sturdy two-masted timber vessels with huge rudders. Flat bottomed, they had round bilges which were double planked and specially designed to allow them to rise when pinched in ice.

Pomors

HISTORICAL NOTES

THE COSSACKS (16TH CENTURY - PRESENT)

They may well have been Khazars, but the origins of this proud, warlike and fiercely independent people are not known. In any event, by the 16th century two Cossack groups had established themselves in Azov Ukraine and along the Don, respectively. In these sparsely populated areas the Cossacks provided Imperial Russia with a buffer zone along its southern borders. Variously in bloody conflict or intermittent alliance with Russia, for more than 300 years the Cossacks were exploited as fighting forces. Their legendary prowess as warriors gained them special status and they fought with Russia in the Napoleonic War, the Crimean War and the First World War, among many others.

In the second half of the 17th century the legendary Cossack hero Stenka (Stepan) Razin led forces up the Volga in an attempt to overthrow centralised control by the Grand Duchy and create a Cossack republic along the entire length of the river. Legend has it that he drowned his betrothed in the Volga, to demonstrate his strength and single-mindedness of purpose. For a time he secured Samara and Saratov, but his army was ultimately defeated. In Russia his memory lives on in popular culture, folk song, and works by Glazunov and Shostakovitch. [Google search - Razin + Springsteen + "Carnival is Over" for more information].

The Cossacks formed the core of the White (anti-Bolshevik) Army. After the victory of the Red Army, many fled to the Balkans. Those who remained faced systematic and brutal repression of their ethnic, political and economic identity. In Russia, public acknowledgement and acceptance of the Cossacks only occurred after the dissolution of the Soviet republic, since which time there has been something of a Cossack renaissance along the Don River, in particular.

Razin monument

THE ROMANOVS

After the death of Ivan the Terrible (1584) and the Time of Troubles, the Romanov dynasty came to power in 1613. Peter the Great, who had himself travelled overland from the White Sea down to Lake Onega, dreamt of of a permanent canal linking the two. This dream was not realised in his lifetime. In any case Archangel'sk, ice-bound for 9 months of the year, would always be an inadequate northern port for Russian trade. Accordingly, having secured extensive east Baltic territories from Sweden, Peter established St Petersburg, which became his new window on Europe and gateway to the Baltic Sea.

Peter the Great dreamt of connecting the Volga and Don Rivers and began construction of two canal systems (in 1700 and again in 1717). Because of engineering and cost problems however, neither system was completed.

It was left to Catherine the Great to extend and formalise Russia's southern borders down to the Black Sea, with her defeat of the Ottomans in Crimea in the late 18th century. Trade from the Volga to the Don and the Black Sea was effected overland by portage between the two rivers.

The Last of the Romanovs

HISTORICAL NOTES

SOVIET RUSSIA

Alive to the enormous commercial benefit and strategic importance of an uninterrupted trade route connecting the Arctic, Baltic and Black Seas, Joseph Stalin forbade access of all foreign vessels to Russia's inland waterways in 1936 (Article 5, Russian Inland Waterways Act 1936). 10 years later he ordered the completion of the final link in the trade route - the connection of the Volga and Don Rivers by canal. For 5 years, more than 100,000 German prisoners of war and Russian gulag inmates laboured to complete this project under brutal conditions, but Stalin did not live to see its grand opening in 1953.

VOLGA RIVER TRAVEL

Nicolas Roerich - Volok portage

Before construction of the barrages and locks the Volga was a fast flowing river with vast shoals, shifting sands (polites) and much variation in river heights according to season and rains. Navigation was very much a hit and miss affair, even in the hands of the most experienced of river pilots.

EARLY PORTAGE

Little is known about the means by which the Vikings moved their vessels from the Baltic and Lake Ladoga to the upper reaches of the Volga. One can only imagine the travails they faced hauling 13metre long timber ships up 1000 feet from Lake Onega then down to the Volga headwaters.

In 2009 Edberg reviewed the experiences of a number of recent re-enactment expeditions which followed Viking river routes. He concludes that "...the notion that Scandinavians brought their own vessels to and across Russia, as sometimes suggested by imaginative scholars, is neither supported by archaeological and historical research, nor by these experiments." In Edberg's view, original sources like the 11th century Russian Primary Chronicle should be interpreted with caution. While Vikings and other early travellers followed rivers, sailing them where possible, they must have completed large sections on foot, on horseback or sleigh. [Experimental Voyages 1983-2006, Rune Edberg]

It is clear that the Vikings did not sail their huge ocean-going longships across the Baltic from Sweden and then log-roll them overland to the Volga before sailing to the Caspian Sea. Almost certainly they designed light-weight rowing boats with auxiliary sail power, purpose-built and capable of being carried by perhaps 20 men.

We have voted this the most disturbing of all the photos

VOLGA RIVER TRAVEL

THE RIVER BARGES

This description by English merchant and traveller Anthony Jenkinson, written in about 1562, can hardly be improved upon:

> "very long builded, broade made and close aboue, flatte bottomed, and drawing aboue foure foote water,and will carrie two hundred tunnes: they have no yron appertaining to them but all of timber, And when the winde serueth, they are made to sayle. Otherwise,they have many men, som to hale and drawe by the neckes with long small ropes made fast to the saide boates, and some set with long poles."

VOLGA BOATMEN

Despite the idealised pictures and their eponymous song there was nothing noble about this calling. The burlaks (burlaki), as they were known, were impoverished and homeless human pack animals whose lives were short and miserably arduous. According to one source (Blum, Princeton University Press 1961) there were over 400,000 of them working the river at the beginning of the 19th century, with an annual death rate in excess of 7,000.

Teams of burlaki, both men and women, were harnessed to long tow lines and hauled shipping upstream against the current. By the 16th century, river barges commonly displaced over 200 tonnes. The journey from Astrakhan to Nizhniy Novgorod took 3 months, sometimes spread over two successive summers. Signed on for an entire trip, usually one per year, those burlaki incapable of proceeding were abandoned along the way. At the end of a tow their meagre pay was often squandered on alcohol.

Burlaki worked along towpaths except when the river was wide or inshore depths too low. Then they took their hauling lines out in small boats, anchored in the stream and hauled the barges and ships from there.

In his book "Daily Life in Russia under the Last Tsar", Henri Troyat describes a journey down the Volga in 1903. At pp 227-9 he gives a technical, vivid and moving description of the work of the burlaki.

Some large river barges carried their own tow-men. A diplomatic envoy (Adam Olearius, 1635) describes encounters with river barges near Kazan, where up to 400 men worked on the deck of these ships. They warped their barges up to anchors which then had to be reset using small boats, so that the whole process could be repeated. This tedious business allowed speeds over the ground in the vicinity of 10-16 km/day.

MASCHINA

While horses were also used to tow vessels, the topography of the shoreline often made their use slow and inefficient. Maschina (mashina) were cumbersome horse-driven precursors of steam tugs. Anchored in the stream, maschina used horses on board to turn huge warping capstans. The mechanics of the winching apparatus were Heath-Robinsonian in their complexity.

5 or 6 barges could be hauled simultaneously by just one of these anchored capstan tugs. Once they had been brought up short to the tug, the cargo barges were themselves anchored. Then the maschina tug was warped upstream to anchors newly set from small boats, after which the whole warping process could begin again. The 5 inch diameter warps were up to 3 miles long and one tug could haul barges of up to 17,000 tons (ref: Scientific American Supplement, No. 484, April 11, 1885)

Up to 100 horses were housed on one hauling vessel. Purchased cheaply in Astrakhan the beasts could be sold at a handsome profit in Nizhniy. The wooden barges themselves were often broken up after a single voyage, their timbers also sold in Nizhniy.

VOLGA RIVER TRAVEL

THE ARRIVAL OF STEAM

The first steamer was afloat on the Volga by 1822, but it was not until after the middle of the century that powered vessels had become established as the primary means of cargo transportation. Until well after the Second World War these vessels were all paddle-wheel steamers.

In 1858 the first steam-powered dredge was launched in Nizhniy Novgorod.

It should be borne in mind that prior to the construction of barrages and locks, ship movement remained slow, arduous and unpredictable. Groundings and wreck were frequent. Eccentric Victorian adventurer Laurence Oliphant described an 1852 journey down the Volga and his account of the trials of river navigation in a powered vessel is well worth reading [see appendix].

By 1903 Alfred Nobel had built some 50 steam-driven vessels in Astrakhan for transportation of oil, and within 10 years his Rybinsk shipyard was producing a steady line of Volga steamers. It was not long before the first diesel-powered vessel was launched by the Nobel Shipyard, with 3 triple cylinder engines each producing around 120 HP. By 1925 there were more than 1,500 powered vessels plying Volga waters, although a great many of these were destroyed during the Russian civil war.

During WW2 German forces destroyed nearly 9,000 vessels on the Volga, along with a great many port facilities, locks and dams. A huge program of repair and reconstruction took place as part of USSR's Fourth Five Year Plan (1946-50). Much of this, together with ambitious plans for reservoir construction along the river, had been on the Soviet drawing board before the war.

USING THIS GUIDE

BOAT CLUB CONTACT DETAILS

We have included as many addresses and telephone numbers as we have been able to find, but offer no guarantees as to their accuracy. Once you have tucked into your first spot, have your local contacts there telephone ahead down river for you, to line up the next port.

An incomplete but possibly helpful site for details of marinas other than than those mentioned in this guide is: http://rusyachting.ru/marinas.php

CONVENTIONS

DIRECTION OF TRAVEL

With few exceptions vessels travelling the Volga-Don seaway will be proceeding from north to south. Thus for the purposes of this guide all directions (right, left, port, starboard, ahead, behind) are referenced to yachts proceeding downstream.

WAYPOINTS

While every care has been taken, waypoints in the text are for general guidance only. In every case, navigators must cross-check these positions against charts and use discretion.

Waypoints generally represent approach positions in clear water. Sometimes there are further waypoints in the text which designate anchorages themselves.

COORDINATES FORMAT

xx xx.xx/0yy yy.yy.
So that 53 deg 12.5 min N, 047 deg 32 min E is written 53 12.5/047 32. 22

PLANS AND CHARTLETS

Again, these are for general guidance only and should not be relied upon for navigational purposes. Our thanks to iSailor staff for allowing us to use their electronic charts in preparation of plans and chartlets. Any errors in reproduction are ours and ours alone.

ANCHORAGES

Most, if not all of Tainui's anchorages are included in the body of this guide. They represent convenient stopovers separated by day sails of various lengths. They are by no means proscriptive or unique, and there are many hundreds of alternatives for you to discover. Indeed, this is one of the delights of the voyage. Anchorages requiring night approach after the longer passages can be assumed uncomplicated and generally straightforward with prudent navigation, radar and GPS assistance.

DISTANCES

Belomorsk to Rybinsk	900 km	562 miles
Rybinsk to Azov	2,763 km	1726 miles
Total	3,672 km	2,295 miles

APPROXIMATE TRAVEL TIMES

For reference, here are Tainui's travel times in 2013

Month	Date	Cumulative days	Location
June	3	0	Dep Vardo
	7	7	Archangel'sk
	11	11	Solovetskiy
	13	13	Belomorsk
	16	16	Medvezegorsk
	20	20	Vytegra
	25	25	Belozyorsk
	27	27	Cherepovets
July	1	31	Rybinsk
	4	34	Yaroslavl
	5	35	Kostroma
	9	39	Nizhniy Novgorod
	21	51	Cheboksary
	22	52	Sviyazshk
	23	53	Kazan
	28	58	Ulyanovsk
	30	60	Tolyatti
	31	61	Samara
August	3	64	Dep Samara
	4	65	Balakhova
	6	67	Saratov
	10	71	Volzhskiy
	26	87	Volgograd
	30	91	Volgodonsk
September	2	94	Rostov-on-Don
	5	97	Obukhovka
	9	101	Azov
	13	105	Kerch Ukraine

DISTANCES AND LOCKS

BELOMOR (BALTIC) CANAL

from Belomorsk to Povenets
distance	219 km
number of locks	19

LAKE ONEGA

from Povenets to Vytegra River
distance	208 km
number of locks	0

VOLGA-BALT WATERWAY

from Vytegra to Rybinsk
distance	459 km
number of locks	8

VOLGA RIVER

from Rybinsk to Volgograd
distance	2153 km
number of locks	7

VOLGA-DON CANAL

from Volgograd to Volgadonsk
distance	300 km
number of locks	13

DON RIVER

from Volgadonsk to Azov
distance	310 km
number of locks	3

Total distance	3672 km - 2295 miles
Total locks	50

CANAL FEES

The inland river system is divided into 3 administrative sections covering the White Sea (Belomor) Canal and Lake Onega, the Volga-Baltic canal, the Volga, the Volga-Don Canal and the Don River. Separate approvals must be obtained from each of these agencies seriatim, with canal fees paid in advance. For some reason there are 5 separate subsections at which the fees must be paid. We never sorted out the relationship between these subsections and the 3 main administrative regions. Canal fees, which depend on ship measurements (L x B x D) are in the vicinity of $500 per section. Calculation and payment was organised by Vladimir Ivankiv, our St Petersburg agent. In 2013 Tainui's total transit fees were 25,200 roubles (about $800).

APPENDIX

RUSSIA - GENERAL INFORMATION

MONEY

In larger stores, service stations and supermarkets, credit card facilities are ubiquitous. Automatic translation into English is available. Note however, that cash payment is necessary in smaller stores and at most boat clubs. Many vendors cannot change large denomination notes and it is important to carry adequate cash in small notes. The rouble equivalent of 500 Euros would be a reasonable amount to keep in hand on the boat.

LANGUAGE

Despite the Russia's huge size and its ethnic, cultural and social diversity, Russian is the first language of 99% of the people. Almost invariably it is the only language spoken regardless of professional status or previous travel overseas. Cyrillic script is ubiquitous and almost nobody can read Roman script. For foreigners travelling in Russia this is a major contributor to the sense of alienation so commonly experienced. The simplest things - buying a bus ticket, finding your way to a street address, shopping - are fiendishly difficult and can be very frustrating.

Tainui's inarticulate skipper, who has no Russian, recommends two other methods of communication which help to ease this sense of alienation - charade acting, and vodka.

It is almost trite to mention here the critical importance of a crew member who speaks and reads Russian fluently. Not only is this vital for practical reasons, but also because it is a formal requirement of entry. On arrival in Belomorsk at the beginning of your journey, canal officials will need to be satisfied about this.

In the Barents Sea and in the Sea of Azov, Russian and Ukrainian coast guard radio operators cannot (? will not) communicate in English. Further, radio operators in Russian commercial vessels can rarely speak English.

Maritime discourse

It is important to ensure that Russian speaking crew have language facility specifically with radio procedures, general maritime discourse and and SAR. The Russian phonetic alphabet must become intuitive - the on-board interpreter will be spelling boat and crew names many times over the radio. Tainui's port of registry in Australia is Mooloolaba. Spelling this out over the radio was difficult. Even the name "Tainui", carefully spoken, spelled phonetically and repeated, was often morphed mysteriously into "Tanya".

Note for Skippers

Unless you speak and read Russian, a journey through Russia's inland waterways poses unusual and frustrating problems for you. Almost nobody speaks a word of English and you will find yourself very much in the hands of your Russian-speaking crew.

Relinquishing all control of ship's business can be disturbing, to say the least. You must have absolute faith in your interpreter, whose competence will be pivotal. Negotiations with customs, immigration, canal authorities, lock keepers, dispatchers and the many other bureaucrats dealt with every day are completely out of your hands. You will be expected to sign endless forms whose contents are quite incomprehensible. Often you will have no alternative but to sit back, tipple and go with the flow. This takes some getting used to.

TELEPHONE (ISD ETC)

Russia's country code is 7. Russia has an internal "federal" entry code: 8. When you phone out to a different city, you first phone 8, then the area code and the home or office number. When you phone a mobile phone, you first dial 8, after the mobile number. But instead of the 8, you can also dial +7 with the same results.

Except in parts of the White Sea (Belomor) Canal and Lake Onega, there is good mobile phone coverage on the internal waterways, although on long stretches there may be no accompanying internet coverage.

One or more of your crew will need a Russian SIM card. These cards are readily available to Russian citizens and residents. Foreigners cannot obtain SIM cards unless/until they are listed on the immigration register. (For more information about the immigration register, see chapter on Visas). The simplest solution is to ask your Russian crew to purchase SIM cards in their own names. We bought prepaid SIM cards for our iPhones and iPad to use for phoning, internet and GPS navigation. While you can keep using a foreign SIM card the expense will be prohibitive. Much more importantly, canal authorities will not be able to contact you.

There are three major service providers - MTS, Beeline and Megafon. MTS is the oldest and, although not the cheapest, it has the most extensive coverage. Shops and service outlets can be found in all towns. SIM cards can be topped up at small automated terminals in most supermarkets, banks, railway stations and larger shops.

Many terminals will ask for a commission which can be rather steep. Sberbank (the country's national savings bank) provides SIM card top-up without commission and also accepts foreign credit cards. Sberbank is and has offices everywhere.

Note that the mobile phone is an important adjunct to VHF communication with lock-keepers and dispatchers. In case of radio problems, communication with them can be set up by phone. Moreover, waterways authorities use telephones to check up on your progress.

APPENDIX

COMPUTERS

Make sure that you have one notebook on board with a Russian keyboard. Without it, your Russian crew will not be able to access and write to Cyrillic websites.

SHORE POWER

220 V shore power, only available at a small number of boat clubs, cannot be relied upon. Expect either 2- or 3- pin standard European plugs.

TAXIS

In many Russian towns you can hold your hand out as if hitch-hiking and someone will stop (Archangel'sk is a notable exception here). Fares are open to negotiation but are generally low by European standards. Licensed taxis have higher rates.

TOILETS, SHOWERS AND LAUNDRY

Sought vigorously and relentlessly by our crew, these facilities are often not available. Specific details are mentioned anchorage by anchorage.

SECURITY

The early years of Yeltsin's reforms, (after the collapse of the Soviet Union in 1991) were characterised by lawlessness and random violence. In Volzshkiy the crew of yacht Aenigma were robbed at gunpoint. Things have settled down since then. In our entire trip we did not experience a single threat to personal or yacht security. Before going ashore we locked the main hatch but did not strip the decks of all removable items of value.

Without exception the Russians we met went out of their way to assist us. They were always happy to keep an eye on the boat while we were ashore. It seemed they would have felt personally responsible for any mishap or misadventure which befell us.

TRADITIONS AND CUSTOMS

Dress: Women are expected to cover their head when entering a church. Carry a small headscarf in your handbag. In monasteries you may be expected to cover your legs too, even if you are wearing slacks, but wrap-around skirts will usually be provided at the entrance.

A few miscellaneous points to note:

- Women do not usually shake hands.
- Friendly embrace between men is normal and can be expected.
- Remove shoes before entering a private house, especially in winter.
- Always bring a small gift when visiting private dwellings.
- Expect your visitors to step cheerfully aboard without formal invitation.
- Once a bottle of alcohol has been opened, it must be emptied.
- Visitors to your boat may be unwilling to sit in a corner of the cockpit.

FOOD

In Russia, restaurant food is at best variable in quality. Supermarkets are well-stocked however, and our most memorable meals on the Volga were home-cooked.

DRINK

A huge variety of alcoholic beverages is available in all supermarkets. Vodka prices are excitingly low but wine can be expensive and its quality variable.. Most challenging is the ordeal of keeping up with your cockpit guests, drink for drink. With effort we managed, but at times it was difficult.

MEDICAL MATTERS

Russia does not have general practitioners working in solo practice. Most primary care is obtained through polyclinics with mixed nursing general and specialist practitioners. Facilities available depend on the size of the polyclinic. With serious illness requiring hospitalisation, you will need to try and arrange transfer to a larger town or, heaven forbid, repatriation.

Ambulance transport, especially in rural areas, can be rather primitive. If you can walk, it will be better to seek out taxi transport.

It is unlikely that medical staff will speak English, so take your interpreter with you. You may be asked quietly for payment at the medical centre. This will always be an under-the-table cash transaction, the sum of which will be open to negotiation. This is unlikely to be claimable under your health insurance policy.

Pharmacies (Аптека) can be found everywhere. In larger centres these are often open 24 hours a day. Many medicines (steroids and antibiotics, for example) requiring prescription elsewhere can be bought over the counter the counter in Russia.

VISAS, ENTRY FORMALITIES AND REGISTRATION

VISAS

There are two Russian visas to consider for this trip - the 90 day business visa and the 30 day tourist visa. With each you need first to obtain a visa invitation from within Russia. In both cases this requires you to make formal application to the appropriate authority. Once that invitation has been granted, you take the invitation and your visa application to your friendly local Russian embassy or consulate, where visa issue is relatively straightforward.

Tourist visa - It is quite easy to obtain tourist visas. Any tourist agency with Russian visa experience can organise the visa invitation and arrange the necessary paperwork for you.

Business visa

Getting a business visa takes a bit more effort. Both single and double entry visas are available. The latter are more expensive but may be useful if you have to leave Russia in emergency circumstances, or if you have crew who wish to spend two separate periods on the boat. For business visas the formal visa invitation is more difficult to obtain. It is a document in established form issued by a Russian government department (eg Ministry of the Interior) or a specially licensed private organisation or company. You would do well to enlist the services of a tourist agency with relevant experience to ease this process for you. "Reason for travel" needs to be defined in the application for the visa invitation. In Tainui's case, this was "author's research into the history of Volga Vikings"

One year business visa

These are of no practical value because they do not allow you to remain in Russia for more than 90 days out of every 180, which rather defeats their purpose.

Working Visa

This a visa for foreign employees working in Russia. Maxine had one of these and was therefore spared the difficulties which foreign skippers and crew are likely to face.

And so...

You need to plan ahead!

The travel window is determined by spring breakup of ice in the White Sea (late May or early June) and the onset of autumn gales (October) and freeze in the Sea of Azov (late November).

While the journey is easily possible in 3 months, that leaves little time for stopping and sitting, exploring, visiting Moscow, repairing the engine and other exigencies. We recommend that you allow 4 months for the trip through Russia from Archangel'sk to Azov. You need a visa valid for at least three months. That rules out the tourist visa. You could get a business visa for three months and renew it if you need more time. You will need to abandon your boat on the river for 10 days while you leave Russia to get your second visa in an adjacent capital (Riga, Tallinn or Athens, for example). Kiev may be on the list of choices, but remember to check whether you need a Ukrainian visa to get to Kiev! We left Tainui in Volzhskiy, but Saratov and Samara would probably be safer and more secure choices."

You also could get a business visa for a year which allows to be in the country for up to 182 days (6 months minus 1 day) and you can enter and leave the country as you like. If you want to take your time, then this is the best option.

NEVER EVER allow your visa to expire while you are still in Russia. That may lead to major problems. You are likely to be prevented from leaving the country and will have to apply for a new visa (a so-called exit visa) before you will be allowed to depart. The process is cumbersome and may take more than two weeks. For minor infringements immigration authorities do have a discretion to extend your visa by up to 3 days but that may not be extended to you.

THE TRICK

Living and working in Russia Maxine did not require specific visas for this trip. John however, did. Our early attempts to obtain a business visa were met with silence. Looking back, perhaps our error was to include details of our intended mode of travel - Tainui. The notion of a foreign yacht traversing the inland waterways did not fit within acceptable parameters for the bureaucracy.

Finally, we applied for a random business visa invitation simply omitting any reference at all to our yacht or the inland waterways. For all anyone knew, we were travelling by bus from one port to the next, all the way down the Volga. That visa invitation arrived within 6 days of our request! We infer that the issuing of visas is unrelated to the intended mode of transport.

With the business visa in hand we were able to arrive in Archangel'sk with credible paperwork. But we knew that we had only moved the entry hurdle along, from the visa issuing authorities to the departments of customs and immigration in Archangel'sk. There we could not keep secret the existence of Tainui and our intention to sail her through central Russia.

In Archangel'sk we included with all our papers copies of the 2012 Decrees issued by Prime Minister Medvedev and President Putin (see appendix), announcing the opening up of inland waterways to foreign vessels. In Archangel'sk and Belomorsk we produced these at every opportunity. Whether it was pivotal we do not know. But we got in.

PORTS OF ENTRY

Apart from St Petersburg and Kaliningrad on the Baltic, the two ports of entry in Russia's European north are Murmansk and Archangel'sk. For reasons set out below, we believe the latter is much to be preferred.

Murmansk

We decided by-pass Murmansk, having heard too many horror stories about the place. It is a military port and home to Russia's Arctic Fleet. The Cold War may be gone but the mentality still lingers on. The consequences of a minor navigational mistake, an innocent typographic error in some document or a simple misunderstanding may be far-reaching - fines, vessel arrest (chains, notice on the mast etc). Have no doubt, Soviet bureaucracy is alive and well here.

Of course, things change. By the time you make this trip, Murmansk may have eased its approach, so do check in advance.

Archangel'sk

This is the only other port of entry. While there really isn't any choice for vessels arriving from Norway, we are able to recommend it.

USING A SHIPPING AGENT

Unsure of the requirements here, in Vardo we engaged the services of **Yuri Klyutkin** for our entry into Russia at Archangel'sk. His support was efficient, inexpensive and comprehensive. Yuri also facilitated our entry into the White Sea-Baltic Canal at Belomorsk.

We later learned that vessels entering Russia at Archangel'sk do not require a shipping agent. **Alex Galitsky**, a very experienced local sailor with 40 years' cruising experience in the White Sea, can organise entry for you. Dutch yacht Bestevaer 2 (Gerard Dykstra) had smooth entry into Russia at Archangel'sk in 2013 with Igor's competent assistance.

Vladimir Ivankiv is Russia's RCC representative. Based in St Petersburg, this delightful chap has many years' experience coddling foreign vessels through the bureaucratic difficulties associated with transit through Russia's inland waters, particularly between Belomorsk and St Petersburg. Vladimir took charge of negotiations for our transits through the Belomorsk Canal, the Volga-Balt and Volga-Don regions. His services were essential and his commitment assiduous and cheerful.

APPENDIX

Before you leave Norway (from Vardo or Kirkenes), you must inform your Archangel'sk shipping agent of your departure and your ETA at the Dvina rivermouth in the White Sea. You should email your crew list and boat registration details and specifications (see section "Departing Norway" below), together with scanned copies of all crew passports and visas. This allows your agent to insert you into the system, as it were. By the time you call up the River Traffic Authority at the entrance to the Dvina River, the officials will know who you are. They should already have processed your entry formalities and will let you know when you may enter the river.

We were instructed to proceed to Ekonomia wharf, about 3 hours upstream from the river mouth in Archangel'sk port. This is where immigration and customs formalities are taken care of. Our agent had arranged for the officials to meet us, as he did himself. We found both customs and immigration officers professional and reasonable.

CUSTOMS AND THE BOAT

Customs in Russia seem to have authority to grant foreign vessels entry for up to 12 months, regardless of your visa restrictions. The law is written mainly with cars in mind but the wording covers all modes of transport, including pleasure yachts. We explained that our trip would take longer than the 3 months covered by John's initial business visa. We sought, and were given a 4 month entry permit on the basis that he would be applying for a new visa to cover the latter part of the journey. Customs went along with that.

A special document

Before we set out on this trip Maxine had informal discussions with various agencies within the Ministry of Transport, following which she had become concerned that the intention of the 2012 decrees (opening inland waterways to foreign yachts) may not have filtered down to local authorities. As a result, we decided to try and create a series of documents which would expressly set down our itinerary and general intentions while in Russia, to constitute some sort of evidence on paper that we had permission to be wherever we were.

With the assistance of an understanding customs official in Archangel'sk we prepared a document defining our route through Russia to Azov, listing all the ports to be visited with approximate dates. This was stamped and signed by the customs officer, although we have no idea what became of his copy of it. We presented our copy of the document to the Captain of the Belomor Canal to satisfy him that Customs were clearly aware of our plans and it was he who granted us entry into the inland waterways. We also presented the document to the Customs authorities in Azov on our departure from Russia.

In the end we probably needn't have worried about this. The relevant authorities en route knew about the Presidential and Prime Ministerial decrees and welcomed us with open arms. The relevant authorities did not cause us any trouble. And now, after Tainui's journey, all authorities are aware of the lifting of restrictions in foreign vessel travel on the inland waterways.

You will however, need an itinerary of ports to be visited and approximate dates. We sent regular updates of ours to Vladimir Ivankiv, who forwarded them to the relevant authorities.

Customs will need photocopies of your ship's papers, ship specifications (safety equipment etc), passports, visas and crew lists. All documents other than passport photocopies should be provided both in English and in Russian translation. As we have said, you should carry with you multiple copies of these (a dozen, perhaps). We were asked to stamp each of these photocopies with our ship's stamp.

Note that Russia has absolutely no tolerance for illicit drugs. If you are found with them, arrest and imprisonment are likely. The customs officials with whom we dealt showed no interest in our ship's medical supplies however, nor the ample size of our drinks cabinet.

IMMIGRATION

You will be asked to complete two copies of a so-called "migration card". One copy is retained by the immigration department and one stays with your passport. DO NOT LOSE YOUR COPY! You will be need to produce it when you complete your departure formalities when you leave Russia.

Special advice for your Russian speaking crew

Check very carefully that all forms are completed correctly. Check all names for correct spelling and compare passport numbers with the original documents. This is boring and should not be necessary, but we suffered for want of this level of pedantry (but only once). We encountered problems departing Russia when we found that there was an accidental, one digit discrepancy between a passport number and the number transcribed to the customs form.

CLEARING OUT OF RUSSIA

Caution: Recent events in Crimea create uncertainty about the entire process of exit from Russia. It may be that all clearance formalities will be transferred from Azov to Kerch in Crimea. You will need to clarify this prior to entering Russia.

In Arkhangelsk and St Petersburg there are good and reliable shipping agents willing to work for a reasonable fee. In Azov things were different. We couldn't find an agent willing to charge less than $1,500 so we handled the exit procedure ourselves. We do not recommend this.

For further details, see Azov section.

REGISTRATION OF FOREIGN VISITORS IN RUSSIA

This ridiculous piece of legislation is complicated and self-defeating.

In Russia every foreigner is obliged to register with the immigration department within 7 days of arrival. The process is cumbersome and may require you to sit in a queue for 2 days. It is quite impossible for an ignorant foreigner to manage. Hotels will take care of registration for you if you stay with them. Indeed they are legally obliged to register all foreigners who stay with them, but they will onlyprovide registration for the duration of your stay at the hotel.

In theory, each time a foreigner travels to a different location within Russia he has to register again in that new place. But because of the 7 day clause, you only have to register if you stay in one place for more than a week. For much, if not all of your voyage the rule will not apply to you. You can travel quite legally down the inland waterways without registration. But after 7 days of non-registration only the Immigration Service can provide you with registration documents.

The problem becomes a practical one when you decide to check into a hotel en route, for a hot shower, clean sheets and general R & R. The hotel must register you when they accept you as their guest, but they can only do that if you can produce proof of registration somewhere else within the preceding week. Hotels which provide accommodation for foreigners without confirming their registration history face very heavy fines and so they will not do it. We did find one hotel which was kind enough to book us in under Russian names. We paid in cash and tipped the receptionist handsomely for her efforts.

Proof of registration is not needed for clearance out of the Russia.

Registration legislation is not aimed at foreigners who enter Russia with legitimate visas. It it is directed at immigrants from the former Soviet republics who come in droves to work in Russia. They don't need visas and registration is the method by which the authorities try and ensure that they do not overstay their welcome and work illegally. As it happens, it is not working.

For hot showers and clean sheets you will need to improvise until these regulations are either abolished or amended. As Maxine says, if all else fails, throw a scene.

PREPARATION

CHARTS

Paper charts

There being no offshore hazards between Vardo and the approach to Archangel'sk, you can get by with Cmap until you reach the North Dvina River. However you do need paper charts for the North Dvina River approach to Archangel'sk and also the Solovetskiy Islands.

There are more than 270 ENCs covering 2,600 kilometres of Russia's inland waterways. A series of 7 chart books covers the length of the waterway the subject of this guide, from Belomorsk (White Sea) to Azov (eastern end of Sea of Azov).

These chart folios are expensive. In March 2013 we paid some 55,000 roubles (about 1,500 Euros) for our set. They are excellent charts and quite essential. Indeed, you will not be allowed to proceed south from Belomorsk until the canal authorities have sighted your collection.
All text is Cyrillic but for navigational purposes the rudiments can easily be followed by non-Russian speakers.

There were three gaps in our folio coverage - Lake Onega, Rybinsk Reservoir and Volgograd waters. We relied on our electronic charts in these places and found them quite adequate.

Paper charts of Lake Onega are readily available. Rybinsk Reservoir is included in a separate chart folio covering the Volga headwaters, while Volgograd waters are covered in the chart folio for the lower reaches of the Volga from Volgograd to the Caspian Sea. For reason of cost we did not buy these.

If the chart folios have one failing, it is that they do not show latitudes and longitudes. This is only a nuisance if you are trying to write a cruising guide and want easily to coordinate the many hundreds of waypoints.

Note that the book covering the White Sea (Belomorsk) Canal is organised from south to north (with water flow). This is the only section you follow in reverse order of charts.

As mentioned above, you also will need paper charts covering the southern White Sea, Archangel'sk and approaches, the Solovetskiy Islands and approaches to Belomorsk.

A quirk of the Volga-Don Canal folio is that the charts are all upside down (north is at the bottom). You get used to this quickly.

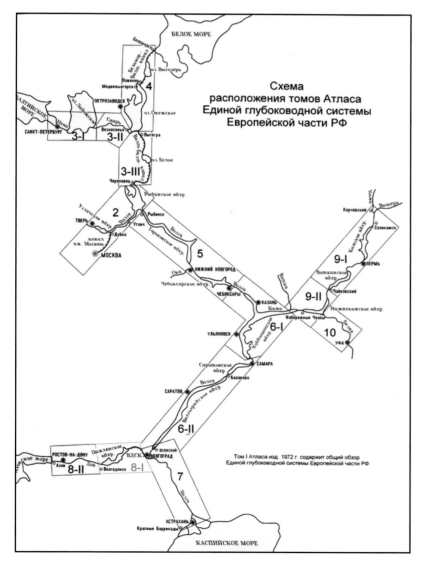

Russian chart folios

APPENDIX

Purchasing chart folios

Inland waterways paper charts are produced and updated by several publishers, most notably VolgoBalt, a Russian State organisation in St Petersburg https://www.volgo-balt.ru

Offshore sea charts (approaches to Belomorsk etc) can be obtained at Chart Pilot, also based in St Petersburg www.chartpilot.ru. Note that this company does not sell the inland waterway charts.

We bought our inland waterways chart folios from Morkniga, www.morkniga.ru, a nautical shop in Mitino, on the outskirts in Moscow. Some of the charts had to be ordered in from St Petersburg, which took about two weeks.

Vladimir Ivankiv will advise you about charts atlases for St Petersburg to Lake Onega. He is also able to provide all atlases for you if you are starting your trip from St Petersburg.

Chart Atlas coverage

Volume 4	Belomorsk to Povenets (runs from south to north)
Volume 3, part III	Vytegra to Cherepovets
Volume 5	Rybinsk to Cheboksary
Volume 6, part I	Cheboksary to Samara
Volume 6, part II	Samara to Volgograd
Volume 8, part I	Volograd to Volgadonsk
Volume 8, part II	Volgadonsk to Don River mouth
Volume 8, part II supplement	From km 3121 to Don River mouth

Note - Volume 8 part 11 supplement covers waters where IALA buoyage Rules apply. Note this is also where you need to change back to your international channel VHF transmitter.

Electronic charts

These are an essential adjunct. Our paper chart books did not cover Lake Onega, and on exit from the Belomor Canal there are multiple cardinal marks to navigate. Electronic charting filled this gap for us and it was also very convenient for cockpit navigation.

We used the IOS program iSailor and found it clear and accurate. An altogether excellent program. iSailor's Russia inland waterways charts can be downloaded from the iSailor app store. We downloaded iSailor onto both iPhones and iPad. While their internal GPS worked quite well, we used an external bluetooth GPS receiver (XGPS150) which performed faultlessly and was of great help.

Navionics has also produced electronic charts of the Russian inland waterways. Tainui carried this program as backup, but crew consensus was that the iSailor interface was preferable, both clearer and easier to use. Navionics charts for iPad are reasonably priced but the Windows notebook version is very expensive.

SHIP'S BUSINESS

Courtesy flags

As in many East European countries, the larger the better.

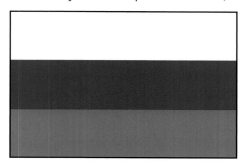

The Merchant Ensign of the Russian Federation is the white/blue/red tricolor. The white signifies nobility, the blue honesty and the red, love. This flag was adopted in 1705.

Legend has it that Peter the Great ordered construction of a frigate in Holland. When it was delivered to Archangel'sk he was so taken with the Dutch ensign at its stern that he modified it into this horizontal tricolor. In 1896, before the coronation of Tsar Nicholas 11, it became the official Russian ensign. The tricolor was abandoned in 1917 but reinstated in 1991 as the official flag of the Russian Federation.

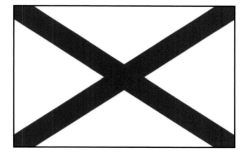

The Naval Ensign is the St Andrew's cross. Adopted in 1722, it was decommissioned at the time of the Russian Revolution in 1917 but is now once again the official naval ensign.

Ship's papers and declarations

You will require multiple copies, in both English and Cyrillic, of each of the following documents. A dozen copies of each would be safe. Copies in Russian should be stamped and verified as true copies.

1. crew list, including nationalities and dates of birth
2. passport details for each crew member, including passport number, place of issue, date of issue, date of expiry
3. ship registration papers
4. captain's CV, covering experience and all maritime qualifications
5. vessel insurance papers (we had 3rd party person and property insurance only)
6. personal health insurance (proof of this is required with visa application)
7. vessel route outline covering all intended stops, with dates and times

8. full dossier of vessel specifications including safety equipment, electronic and other navaids
9. engine specifications and details, including age, make, model and serial numbers

Item 7 above is problematic insofar that it will involve significant guesswork. The document can be updated along the way however, and your agent will keep the authorities abreast of changes you make to it. We listed all ports along the entire waterway system and estimated roughly our expected times of arrival and departure from each. We do not think this list was ever examined critically, although it is an important document.

Item 9 is necessary because, as we were told, there have been examples of vessels doing quiet, unoffical engine exchanges and bypassing duties and taxes in the process. Our venerable 80 HP Ford diesel has no serial number that we have ever been able to find. In Azov this caused considerable anxiety for the customs officials charged with finalising our clearance out of Russia. Ultimately they took a whole series of photographs and seemed satisfied that we had not engaged in any nefarious activity. A simple glance at our engine might have led a disinterested observer to the same conclusion.

Ship's stamp

In Russia the bureaucracy is very fond of rubber stamps. Ours was in constant use in all dealings with customs, immigration, health, canal authorities, and other officials. The stamp should be self-inking and include ship name, official registration number, international call sign and port of registry. This is an essential item.

Insurance

For Tainui we had 3rd party person and property insurance only. Proof of personal health insurance expressly covering Russia is required with visa applications. You should check the fine print of your personal health policy - can you claim without a formal receipt? Are there specific issues as regards choice of hospital?

Maritime qualifications

For the moment, this is a moveable feast.

The rules state that on the inland waterways there must be at least one person on board who speaks Russian. That person also must have sufficient Russian maritime qualifications.

In Tainui we had commercial masters tickets, CEVNI, ICC and RYA qualifications. The skipper's qualifications, having been issued outside Russia, are completely irrelevant. The ICC is not valid and, while Russia is a signatory to CEVNI, no-one seems to be aware of that fact.

The rules imply that your Russian speaking crew is Russian and hence holds Russian maritime qualifications. Fortunately, when we entered Belomor canal we had on board one Russian crew member with the right qualifications. His were time-expired, but only because some bureaucratic quirk meant that renewal at that time was impossible (apparently a not unusual state of affairs in Russia). Our inspector knew of this gap in the law and was happy to accept his expired papers.

Because of illness our vaguely licensed crew member left Tainui 3 days later. For the remainder of our voyage Maxine was our nominated Russian-speaking crew member but she only had foreign maritime qualifications. The water police checked our papers only once but they were so shaken by being on a foreign-flagged yacht that they were happy to accept anything formal-looking, as long it came with translation. We had had all our foreign maritime qualifications translated into Russian.

Radio transmitters

International VHF channels are used in the White Sea (up to and including Archangel'sk, Solovetskiy and Belomorsk). After the entrance to the Belomorsk Canal however, Russia's internal waterway VHF channels are used all the way down to (but not including) Azov, so you will need a special transmitter. Russian hand-held VHF radios can be purchased over the internet but deliveries can be made only in Russia.

With your transmitter purchase you will receive a radio equipment license. The authorities are very fond these, so keep that piece of paper in a safe place in case you and your yacht get checked.

There is a useful little booklet about radio communications (in Russian, obviously) which can be ordered at http://www.morkniga.ru

Gifts

Russians are a wonderfully generous people. It is normal for visitors to the boat to bring food and drink with them. Repaying kindnesses is difficult. We carried a supply of small Australian mementoes which the children loved. But quality A4 photos of Tainui, specifically inscribed for recipients, were appreciated and much prized. We were glad to have brought a pile of photos with us.

ESSENTIAL EQUIPMENT

Most elements under this heading apply to any vessel exploring less commonly frequented cruising grounds. This is no more than a checklist, highlighting issues which may require special consideration in Russia's inland waterways.

Fuel

Diesel is readily available and of good quality. Cost in 2013 - around 30 roubles (1 USD) per litre. The quality was generally good and we did not take the precaution of double filtering before filling the tanks. We did increase the frequency of filter replacement though. Our two stage in-line filters (changed every 50 engine hours) were no more clogged than usual.

Diesel is usually bought at local service stations and transported tediously by the taxi/jerrycan method. At some boat clubs you can arrange for delivery of fuel by truck.

APPENDIX

FUELLING AND PROVISIONING : JOHN

I will mention this tedious business once, for completeness.

All refuelling in Russia is by drum. Our 7 or 8 five gallon jerrycans are loaded into a rusty Lada taxi and we clamber in on top of them. It is hot and the windows are closed. There follows a long conversation between Maxine and the driver, in Cyrillic of course, while I relinquish all control once more and dream of cold beer. Then the radio is turned up to shriek levels, and off we bump along a dirt road to a petrol station miles out of town. We join a long queue of old soviet trucks, Ladas and Hummers. We sit and wait. So far we have found clean-looking diesel and I have not, for my sins, been filtering it at source. Fuel is cheap. Eventually, after the jerrycans have been refilled, we return to the boat and load them on board.

The much easier alternative, if we're lucky, is to line up a local entrepreneur to bring down some big drums of diesel and a pump. Then the process is less stressful.

Tainui's tankage is about 400 litres, in 3 separate stainless tanks. Transferring fuel is messy despite the most careful preparation. Our tank air breathers are small, so as levels rise invariably there is a great eructation of foamy diesel up the filler, all over me and the deck. Also, I can only tell how full they are by computation since last fill (3.8 litres per hour x engine hours run) and the sound at the filler as I pour. Despite a reasonably musical ear I do not find this foolproof. The other problem is movement of the yacht. The tanks are baffled of course, but any rolling motion makes a nearly filled tank regurgitate like an overfed baby. But the job is at last done. It is a pain, but the job is certainly easier here in flat water than at sea.

At the supermarkets, most of which seem plentiful and well-stocked, we wander about and grab anything which takes our fancy. This method is slapdash, more expensive but quick. Long gone are the days when I would itemise purchases and buy judiciously according to the week's menus.

There are good vegetables, breads, meat and dairy products. I recall a Brazilian fresh meat market which David and I visited once in Bahia de Salvador. I still have dreams about those whole goat heads with eyes looking up at me pleadingly, floating in buckets of bloody water, and the trotters and knuckles lazing about in 100 gallon drums of oily sludge.

At the checkout an obese, haemorrhoidal woman behind us in the queue looks at our 6 bottles of vodka, 6 cartons of beer and the white wine cask with barely concealed distaste. Using eloquent charades I explain to her that Maxine has a drinking problem and this is the beginning of her slow withdrawal. She isn't amused, nor is Maxine.

Water

Bottled water in 2-5 litre containers is available everywhere. While hose water at marinas is generally deemed "not potable" we were casual in our observance of this warning and suffered no gastrointestinal problems. The waters of Lake Onega are pristine and can be pumped (by deck wash pump with additional hose, or bucket). On the Volga we purchased 2-5 gallon plastic containers of drinking water. These are available everywhere.

Gas

Russian propane containers have unique reduction valves and hose fittings. It would be wise to carry enough gas for the entire journey. We ran out of gas at the southern end of the Don and purchased a single large replacement tank in Obukhovka. Like most long distance offshore cruisers, Tainui carries a range of adapters, regulators and hose fittings. Something can usually be cobbled together from this chaotic storehouse.

Electricity

220 volt shore power is only available at a few boat clubs and should not be relied upon. A supply of two- and three-pin round plugs and sockets terminals should be carried.

Service and spares

Importation of spare parts into Russia can be an expensive, slow and uncertain business. Given the time constraints imposed by visa limitations and the length of the river passage, any delay waiting for the arrival of parts can play havoc with your plans. This is best avoided if at all possible, by preparing and maintaining a generous stockpile of engine, steering, plumbing, electronic parts and other supplies prior to entry into Russia.

Engine cooling issues

Fine weed is a problem, especially in the lower reaches of the Don River. We twice suffered overheating problems caused by a blocked salt water intake hose. Keep an eagle eye on your temperature gauge and salt water flow.

Hull anodes

There is much discussion online about the choice of anodes for extended cruising in fresh water. Zinc anodes tend to become inactive after 2 months or so, because of a build up of an insulating layer of zinc hydroxide, whereas aluminum anodes will remain active. For fibreglass hulls, Navalloy™ (aluminium/zinc/indium alloy) anodes are recommended over zinc.

Perhaps out of an excess of laziness we stuck with our usual zinc anodic protection. After 4 months in fresh water our anodes did not seem to have deteriorated any more than they would have done in sea water.

Holding tanks

These are mandatory for all commercial vessels but Russian yachts do not have them. In Belomorsk the issue was raised with us but was not pursued. Tainui did not have a holding tank. It would not be wise to assume that entry of yachts in future will be granted without tankage.

APPENDIX

Refrigeration

With increasing age Tainui's skipper has found this, along with other complexities of shipboard life, more and more useful. He still draws the line at underfloor heating, to the annoyance of some of his crew!

Tainui's 5.3 cu ft fridge employs a Waeco CU-84 condensing unit and a Waeco VD-15 forced air evaporator. Kept full, it disgorges chilled wines and juices reliably. We do not have a freezer.

Fresh provisions, including quite good fruit and vegetables, are reliably available from well-stocked supermarkets in all ports and towns.

Insect screens

These are very important, especially in the channels south of Vytegra. Only intermittently were they needed as we progressed further south.

In White Sea (Belomor) Canal and the long section between Vytegra and the Volga mosquitoes were a problem at dawn and dusk at all anchorages. In the Volga-Balt Canal we were intermittently troubled also by huge numbers of march flies. Slow and stupid they may be, but they are persistent creatures. Maxine got significant allergic responses to the bites. Insect screens are essential. DEET skin sprays didn't seem very effective.

On the Volga itself, the insect problem was insignificant.

Fenders

For lock work, adequate fenders are of course essential. We carried 3 of those large, flourescent pink spherical fenders (600 cm diameter) and 6 of the common cylindrical yacht fenders. All were used routinely in the locks.

Ground tackle

Anchoring demands no specific skills. The waters are shallow and there is generally good holding, usually in soft mud. In narrower sections of the waterways it is often necessary to set a stern anchor. Our bower was a 60 lb Spade with 3/8" chain rode and our kedge a 44 lb Danforth. We never dragged.

Other equipment

cockpit shading
binoculars
phones
wind scoop

GENERAL INFORMATION

Crew changes

It is very difficult if not impossible for crew who do not speak and read Russian to travel by train or bus in Russia. The language barrier is simply prohibitive. Air travel is manageable however, so crew changes need to take place in towns which have air connections with Moscow. Note that there are several airports in Moscow and connections there should be organised in and out of just one of them.

Guide books

There is a plethora of literature available, overwhelming in its complexity and variety. We found simple travel guides like Lonely Planet Russia very helpful. First-hand accounts of Volga travel by authors such as Troyat and Oliphant (see bibliography) were of great interest. In addition to Google maps, a paper atlas showing airports, rail and road networks is very helpful when planning crew changes.

WEATHER

1. Barents Sea

Warmed by the last eastward vestiges of the Gulf Stream, the Barents Sea remains ice free all year. While winter weather can be very severe, tough inshore fishing boats continue to work off the Norwegian and Russian coasts. During the long trip east along the Kola Peninsula we had generally fresh breeze from the east and north-east, easing at night. This is usual.

2. White Sea

The White Sea freezes and ice may be encountered there until the first week in June. Sailing east from Vardo or Kirkenes, vessels should plan to arrive in Archangel'sk no earlier than that. Ice breakers offer service for commercial shipping but cannot be relied upon by yachts. We encountered a fresh, icy northerly wind and sleet between the Dvina river mouth and the Solovetskiy Islands. We had been warned about uncomfortable seas on approach to the islands and those warnings were borne out.

3. Inland waterways

The weather improves steadily as you proceed south and summer progresses. From Lake Onega onwards we swam comfortably everywhere. By the time we entered the Volga (3 July) the weather had become hot and quite humid. Cockpit shading and cabin fans were de rigeur.

Our weather generally was clear. Predominant winds were light, from the southern quarter. Crossing Rybinsky Reservoir we had 25 knot headwinds which, with a 40 mile fetch in 8 m of water gave a very uncomfortable sea. We did not ever experience winds in excess of 36 knots.

Perhaps we were lucky. Certainly Wild Goose had much worse weather until well south. We were particularly grateful for the sunny calm weather we experienced on Lake Onega and White Lake, each of which has a fearsome reputation for gales and nasty seas. We were alive to the real dangers of storms on the exposed waters of the large reservoirs and planned our longer passages with care and careful attention to safe refuges along the way.

APPENDIX

While river waters are often confined, the long fetches and shallow waters of the big reservoirs deserve real respect. For example, "Aenigma" encountered a vicious storm cell near Saratov, with a short period of hurricane force winds. "Wild Goose" was plagued by cold, wet and squally weather and fresh winds for much of the northern section of its passage.

4. Sea of Azov

This is the shallowest sea in the world, with average depths of only about 9 metres. Prevailing winds tend to be from the western quadrant. When fresh, short steep seas (2-3 metres) kick up quickly and can make progress arduous at best. The sea is freezes in December and ice breakers are active until the beginning of April.

5. Seasonal weather limitations

The limiting factor is ice. During winter, when temperatures may fall as low as - 35 C, the entire river system is frozen over and all commercial shipping ceases. In the upper sections, shipping commences in late April each year and continues until November. The season is understandably longer further south, beginning in April and extending into early December.

We have no idea how many buoys there along the river but suspect the number may be 15-20,000. All of these are removed before the river freezes, then re-set each year with the thaw. A mammoth task!

6. Weather reports

In typical, lazy Tainui fashion we used weather eye and gut sense as our main forecast assets. Perhaps we were just lucky, but they did not let us down.

Weather report times and channels are announced regularly on VHF channel 5. They are also listed in the VHF radio handbook mentioned above. Weather reports are also obtainable on telephone request to the waterway despatchers.

Buoyage, lights, distance marks

Travelling south in the White Sea (Belomor) Canal, spar buoys are usual - port hand marks are red cans and starboard marks are white cones. Most are unlit. Some of these, especially the starboard spars for some reason, are slender and quite difficult to locate.

In the Belomor (Baltic) Canal the numerous land-based transit leads (white lattice squares) are generally unlit, often unpainted and ill-defined.

Belomor (Baltic) Canal authorities are in the process of installing AIS transmitters on many of the major buoys, which will significantly assist with navigation in thick weather.

After Vytegra the buoyage convention changes - for vessels heading south the starboard marks are red cans and port marks are white cones. These buoys are large, clearly numbered and lit. They are often laid in duplicate.

One very useful annotation on the paper charts (and on both the Navionics and iSailor programs) is the marking of km distances from Moscow. Beginning in Belomorsk at lock 19 for example, the distance mark on both electronic and paper charts is 1,334 km and the distance marks reduce seriatim as you proceed south until Rybinsk. From there, as you are now sailing away from Moscow, they increase again to 3183 km at the Sea of Azov.

Working the radio

On the inland waterways:

__channel 5__ - this is the general ship-to-ship calling channel. All commercial vessels maintain continuous listening watch on channel 5

__channel 3__ - lock traffic calling and working channel. Use channel 3 to establish contact with lock-keeper on approach. Radio control of vessel movement in and out of locks takes place on channel 3. Communication is brisk and business-like. Because locks are sometimes multiple (notably at Povenets, Vytegra and in the Volga-Don Canal), there may be confusing overlap here. You have to listen very carefully.

__Working channels__ - Note that channel 3 is for lock movements only. Lock-keepers will also need to discuss ship business with you - your yacht identity, crew details, fee payments and the like - they may direct you to another working channel for this purpose. Alternatively, they may ask you to contact them by mobile phone to work through this often lengthy process.

We encountered very few local yachts on route. For them, communication with locks is comparatively simple. They commonly do not carry VHF transmitters and handle all their lock communication by mobile telephone.

Because small yachts do not often have VHF radios, if you call commercial vessels on channel 5 they will be looking to establish visual contact with another commercial vessel. You need to be explicit in describing your diminutive vessel, its range and bearing from the ship you are calling.

Russian radio language is simple and very informal. When there are not many vessels about, channel 5 (general) and channel 3 (locks) are used for all sorts of banal and non-maritime conversation. Hence at Lock No 13 on the Volga-Don Canal we used channel 3 with the lock-keeper to discuss our supermarket shopping needs. On another occasion, when Tainui's crew were largely of the female persuasion, we were asked by an incredulous lock-keeper why he could not see any men working our lines and fenders (the crew's response - "So what?" - silenced him). Also noteworthy was the astonished response of Vytegra Radio as we sought permission to enter the river from Lake Onega - "Oh no, not a yacht!" And when we reported that we were sailing under Australian flag: "And as if that isn't enough"!!!! (Нам это еще не хватает!)

When the navigation buoys en route change from inland (red and white) to IALA (red and green) it is time to switch VHF radios.

Working the locks

Small vessels are a novelty, if not an inconvenience for both lock-keepers and commercial traffic alike. Nonetheless, we found the locking process smooth and our reception by the keepers warm, professional and helpful.

By any European standard the large locks on the Balt-Volga-Don system are efficient, smooth and well-run. Built to accommodate two or three 5,000 tonne vessels at once, they appear daunting at first glance but the locking process is in fact quite straightforward.

First, choose a favoured side for tying off. Then you can leave your fenders and lines in situ between locks, which saves a good deal of fiddling about. The lock keepers will usually allow you to take your chosen side but you must remember to specify your needs during initial VHF contact.

While deck crew of small vessels are supposed to wear life jackets in the locks this rule was only occasionally enforced.

Large steel hooks sit atop floats recessed into the lock walls. These rise and fall with the water level and it is only necessary to attach to one hook. The hooks are numbered and you will be told which hook to use.

We used a single, looped breast rope, with a second one we attached later, as backup. A bight of the line was led through a stout fairlead amidships and laid on deck prior to arrival at the designated hook. In some locks the hook is quite high and some easy lassoing may be required, but in 56 locks we did not encounter significant difficulty.

We led the breast rope to a cockpit winch and hauled it in tight. It requires constant attention, particularly in descent locks, as the hook flotation device sometimes grounds out before the boat does. Thus the line needs to be paid out as the vessel settles further.

Don't forget to thank the lock keepers for their work once you are leaving the lock! If you are in a series of locks, on departure from each you should radio ahead to forewarn the next lock of your imminent arrival.

ARCTIC PILOT REPORTING WAYPOINTS

The full list of waypoints for mandatory position reports to Russia Coast Guard is as follows. Our agent told us that only those in the Barents-White Sea channel (the D series) are needed for cruising yachts.

D4	Mys Svyatoy Nos	68°04.00'N,	40°31.50'E
D5	Mys Orlov Terskiy Tonkiy	67°37.00'N,	41°16.80'E
D6	Mys Bolshoy Gorodetsky	67°25.40'N,	41°27.00'E
D7	Mys Zimnegorskiy	65°32.70'N,	39°28.00'E
D8	Mys Zimnegorskiy	65°18.20'N,	39°35.60'E
D9	Ostrov Mudyugskiy	65°00.00'N,	39°57.80'E
D10	Ostrov Mudyugskiy	65°01.00'N,	40°02.00'E
D11	Mys Orlov Terskiy Tonkiy	66°51.80'N,	41°33.00'E
E1	Mys Nikodimskiy	66°11.20'N,	40°01.90'E
E2	Mys Nikodimskiy	65°57.40'N,	38°23.00'E
E3	Ostrov Zhizhginskiy	65°20.10'N,	37°00.00'E
E5	Ostrov Zhizhginskiy	65°06.00'N,	36°35.00'E
P0	Mys Zemlyanoy	69°54.60'N,	31°00.00'E
P1	Mys Zemlyanoy	70°07.20'N,	31°38.00'E

HAZARDS

Logs

Timber, both floating and semi-submerged, is a significant hazard. Logs are most common in Kovzha River, above the Vytegra ladder.

APPENDIX

Fishing traps

Traps are often marked with no more than one or more empty plastic bottles. These are usually, but not always near the edge of the channel, or around the mouths of inlets. Occasionally we came across streamed polypropylene line whose floats had presumably come adrift. You need to keep an eagle eye out for these.

Weed

fine weed can be a problem, especially in the Volga-Don Canal and in the Don itself (see Azov section in the guide). Salt water flow should be checked regularly (more often than we did - twice we had overheating problems caused by weed blockage of either the sea water inlet or the hose above the cock).

Sailing at night

We enjoyed our night passages. Because the waterways are so well buoyed and lit, sailing at night presents no particular problem. All commercial ships are appropriately lit and colregs are observed. Given the volume of traffic this is obviously of vital importance. It goes without saying that scrupulous watch-keeping is vital.

We did not once encounter a close quarters situation in which a stand-on and give-way vessels behaved unexpectedly or inappropriately. Given the size of some vessels - particularly those huge and cumbersome double barges with push tugs - we took pains to keep well out of the way, even if that meant moving outside the channel.

In narrow channels it can be off-putting though, if you are off watch down below and happen to glance out a porthole to see the slab side of a 5,000 tanker sliding past only 10 metres away.

Strobe lights

All ships have a strobe light on the bridge deck. When an approaching vessel saw us it set the strobe flashing. We responded with our own light and then both lights are doused. A nice way of saying hello, lovely evening, we can see you, we know you can see us, let us be careful of one another, and have a safe passage.

Using the locks at night

For commercial shipping, locks operate 24 hours daily. Except in White Sea (Belomor) Canal where darkness at night is incomplete, small vessels are generally not allowed transit locks at night. The locks are so well-lit that this rule seems unnecessary. Enforcement is at the discretion of the lock-keeper, and we were allowed to use the Volga-Don locks at night. If you are not allowed to proceed the lock-keeper will generally tell you where to anchor for the night and may call you in the morning to advise about your slot in the morning queue. Of course that means that your Russian crew will have to maintain radio watch.

Swimming

From White Lake onwards we swam everywhere except in the immediate vicinity of ports. In reservoirs those rich green algal blooms can be a bit off-putting, but we paid less and less attention to this as our journey progressed.

Photography

There is an incomparable richness of opportunity for photography on the inland waterways. We are not by any means professional photographers, but we found that most photographs composed and took themselves. Our basic equipment included:

Canon 95S -This little hand held camera has been a gem. Always available in the cockpit for immediate use, it was our mainstay. Ashore, we found its low light capability exceptional and almost never used flash.

Nikon D300 - This reliable brick was brought out to capture those magic moments. Our basic lens was a top-of-the-line 18-200mm zoom. We carried a number of prime lenses also (loving heritage from my old FM2) but almost never used them. We carried a backup D300 body also, but never needed it.

APPENDIX

PRIME MINISTER MEDVEDEV DECREE 2012

GOVERNMENT OF THE RUSSIAN FEDERATION DECREE
from May 12, 2012 N 472

About the adoption of the Regulations of the inland waterways sailing of the Russian Federation - sports sailboats and pleasure crafts under the banner of foreign countries.
In accordance with Article 23.1 of the Code of Inland Water Transport of the Russian Federation, the Government of the Russian Federation decrees:

1. To adopt the following regulations of navigation on inland waterways of the Russian Federation of sports sailboats and pleasure craft under foreign flags.
2. To establish that this resolution comes into force on May 25, 2012

Prime Minister of Russian Federation
DMITRY MEDVEDEV
Approved by the Government of Russian Federation
on May 12, 2012 N 472

Regulations of navigation along the inland waterways of the Russian Federation of sports sailboats and pleasure craft under the banner of foreign countries.

1. These Regulations shall govern navigation on inland waterways of the Russian Federation of sports sailboats and pleasure crafts under the banner of foreign countries (hereinafter - the water crafts).

   In the part which are not covered by these Regulations, the water crafts navigating along the inland waterways of the Russian Federation according with the requirements under the Regulations of navigation along inland waterways of the Russian Federation, approved by the Ministry of Transport of the Russian Federation in accordance with the Code of Inland Water Transport of the Russian Federation (hereinafter - the Code).

2. The water crafts are allowed to navigate along inland waterways of the Russian Federation and port visits, which are included in the list of inland waterways of the Russian Federation which are allowed to sail ships under foreign flags, and a list of ports open for the water crafts navigating under the banners of foreign countries approved by the Russian Government.

3. The water crafts, navigating along the inland waterways of the Russian Federation with the crossing of the Russian Federation border, and people who are on the water crafts are under Immigration, customs, veterinary, quarantine, phytosanitary, sanitary and quarantine control and other controls in order prescribed by legal system of The Russian Federation and international treaties of the Russian Federation, at the crossing point on the state border of the Russian Federation, which are open on sea ports of the Russian Federation, the waters of which have access to the inland waterways of the Russian Federation.

4. At the border control Captain (owner) of the water craft shall submit information on the planned route of navigation on inland waterways of the Russian Federation and state assumed ports of call and estimated dates of call in these ports.

5. The following documents should be at the water craft:

   a) documents, confirming the type and nomination of the water craft, its right to navigate under the banner of the State in which water craft is registered, and the compliance of the water craft with set international technical specifications and technical requirements of the state where the water craft is registered;

   b) a crew list, made by the captain of the water craft;

   c) a ship's journal (a ship's log book or a united ship's log book);

   d) duly certified copies of documents confirming the ownership of the water craft;

e) the rules of navigation along inland waterways of the Russian Federation, approved by the Decree of the Ministry of Transport of the Russian Federation in accordance with the Code, and this Regulation;

f) a list of inland waterways of the Russian Federation, along which navigation of water crafts under the banners of foreign countries is allowed. This list must be set by the Government of the Russian Federation;

g) a list of the ports open for water crafts navigating under the banners of the foreign countries, set by the Government of the Russian Federation.

6. Water crafts remain their identification beacons, according to the requirements set by the State of registration of the water craft.

7. Pilot navigates water crafts:

on parts of the inland waterways of the Russian Federation, established in accordance with paragraph 3 of Article 41 of the Code as a compulsory pilotage area; on parts of the inland waterways of the Russian Federation, which are not included in the number of compulsory pilotage areas established in accordance with paragraph 3 of Article 41 of the Code, which sailing conditions due to navigation, weather conditions, heavy traffic, the nature of traffic and other reasons are of increasing complexity.

The lists of such inland waterways of the Russian Federation shall be established by the Ministry of Transport of the Russian Federation.

8. A pilot does not navigate water crafts on parts of the inland waterways of the Russian Federation which are not stated in paragraph 7 of this Regulation, under the following conditions:

- total transit time between stops does not exceed 12 hours in one day, while there should be at least one member of crew who speaks the Russian language and has a document confirming power endorsement of appropriate category for having negotiations with control and port services, as well as the negotiations between the water crafts in passing and overtaking;

- total transit time between stops is more than 12 hours in one day, while there should be at least two members of crew who speak the Russian language and have documents confirming power endorsement of appropriate category for having negotiations with control and port services, as well as the negotiations between the water crafts in passing and overtaking.

In case of default of these conditions the water craft must be navigated by a pilot.

9. Pilots navigating the water crafts along inland waterways of the Russian Federation for a fee must have pilot certificates issued in accordance with established order.

10. Certain categories of water crafts may be exempted from compulsory pilotage on the some parts of inland waterways referred to paragraph 7 of these Regulations, upon the decision of the Ministry of Transport of the Russian Federation, adopted on the basis of design features and specifications of such water crafts and sailing conditions.

PRESIDENT VLADIMIR PUTIN DECREE 2012

Распоряжение Правительства РФ от 05.05.2012 N 734-р

<Об утверждении перечня портов, открытых для захода судов под флагами иностранных государств и перечня внутренних водных путей Российской Федерации, по которым разрешено плавание судов под флагами иностранных государств>

APPENDIX

List of approved ports for foreign vessels

This list is made by order of the Government of the Russian Federation dated May 5, 2012 N 734-p Moscow. Official date of publication: May 16, 2012

Ports open to ships flying foreign flags:

1. Arkhangelsk (Arkhangelsk region)
2. Barnaul (Altai Territory)
3. Volgograd (Volgograd region)
4. Kazan (Tatarstan)
5. Kirensk (Irkutsk region, district of Cyrene)
6. Kolpashevo (Tomsk, Kolpashevsky district)
7. Komsomolsk-on-Amur (Khabarovsk, Komsomolsk region)
8. Krasnoyarsk (Krasnoyarsk Territory)
9. Labytnangi (Yamal-Nenets Autonomous District, Priuralsky district)
10. Lensky (Republic of Sakha (Yakutia), Lensky District)
11. Lesosibirsk (Krasnoyarsk Territory, the Yenisei region)
12. Moscow. West Port (Moscow)
13. Moscow. North river cargo port (Moscow)
14. Moscow. North River Passenger Terminal (Moscow)
15. Moscow. Southern river cargo port (Moscow)
16. Moscow. South River Passenger Terminal (Moscow)
17. Nizhnevartovsk (Khanty-Mansi Autonomous District, Nizhnevartovsk district)
18. Nizhny Novgorod (Nizhny Novgorod region)
19. Novosibirsk (Novosibirsk region)
20. Olekminsk (Republic of Sakha (Yakutia), Olekminsky ulus)
21. Omsk (Omsk region)
22. Sturgeon (Ust-Kut) (Irkutsk region, Ust-Kut district)
23. Perm (Perm)
24. Petrozavodsk (Republic of Karelia)
25. Podporozhsky (Podporozhye) (Leningrad region, Podporozhsky district)
26. Salekhard (the Yamal-Nenets Autonomous District)
27. Samara (Samara Region)
28. St. Petersburg-passenger (St. Petersburg)
29. Saratov (Saratov region)
30. Sovetsk (Kaliningrad)
31. Surgut (Khanty-Mansi Autonomous Area - Yugra, Surgut district)
32. Tver (Tver region)
33. Tobolsk (Tyumen Region, Tobolsk district)
34. Ulyanovsk (Ulyanovsk region)
35. Ust-Donetsk (Rostov region, Ust-Donetsk region)
36. Khabarovsk (Khabarovsk Territory)
37. Khanty-Mansiysk (Khanty-Mansi Autonomous Area - Yugra)
38. Cherepovets (Vologda region)
39. Yakutsk (Sakha Republic (Yakutia))
40. Yaroslavl (Yaroslavl region)

Reference, guide books and reading

"Sailing Round Russia" - Wallace Clark (Wallace Clark Book Sales)

"Russia and the Russians" - 2nd edition 2012 Penguin

Alan Logan notes - OCC Flying Fish archive

"Lord and Peasant in Russia", Blum, J, Princeton 1961

Aenigma journey - Royal Cruising Club Roving Commissions

"Russian Primary Chronicle"

"Daily Life in Russia under the Last Tsar", Troyat 1959, Stanford University Press

"Last Boat to Astrakhan", Haupt, Random House 1998

"The Volga River" McNeese, Chelsea House Philadelphia, 2005

"In Our Time - Volga Vikings", Podcast Melvyn Bragg BBC 4 series

"Experimental Voyages 1983-2006", Edberg, Marinarkeologisk tidskrift, No. 1, 2008.

 Edberg, Södertörn Academic Studies 2003

"Rivers of Europe", Klement Tockner et al, Academic Press 2009

"Trip up the Volga to the Fair of Nijni-Novgorod", Munro-Butler-Johnstone 1875

"The Russian Empire: Its People, Institutions and Resources", von Haxthausen, 1856

"Russian Shores of the Black Sea", Oliphant, 1850, Konemann Classics 1998

APPENDIX

TAINUI ON THE VOLGA : SKIPPER'S COMMENTS

Without sentimentality I must say that Tainui has served us well indeed. As usual, she has never given me a moment's anxiety, although she cannot say the same of me. Much of the novelty on this trip has to do with the conversion of a high latitude cold weather boat into one suited to tropical climates. I find that takes time - March fly screens, mosquito netting, sun awnings and shades, adequate ventilation, swim boarding ladders, cockpit bedding, engine cooling etc all need review.

The waters of the Volga River are pristine only in a relative sense. Our epoxy topsides are going powdery and they have absorbed much of the river's oily pollutants. A paint job is in the offing and I will do that in Izmir at the end of the season.

The other novelty for me is having the mast on deck. Dock work with 10' of mast sticking forward of the bows and another 7' behind us is not hard but needs care. In any sort of seaway the motion is not natural and I do not like having to be totally dependent on our engine. Fortunately the river is only 12-20' deep on average, so that anchoring is always the solution in an emergency. But there is a lot of commercial traffic - huge barges, Volga cruise ships and bulk carriers - and I can imagine an awkward emergency arising.

Our mast stands 19 metres off the water and there was no question about our need to pull it in Vytegra. I made three 6 x 1" cross frames to support the beast above the cockpit dodger and it slotted in neatly below the solar panel arch aft. The cross frames are through bolted and also lashed at the cross. Fore and aft support for the whole structure is by way of six 5/8" lines. Despite all that, we have found that there is still fore-and-aft movement when some clown rushes across our bows at speed. Then the whole mess creaks and groans and I grit my teeth. I envy Fremantle sailors with their ready-drop mast step arrangements.There are many 20 mile stretches of river on which a mast and genniker would make for delightful sailing.

Miles Clark ("Wild Goose"), who pioneered this route for foreign yachts, rebuilt his mast so they could fit under the bridges and aerial cables. But she was only 34' and it was not a big job, I gather. Cruisers doing this route in future should consider how best to deal with the 15 metre height restriction.

Compared with Gota Canal, the huge commercial locks on the Belomorsk and Volga-Balt Canals are straightforward. There are enormous mooring hooks which rise and fall with water level, and it is an easy matter to lash firmly to them with a tight breast rope. For topsides protection, big round fenders are a must. Water movement is sedate even though the level changes are at times spectacular, and there is always plenty of room. I could not imagine how you could transit the locks without a competent Russian speaker though. There is much obligatory VHF communication during the process and you often share the locks with 5,000 tonne tankers.

Our one big problem with Tainui has been persistent fresh water coolant loss. We are all baffled by it. I have pressure tested the header tank and the exhaust manifold hot and cold, replaced the water pump, removed the head and had it pressure tested and honed. I have replaced the head gasket. The engine itself runs faultlessly and there is no milkiness or rise in levels of oil. The header tank fluid does not bubble. I have cordoned off the calorifier exchanger and the bus radiator circuits and there is no external loss. But we continue to lose about a pint of coolant per hour, and much more if I tighten the radiator cap and run the engine at more than 1300 rpm. The only possibility I have not been able to investigate is a leak from the welch plug at the aft end of the block, inside the gearbox bell housing, but there is no external loss from the housing. Anyone who can find the source of our leak will win a large prize.

The distances are huge.

ABOUT TAINUI

Tainui is a venerable 46 foot cruising cutter. Nearly 40 years old, she is heavily laid up in fibreglass, with timber decks. A fine centre-cockpit ocean cruising boat, Tainui has never given us a moment's worry, although the reverse is not true.

Tainui was built (as "Vela") in Taiwan in 1976 to a modified Doug Peterson design. A number of these Formosa 46 yachts were built and, along with the original Peterson 46's and Kelly Peterson 46's, they have explored all the world's oceans and coastal waterways.

By modern standards she is a small yacht, without the excessive freeboard, broad beam and cavernous interior spaces typical of modern designs. With long fin keel, cut away forefoot and skeg hung rudder her hull shape is best described as moderate in all respects. She is a well-mannered, comfortable and dry boat. The cockpit has only rarely been filled with water.

She has a heavy mast and rig. Our standard cruising sails are Profurl furling yankee, hanked staysails, two loose-footed fully battened mains, with storm trysail on a separate mast track. Her 40 year old 80hp Ford Bowman diesel is noisy but reliable and does not complain too much.

Because we have so much cruising gear on board there is limited space below although the solid teak interior layout is comfortable and very functional. We do not have a hot shower, microwave, washing machine or TV. But the galley is well laid out, the music system excellent and the cabin heating system adequate (but in high latitudes, only just). All navigation systems, radar, etc are to a high standard, although I have avoided interfaced electronic systems.

Tainui is sailed easily by two and and is easy to manage single-handed. On passage her daily runs can comfortably exceed 200 nautical miles. These days however, both Tainui and I have slowed down a bit - advancing age, laziness and an excess of prudence have her skipper shortening sail earlier than he used to.

We don't steer much – that onerous task has been delegated to our excellent Aries servo wind vane and a robust but very amp-hungry autopilot. Tainui tracks well under Aries, even under bare poles. Close fetching she has steered herself for days at a time without any self steering at all.

APPENDIX

ACKNOWLEDGEMENT

We would like to thank iSailor for its generous support with this project. In particular, we are grateful for permission to reproduce iSailor chartlets in the text. Please note that these maps remain the property of iSailor and are not to be reproduced without specific permission. It goes without saying, that the charlets are for general guidance only and are not to be used for navigation. While we have made every effort to ensure the accuracy of waypoints reproduced in the chartlets, any errors are ours and not iSailor's.

CREDITS AND THANKS

Libby Blainey

Editor and graphic designer extraordinaire. Without her help, none of this would have happened!

Vladimir Ivankiv

Based in St Petersburg, "Vladski" is among many things the Russian representative of the RCC. Gentle, patient and always professional, he was an invaluable intermediary in our dealings with so many bureaucracies. He knows the Volga-Don waterways like few others. Day and night he was available at the end of the phone with reassuring advice - smoothing our dealings with intransigent officials, getting us permission to enter so-called closed ports and arranging payment to canal and lock authorities. It is difficult to imagine this trip without Vladski hovering in the wings.

> phone: +7 921 932 5831
> email: vladimir@sailrussia.spb.ru
> vladimirivankiv@yahoo.com

Konstantin Timonin

Captain of the Belomor Canal and Lake Onega, Kostya is a foreign going master mariner. Thorough and professional, he has a keen interest in seeing foreign vessels safely through his domain. We found him efficient, helpful and hospitable.

> www.bbkanal.ru
> email: ktimonin@yahoo.com
> mobile +7 921 461 4247

Yuriy Klyukvin

Yuriy was our shipping agent in Archangel'sk. A delightful bloke, we were very grateful for his assistance and advice. His fees were low.

> email: klyu@nekgroup.com
> office: +7 911 592 0177
> mobile: +7 818 229 6047

Alexander Galitsky

(Archangel'sk)

Archangel'sk resident Alex has been sailing in the White Sea for 40 years. His expertise and helpfulness are second to none. He is not a licensed shipping agent but, as we discovered after the event, Alex is willing to manage your entry into Russia from Norway.

```
home   +7 818 224 0061
mobile +7 921 720 1568
email: snark1@atnet.ru
```

Barry Martin

(The Russia House, London)

Barry took on our unusual plans with unbridled enthusiasm. His advice and assistance with visa issues during the long and frustrating gestation period were most helpful.

```
The Russia House
Chapel Street Court
Borough High Street
London SE1 1HH
phone: +44 20 7403 9922
email: barrymartin2@btconnect.com
www.therussiahouse.co.uk
```

Among the many others who helped us along the way, the following deserve specific mention:

Marat Kayumov (iSailor Charting, Moscow)
Sasha Laschenko (Archangel'sk)
Sandro Gurchiani (Yaroslavl)
Oleg Tyurin (Lokomotiv YC, Kazan)
Crew of "Credo" (Kazan)
Sergey Kazakov and Maxim Zakrzhyevskiy (Ulyanovsk Yachting Federation)
Dmitry Gulbitsky (Tolyatti)
Oleg Otchenashev (Russian Yachting Federation Volgograd Region Volzhskiy)
Alexei Chirkin (Volgodonsk)
Ivan Parada (Obukhova)
Helen Womack
Floyd Rudmin (Professor of Social & Community Psychology at the University of Tromsø -
the Abdulla Dubin (postcard archive, Kazan)
Jane Vallentine (editor extraordinaire)
Tony Gooch (OCC)
Gerry Dykstra (Bestevaer 2)